Reminiscences

of

Vice Admiral John L. McCrea

U.S. Navy (Retired)

Copyright © 1990

U.S. Naval Institute

Annapolis, Maryland

Preface

John McCrea was a remarkable human being. I first encountered him in the summer of 1980 when I was working on a book about Pearl Harbor. I went to see him at his home in Chestnut Hill, Massachusetts, and found him a delightful individual with whom to talk. He had a marvelous sense of humor and a captivating way of telling stories. In addition to the interview, he provided me with a detailed report he had written in 1940 about a trip to deliver new war plans to U.S. Navy commanders in the Pacific. It's a remarkable document, included as Appendix B in this volume.

Even though he was nearly 90 when I first met him, Admiral McCrea had a remarkable memory for people and events of long ago. When some subject was brought up, he would not only describe his recollections but also make sure that he provided thorough background on the topic. When checked against documentary sources, his recollections proved to be on the mark. Based on my encounter with the admiral, I recommended him as an interviewee to my predecessor, Dr.

John Mason. Dr. Mason conducted one interview toward this oral history, and I subsequently conducted two more.

Time didn't permit covering his career as thoroughly as I might have wished, which meant that some tours of duty were discussed only briefly and a few not at all. That shortcoming was rectified a few years later when Ms. Julia C. Tobey, the admiral's stepdaughter, reported that Admiral McCrea had previously dictated about four dozen tapes about his career, covering it in great detail. She donated copies of those tapes to the Naval Institute; some of them have been transcribed, others have not. In the meantime, we are issuing this first volume of Admiral McCrea's oral history: the transcripts of the three interviews with the Naval Institute.

Admiral McCrea's naval career began before World War I. Indeed, he tells in his oral history of having his 1914 midshipman cruise interrupted because the ship in which he was serving was sold to the Greek Navy. He subsequently served in the battleship New York (BB-34) during that war and wrote the deck log when the German High Seas Fleet surrendered at Scapa Flow in 1918 (see Appendix A).

In the 1920s and 1930s, McCrea developed and matured as a naval officer. He especially enjoyed command at sea. He also took time to get a law degree, and that experience made him eligible to serve a tour of duty in Guam in the 1930s. As the decade drew to a close, he was executive officer of the USS Pennsylvania (BB-38), flagship of the U.S. Fleet, then he went to Washington, D.C., to serve as an aide to Admiral Harold R. Stark, Chief of Naval Operations. From there he went to the White House as naval aide to President Franklin D. Roosevelt. Many of the stories in this volume illustrate his fondness for FDR. In Herman Wouk's epic novel, War and Remembrance, Pug Henry, the fictitious protagonist, served as naval aide to the President, then became first commanding officer of the battleship Iowa (BB-61). McCrea had had those same two billets in that sequence. He has a good deal to say about the Iowa, her commissioning, and her war service.

Before he retired from the Navy in 1953 and began a second career with the John Hancock Life Insurance Company, Admiral McCrea held a series of responsible positions, including Deputy Chief of Naval Operations (Administration) and Deputy Commander in Chief, U.S. Pacific Fleet. While at John Hancock, he courted and married a second wife following the death of the first Mrs. McCrea. Julia C. Tobey has written a charming account of that courtship, and it is included as Appendix C in this volume.

That description helps explain why John McCrea was such a delightful person to know. Even though he had a winning personality and a self-deprecating wit, McCrea was a man of real substance. The responsibilities entrusted to him by the Navy bear witness to that. At his funeral in Arlington in January of this year, the presiding chaplain described him as "an oak of righteousness." Former shipmates from the USS Iowa were moved to tears over the loss of their old skipper. He was a man of both dignity and warmth. The recollections that follow convey some of both of those qualities.

The transcription of the interview tapes was done by Mrs. Grace White. Admiral McCrea did some editing of the first interview, and I edited the other two. Even so, they are substantially as he spoke during the interviews themselves. Ms. Joanne Patmore produced the smooth-typed version, and Ms. Linda O'Doughda put together the detailed index at the end of the volume.

                                          Paul Stillwell
                                          Director of Oral History
                                          U. S. Naval Institute
                                          May 1990

VICE ADMIRAL JOHN LIVINGTONE McCREA, U.S. NAVY (RETIRED)

FAMILY

Vice Admiral McCrea was born in Marlette, Michigan, on 29 May 1891, son of Dr. Henry McCrea and Lillie Livingstone McCrea. He married Estelle Murphy (now deceased) of St. Louis, Missouri, at Manila, Philippine Islands, in November 1925. His second wife was the former Martha Houser Tobey. He had two daughters: Meredith (Mrs. Christopher Coyne) and Anne Lambert (Mrs. Edward Sullivan). Admiral McCrea died at his home in Needham, Massachusetts, on 25 January 1990.

EDUCATION

Vice Admiral McCrea was graduated from the U.S. Naval Academy on 4 June 1915 and from the Naval War College, Newport, Rhode Island, in May 1924. He later received degrees of bachelor of laws and master of laws from George Washington University, Washington, D.C., in 1929 and 1934, respectively.

He was a member of the bars of the District of Columbia and the Supreme Court of the United States, as well as a member of the American Bar Association and the Boston Bar Association.

NAVAL SERVICE

Prior to and during World War I, Vice Admiral McCrea served in the battleship New York (BB-34), which as a unit of the Sixth Battle Squadron operated with the British Grand Fleet throughout the last year of the war. Following the Armistice, he had duty in the battleship New Mexico (BB-40), flagship of Commander in Chief Pacific Fleet, and later as aide to Commander in Chief Hugh Rodman. He continued duty afloat for several years in the destroyers Burns (DD-171), Babbitt (DD-128), and Zeilin (DD-313), and as executive officer of the oiler Ramapo (AO-12).

In 1924 he went to the Asiatic Station, and while in command of the minesweeper Bittern (AM-36), he assisted in the rescue of a Chinese merchant man aground near Chefoo Harbor. He was aide and flag secretary to the Commander, Special Service Squadron in Central American waters, in 1930-31, and the next year he commanded the destroyer Trever

(DD-339). He served as navigator of the cruiser Astoria (CA-34) from June 1934 until February 1936, and during the period November 1938 to September 1940 he was executive officer of the battleship Pennsylvania (BB-38).

Between wars, on regular rotation of duty between sea and shore, he had three tours in the Office of the Judge Advocate General, Navy Department, and was aide to the Chief of Naval Operations in 1940-41. During the visit of Prime Minister Winston Churchill to this country, he served as naval secretary at the first meetings of the Combined Chiefs of Staff.

Early in World War II, he was appointed Naval Aide to the President of the United States, and as such, he accompanied Roosevelt to the Casablanca Conference. He commanded the battleship Iowa (BB-61) from her commissioning in February 1943 until August 1944, during which period she transported the President and Joint Chiefs of Staff to Oran for the Cairo and Teheran Conferences in November 1943, returning them from Dakar in December. Under his command the Iowa participated in operations at Kwajalein, Truk, Saipan, Palau, and Hollandia; the Battle of the Philippine Sea; and bombardments of Mili, Ponape, Saipan, and Tinian. Off Guam in February 1944 in daylight action, while a member of a task group, the Iowa engaged and sank a Japanese cruiser. McCrea was awarded the Legion of Merit, with Combat V, for exceptionally meritorious service in that command.

In the rank of rear admiral, he commanded Cruiser Division One and a task force in Aleutian waters in the North Pacific. He was awarded a gold star in lieu of the second Legion of Merit with Combat V for outstanding service in the vicinity of the Kurile Islands from August 1944 to April 1945. Upon his return to the Navy Department, he was appointed Director of the Central Division, Office of the Chief of Naval Operations, his title later changing to Assistant Chief of Naval Operations for Administration. On 31 August 1946 he was appointed Deputy Chief of Naval Operations for Administration and advanced to the rank of vice admiral.

In the rank of vice admiral he served as Deputy Commander in Chief, Pacific Command and U.S. Pacific Fleet, January 1948 to June 1949, and from June 1949 to January 1952 he was Director of the Staff (later Deputy Director)

Personnel Policy, Office of the Secretary of Defense. On 29 February 1952 he assumed the duties of Commandant First Naval District in his permanent rank of rear admiral. He was transferred to the retired list of the U.S. Navy in June 1953, and was advanced to the rank of vice admiral, the highest rank held while on active duty.

CIVILIAN EMPLOYMENT

From 1953 through 1966, Admiral McCrea was vice president for client relations at John Hancock Mutual Life Insurance Company in Boston. He served as liaison to corporate clients and also handled public relations.

U.S. DECORATIONS

    Legion of Merit (two awards) with Combat V
    Marine Expeditionary Medal
    Second Nicaraguan Campaign Medal
    Victory Medals for World War I and World War II
    American Defense Service Medal, Fleet Clasp
    American, Pacific, and European-African-Middle
    Eastern Campaign medals

FOREIGN DECORATIONS

    Order of Leopold, grade of Chevalier (Belgium)
    Order of Al Merito, Second Class (Chile)
    Order of George I with Sword (Greece)
    Order of Ouissam Alaouite Cherifien (French Morocco)
    Legion d'Honneur (France)

Authorization

The U.S. Naval Institute is hereby authorized to make available to libraries and other repositories of its choosing the transcripts of three oral history interviews concerning the life and career of Vice Admiral John L. McCrea. The three interviews were recorded on 1 May 1981 in collaboration with Dr. John T. Mason, Jr.; 26 and 27 October 1982 in collaboration with Mr. Paul Stillwell, for the U.S. Naval Institute.

The undersigned does hereby release and assign to the U. S. Naval Institute all right, title, restrictions, and interest in the interviews. The copyright in both the oral and transcribed versions shall be the sole property of the U. S. Naval Institute. The tape recordings of the interviews are and will remain the property of the U. S. Naval Institute.

Signed and sealed this ___1st___ day of _October_ 1989.

John L. McCrea
Vice Admiral John L. McCrea
U.S. Navy (Retired)

J. L. McCrea #1 - 1

Interview Number 1 with Vice Admiral John L. McCrea,
U.S. Navy (Retired)

Place: Admiral McCrea's home in Chestnut Hill,
                              Massachusetts

Date: Friday, 1 May 1981

Interviewer: Dr. John T. Mason, Jr.

Q: Admiral, I am delighted that you consented to see me and that you will talk a little about your fabulous career in the Navy. Tell me about the early days, about what induced you to go to the Naval Academy, how you happened to have a naval career.

Admiral McCrea: Well, first off, I must register a caveat about the word "fabulous," because my career wasn't fabulous at all; I was just lucky in my first assignment.

Q: That's an element in the naval career--luck.

Admiral McCrea: It just so happened that when I left the Naval Academy, I went to a fine ship, and in that ship I had five captains in the four years and a few weeks that I was in it. The ship was the USS New York.

Q: That is a matter of luck then, but let's go back now to what induced you to seek a naval career in the first place. And first, begin and give me the date of your birth.

J. L. McCrea #1 - 2

Admiral McCrea: I was born on 29 May 1891 in a little town, Marlette, Michigan, which is about 60-odd miles north of Detroit, in the "thumb" of the state. My father was a medical doctor. He was a Canadian; he was born in October 1844, the youngest of eight children of a Scotch Presbyterian minister by the name of John McCrea. My father married, and a year or so later his wife died in childbirth when my half sister was born.

My father suddenly found himself looking out for an infant. His mother was widowed in 1846, and he had two maiden sisters, so he had a family and responsibilities. He had taught school in Canada at the Middlesex Seminary, saved his money, went to the University of Michigan, and graduated from the University of Michigan Medical School in June of 1875. He was very close to 32 years old when he graduated because of the fact that he had to earn his money to get there in the first place.

Q: He had all those family responsibilities.

Admiral McCrea: Yes. After graduation from medical school, he went to New York and did his intern work at Bellevue Hospital, which, in those days, was tops and still is, I suppose, one of the great hospitals of this country. The sheepskin he received from Bellevue bears the signature of Austin Flint, Sr., and Austin Flint, Jr., and any member of the medical profession will assure you that the name of Austin Flint, Jr., is most prominent, because he was a heart specialist and he came up with what is known as the Flint Murmur; I am told it is known to this day as the Flint Murmur. So my father sat at the feet of these fellows. Incidentally, I suppose I should tell you right now that my father was thoroughly convinced that nobody was well educated unless it was based on a solid foundation of Latin and Greek.

Q: I approve of that.

Admiral McCrea: Well, I can recall seeing him, six-feet-four tall, curled up reading the classics in our little library at home. He was concerned about the use of words. He was exceedingly well educated. One of our neighbors, who lived a couple of doors from us, was a lawyer by the name of Donald Stuart McClure, and he, incidentally, was a Canadian too. He and my father were close, close friends. Mr. McClure took a Paris newspaper that impressed me. Now I haven't any idea how old the newspaper was when it got to Marlette, Michigan. It crossed the Atlantic and finally found its way to Marlette.

Q: A few months.

Admiral McCrea: Mr. McClure was a rose and pigeon fancier and had a fine collection of both carrier and tumbler pigeons. They made a great impression on me.

But McCrea and McClure were close, close friends. Once, after I had somewhat grown up, I remarked to my father that I was amazed that he had chosen to stay up there in that country town, and I'll never forget his reply.

I said, "You haven't anything in common with most of these people around here."

"Well," he said, "John, my patients around this little town of ours are people of character, despite the fact that they may be lacking in education. I prefer my neighbors and patients to be people of character."

Meanwhile, after my father lost his wife, he stayed a widower for some 13 years, and at the ripe age of 47 he married my mother who was 24. I was the first of six children that they had, and I am the only one of the six that's living.

Q: That's a very interesting background. That emphasis that your father always made on education spilled out and made some impact on you.

Admiral McCrea: My father, as I grew up and in my high

school days, thought that I was a whippersnapper that would never amount to anything, and in that respect he was somewhat correct. Then I looked on him as an old fogy, but the longer I live, the more convinced I am that his appraisal of me was more nearly correct than mine was of him.

One of his letters, which I treasure, he wrote early in the summer of 1914, the year he died. He died, as a matter of fact, of the ravages of diabetes before the days of insulin. (I, incidentally, am an old-age diabetic myself, but I have it pretty much under control.) The last letter that I had from him, I received just before going on a midshipman cruise to the Mediterranean in the summer of 1914, and he pointed out the items of interest that I should see in Rome. I'll never forget that. He had never been to Rome, but he pointed out the things I should see. He died in July 1914, so I never had the pleasure of telling him of my Rome adventure--the galleries we saw, the audience we had with the Pope, visit to the Colosseum, etcetera, etcetera.

Q: But he read so much about it.

Admiral McCrea: Yes, and each summer he would require me to read something worthwhile. I remember one summer when I was in high school, he assigned for my summer reading The

<u>Decline and Fall of the Roman Empire</u>, and I was to give him a memorandum at the end of the summer as to what I thought of it. Of course . . .

Q: That was quite an assignment.

Admiral McCrea: That was a real assignment, and, of course, what I had to say about it didn't amount to much.

Among other things, he deplored professional athletics. He said, "If we don't watch out, we're heading the way the Romans went."

I have never forgotten that, and every once in a while I think that maybe he was somewhat right about it. He thought we should play football, baseball, etcetera, around high school, amongst ourselves. But as far as packing up and riding in a livery rig to a town 15 or 20 miles away to play another high school team in the same line of sport, just didn't appeal to him at all.

Q: He would be very concerned today, wouldn't he?

Admiral McCrea: Yes, that's right. It so happened that I broke my ankle in one of these high school football games. I was taken home and my father was someplace--I have forgotten--out on a call or something. He came home, and he patched up my ankle as best he could, and he said, "Now, you are a patient of mine, and you will do what I prescribe for you. You are to stay in bed." And then he said, "You are to improve your time staying in bed by doing some reading."

He went out into his little library, and he came back and he handed me a copy of Vanity Fair. I'll never forget that. He said, "You can read this while you are my patient, and then you can give me a memorandum as to what you think about it."

Well, that Vanity Fair interested me in the Napoleonic Wars. As I look back at it now, it was really time well spent, but at the moment I thought it was somewhat of a bore. But I got interested in Vanity Fair, so that I read it with great enthusiasm.

Q: I would think you would.

Admiral McCrea: Well, sure.

Q: It is a fascinating book.

Admiral McCrea: Of course it is.

Q: That sort of thing was helpful in pointing you toward . . .

J. L. McCrea #1 - 8

Admiral McCrea: Well, I suppose, as you remarked about my going to the Naval Academy . . .

Q: Yes, what induced you to do that?

Admiral McCrea: Well, first off, I should tell you, as I told you earlier, that I stood absolutely last in my class at high school, of 19. It was nip and tuck for a time with the daughter of the Methodist minister, a classmate, as to who would stand last. But without being the least bit gallant, I can assure you that I had last place nailed down.

Q: Your father must have been appalled at that.

Admiral McCrea: He was, he was. He made me, absolutely made me, take high school Latin, and I thought that two years would be enough of it. But he found out there was a third year there, and so I had to take that too--this to the dismay of my Latin teacher.

A close friend of mine was Walter Seibert. He stood number two in a class of 12--two classes ahead of me in high school. He got an appointment to the Naval Academy. After one failure of the entrance examinations, he took a second examination and made it. He graduated in the class of 1913 at the Naval Academy. He was a wonderful person to start with and a fine athlete, despite the fact that he never weighed over about 145 pounds. He was a left-handed pitcher, and in his first class year at the Naval Academy, he was not alone the captain of the baseball team, but he pitched a perfect game against Cornell University, which the Naval Academy won, either two or four to nothing--I have forgotten which. A no-hit game and not a man reached first base, striking out, as I recall it, 16 men.

Well, all the newspapers in the East had this thing in the paper the next day about this college athlete. Well, there were more people descending on Annapolis to see what this fellow was like. He stayed in the Navy after he graduated from the Naval Academy, and went through the First World War. And he finally resigned from the Navy and entered business in Pittsburgh, at which he was successful.

Q: You say he is still living?

Admiral McCrea: He is still living in Osterville, Massachusetts, and I see him every once in a while.*

Q: What did you say his name was?

Admiral McCrea: Walter Seibert, and he was one of six or seven kids in his family. And he, too, is the only one

---
*Walter Seibert subsequently died on 9 October 1983 at the age of 94.

J. L. McCrea #1 - 10

that is alive out of that family. Fine people they were; his father and mother were fine, fine people.

Q: But this paved the way, in a sense, for you at the Naval Academy.

Admiral McCrea: Yes, when I graduated from high school, with difficulty as I told you, I was going down the street one day, and Walter Seibert's father stopped me on the street and he said, "Johnny, [everyone called me Johnny] how would you like to go to the Naval Academy where Walter is?"

"Oh," I said, "Mr. Seibert, that would be wonderful. Walter and I are good friends; that would be wonderful."

"Well," he said, "now wait a second. I think you better talk to your father about this."

Q: I think so too.

Admiral McCrea: I said, "All right, I'll do that, Mr. Seibert." I said, "Do you think I could get an appointment?"

"Well," he said, "Mr. McMorran, our congressman, has written to me to the effect that he has been in Congress quite some time now, and everybody that he appoints to the service academies either doesn't make it, and if he does, usually flunks out. But Walter has stuck along and done well down there. And he thinks that this high school of ours may turn out a different product than the rest of them around the thumb of Michigan. So he wants to know if I have anybody in mind that might like to go to the Naval Academy."*

Well, I went home, did as Mr. Seibert said, and talked to my father, and my father listened very carefully. And he said, "John, you thank Mr. Seibert for thinking about you. Mr. McMorran is a machine politician. I am a Republican, and so is he, and if you can get an appointment to the Naval Academy, I will vote for Mr. McMorran. But I want it distinctly understood that I won't work for him."

Q: He, being a Democrat--McMorran?

Admiral McCrea: No, McMorran was a Republican.

Q: Oh, he was too?

Admiral McCrea: Yes, but he was a "machine Republican," so my father said, and that was all there was to it.

But getting the appointment to the Naval Academy wasn't as easy as it may sound. In accordance with Mr.

---
*Representative Henry McMorran, a Republican, of Michigan's seventh congressional district.

J. L. McCrea #1 - 12

Seibert's suggestion, I collected a half dozen or so recommendations from leading citizens. Having had some success as an agent for the Saturday Evening Post, and the owner of a Detroit Tribune (now defunct) newspaper route, I had good recommendations. All these were sent to Mr. McMorran by Mr. Seibert, and I breathlessly awaited an answer.

In due course I received an appointment, but, of all things, it was to West Point. I promptly wrote to Mr. McMorran a letter of appreciation, but explained to him my interest lay in the direction of the Naval Academy. But if he couldn't give me an appointment to the Naval Academy, I would do the best I could to get into West Point. Without further correspondence, I received the Naval Academy appointment for the class of 1915. Had I have gone to West Point and made it, I would have been a classmate of Generals Eisenhower, Bradley, and some 50-odd others of that class who achieved general rank in World War II.*

Well, politics meant a lot in Michigan at that time, and I jump through the years, you know. And when I went to the White House to be naval aide to FDR, I got a letter from my sainted mother in Michigan in which she said that the newspapers in Detroit had called her up about my going to the White House as naval aide, and she just wanted to

---

*General of the Army Dwight D. Eisenhower, USA; General of the Army Omar Bradley, USA.

know whether it was so or not.* She wrote to me, "Remember you were raised Republican, and I don't think your father would like you to do this." My father had been dead 28 years.

I promptly explained to her that I was being sent there as part of my naval job, and that was the end of it.

Q: Nonpolitical.

Admiral McCrea: Yes. Now I go back. I realized that I would only have one crack at the Naval Academy entrance examinations. The entrance years were 16 to 20 at the Naval Academy, and I would get one--the examination in April of 1911, and I would be just a month short of 20 years.

Q: Which would make you ineligible.

Admiral McCrea: Yes. So I explained that carefully to my father, and it was decided that I should go down to Annapolis to one of the two preparatory schools that were in Annapolis that specialized in that sort of training-- training for entrance examinations to the service academies. The local heads wagged. If Walter Seibert, a good student, failed his first try at the Naval Academy

---
*Franklin D. Roosevelt, a Democrat, was President of United States from 1933 to 1945.

J. L. McCrea #1 - 14

entrance examination, how could Johnny McCrea, who stood last in his class, hope to get in the academy?

Q: Which one did you select?

Admiral McCrea: The Robert L. Werntz School.

Q: Oh, yes, Bobby Werntz.

Admiral McCrea: Bobby Werntz, did you know that?

Q: I know about that school, and I know where it was.

Admiral McCrea: Yes, right on King George Street and Maryland Avenue. Well, he had an instructor by the name of Roland M. Teel. He later established that Severn School in Annapolis. Teel was a fine instructor. He encouraged effort, and there were a lot of fellows at Bobby's school. I didn't have time to do anything but study, so I sat in the front row as to be distracted as little as possible.

Q: That was the purpose of it--a certain number of weeks of concentrated study.

Admiral McCrea: And that's what I did, and much to my--I

won't say to my amazement--when I took the entrance exams in April in Washington, D.C., I thought that I did reasonably well in everything excepting algebra. Well, I was living at the Hotel Maryland, a little hotel in the center of Annapolis. Three of us, three candidates, occupied a four-room suite. I knew the night clerk of the hotel well, Mr. John Koehler. He was interested in me, and he wanted to know how I did in the examinations. I told him--I said, "I think I did all right excepting one possible thing, and that is algebra." I said, "I am just worried about that."

Mr. John said, "What did you say, algebra?" He said, "How do you spell that?" So I told him.

The next day, Mr. John (as I always called him) said to me, "Mr. Monahan, the bartender down here, whom you know, tells me that if algebra is the only thing you are worried about, not to worry."

"Well," I said, "what is the basis of that?"

He said, "Well, one of his customers is on the board of examiners at the Naval Academy and he told this chap about you." Incidentally I will tell you his name--he later got to be a flag officer--and his name was James J. Raby.*

Q: Yes, I know the name.

---
*Lieutenant Commander James J. Raby, USN.

Admiral McCrea: ". . . and he said that I was worried about algebra." And Mr. Raby, who was then a lieutenant or lieutenant commander, told Mr. Monahan--when he dropped in for his next beer--that if that was the only thing, to tell me that I had gotten a 2.9 in algebra, and I had done well in all the rest.

So I had advance information, and there I sat. I was delighted, of course, that I found my name posted at the main gate, the Maryland Avenue gate, as one of the successful candidates. But I had to get admitted right away. So on the 11th day of May, I was sworn in as a midshipman in the United States Navy--18 days before I was ineligible. So I got in. There was just one other fellow in the class that was older than I, but he has passed on a long while ago, so I am the dean as far as he goes in my class.

Q: How did you fare during plebe summer?

Admiral McCrea: Plebe summer, I did all right.

Q: It didn't bother you, this regimentation?

Admiral McCrea: No, not a damn bit. I was just delighted that I was able to get in there at the first crack when my

J. L. McCrea #1 - 17

friend Walter Seibert had had to take two cracks at it.

Q: And your father, how did he react to this?

Admiral McCrea: My father? He was delighted; he was delighted.

Q: Thought you might amount to something after all?

Admiral McCrea: Well, he knew that I was in earnest about it all. And, of course, the Naval Academy sends your marks home to your parents or guardian every month, and he was getting my marks and looking them over carefully. He noted with pleasure that I got very few conduct demerits, so that . . .

Q: Well, how did you do scholastically at the academy?

Admiral McCrea: Not well. I didn't do badly either; I never had too much trouble about keeping up. I graduated from the Naval Academy 112 out of a class of 179. That's that.

Q: Tell me something about the summer cruises.

Admiral McCrea: Those cruises were very interesting. The

J. L. McCrea #1 - 18

first cruise that I took from the Naval Academy in the summer of 1912 was on board the USS Massachusetts; my whole class was put on the USS Massachusetts. Well, there is nothing that can be more distraught than living with a bunch of people going to sea on a ship who had never been there before, and we didn't have anybody to ask, because none of the older classmates were in our ship at all.

Q: None of the instructors either?

Admiral McCrea: Oh, we had instructors there, yes, but all the plebes, my class being the ex-plebe class, were put in this one ship, the Massachusetts, and it was quite an interesting experience.

Q: You were, in effect, sailors, weren't you?

Admiral McCrea: Yes, that's right, and we hadn't anybody to ask any questions, any help from, excepting your officers, whom you didn't want to bother, or the boatswain's mate or somebody.

I fell in with a boatswain's mate, who was a real character. He had a red beard; his name was Smith. He was a Norwegian, and he talked with a Norwegian accent. We got to be good friends. He always referred to me as Mr. McCrea, and here I was but 21 years old and being called "mister." I couldn't quite make it. But that was Smith. He was the boatswain's mate of the upper deck, fourth division, and he would let me sit on his chest. Now the boatswain's mate's chest--that's his office--he kept everything in that chest: marlinspike, rope yarn, and marlinspike tools, and everything. And the men in those days made their own clothes. Wednesday afternoons were always known as "rope-yarn Sundays, when men make and mend clothes." Smith had in his chest three sets of patterns. When the chap would go buy his cap cloth (they called it) from the small stores, he would bring it up to Smith, and Smith would take a look at him and he would say, "Well, you take the number two pattern." They would lay down the pattern, and they would cut out the clothes and they would sew them themselves, and the starboard pocket . . .

Q: Not necessarily their own uniform but for somebody else?

Admiral McCrea: Oh no, it's their own uniform. Everybody did his own. And these two pockets up here--these breast pockets--the right pocket was lined with green silk, and the left pocket was lined with red silk: port and starboard running lights.

Q: I see.

Admiral McCrea: Well, Smith was a real character. I remember once him telling me, "You know," he said, "Mr. McCrea, the bluejackets today aren't the way they used to be."

"Well," I said, "that's right, I suppose. And that's one of the penalties, that as people get older they think that about the young." And I said, "In what respect are these fellows different now than they were in your time?"

"Well, I'll tell you what," he said, "too damn many of them can read and write."

Q: Quite the opposite from your father.

Admiral McCrea: "Too many of them can read and write. Well," he said, "one of the best things I know to do is to do a cruise in the Chilean Navy." He said, "I did seven years in the Chilean Navy before I got in the United States Navy."

Well, in the early 1900s, under the administration of Theodore Roosevelt, it came to his attention that a great many of the sailors in our service were foreigners, so he got a bill through Congress that provided for extra pay--I think it was six or seven dollars a month or something like that--if one could prove his American citizenship. And it was put in his enlistment record. There was a rubber stamp

J. L. McCrea #1 - 21

put in there--"Proof of American Citizenship was been provided." And that's the way it was.

About that time, or maybe just a little earlier, there had been introduced in the Navy the system of payment of the men. It used to be that on payday the paymaster sat at a mess table, and these fellows came back when their name was called off, and so many dollars were passed to them. And that was the end of it. Well, obviously that was a rather loose way of doing things, so somebody decided that everybody should have a pay receipt in which he acknowledged the receipt from the paymaster of so many dollars and signed his name. My job as a midshipman was to sit there and witness the "mark"--mind you, the "mark" of many, many sailors because they didn't know how to sign their own name. I'll never forget it.

Q: I would think so.

Admiral McCrea: And we have come a long, long way since then, a long way. But this goes back to 1912. And we arrived here in the Boston Navy Yard.

Q: What was your cruise that summer? Just up the coast?

Admiral McCrea: Up the coast. We were down off Long Island Sound and up in Gloucester, and as I recall it, up near Portland too, but we stayed off the shore a good bit. We came to Boston, and we made a tour, of course, of the Boston Shipyard, and it never once occurred to me that I would ever go back there, but I did ultimately. That was my last active duty, being the commandant of this naval district, and I lived in those quarters there, with which you are familiar.

Q: Were you involved in coaling operations?

Admiral McCrea: Oh yes, we coaled the ship, yes.

Q: That's one of the less pleasant aspects of the cruise.

Admiral McCrea: Oh yes, we coaled ship and, gracious, we certainly--we thought that was the life, I suppose. If it was going to be that tough, we were glad we didn't have to coal ship always. As I say, when we toured the Navy yard here we first saw the Constitution. It was pretty much of a wreck in those days; nothing had been done about restoring her for a long time. They just kept her together; that was all there was to it. She ultimately turned into something well worth looking at now. I remember going through the chain shop in the shipyard. All the big battleship chain was made by hand over there, and the big South Boston, Irish bullies were out there whacking these red-hot chains. And every so often everything would stop, and the bucket was passed around. It was beer; it was beer.

Q: But that was hard work.

Admiral McCrea: Yes, of course it was hard work. That was my introduction to Boston.

There was a newspaper that was published here about that time--I have forgotten the name of it. Maybe it was the <u>Post</u>, but at any rate, they were conducting a recruiting drive for subscribers and one thing and another, and Revere Beach was going in those days. And they had something on the front page of the paper. You were to accost a girl dressed in red and come up with this particular line: "Are you the <u>Boston Post</u> lady in red--looking for subscriptions to the paper?" or something like that. And you had to have it exactly right. The Sunday we were there, I remember we went down to Revere Beach, a number of us, and there were more little girls running around there dressed in red than you could shake a stick at, all wanting to be asked if they were the lady in red. We had a great time. That was my first introduction.

Years and years later I came up here. I had married a gal from St. Louis and she had never been to the East, and we came up here. We went out to the Bunker Hill Monument--

I wanted her to see it. And on the way back, I wanted to get back in town, and I didn't know how to get back. I had my car there and I saw this policeman, and I stopped and told him I just wanted to get back to Boston and he started telling me how to do it. And finally, he said, "You're not taking it; you don't understand."

And I said, "No, I don't; I don't think I follow."

He said, "I'll take you there."

So I opened the door of the car and he got in, and I politely said to this fellow, "My name is McCrea." I was in civilian clothes, of course, and I just said, "My name is McCrea."

He said, "I'm Officer Murphy."

"Well," I said, "there's one sitting in the back seat," because my wife's family name was Murphy.

And he turned to my wife and he said, "Madam, you should have been here last Sunday. We had the Murphy picnic at Revere Beach, and there were 10,000 of us there."

I always had a good laugh about my first summer cruise around here and also my later contact with the Murphys.

Q: Where did your other cruises take you?

Admiral McCrea: The second year from the Naval Academy, we were parcelled out and sent in various small groups to the battleships of the Atlantic Fleet.

Q: The active duty?

Admiral McCrea: On active duty. The ship that I was sent to--I suppose we had 25 or 30 midshipmen in the ship--was the USS Connecticut. We went to Veracruz. We arrived in Veracruz in a half gale one Sunday morning and were transferred right away to the South Carolina. The South Carolina was going up to the Philadelphia Navy Yard for an overhaul. We never got ashore in Veracruz. We were only there at anchor for five or six hours; then we were started back north for the Philadelphia Navy Yard. When we got in the Philadelphia Navy Yard, we were promptly sent to the USS Ohio that had just finished a Navy yard overhaul, and then again we joined the Atlantic Fleet. That was what happened to us that summer.

Q: Why the sudden switch down off Veracruz?

Admiral McCrea: Because the South Carolina was due for an overhaul, and they had to get the ship up to Philadelphia, and there was the USS Ohio just finishing her overhaul in the Philadelphia Navy Yard, so we were transferred to the Ohio and away we went. But it was all very interesting, and that principally was my second class cruise.

J. L. McCrea #1 - 26

Q: You had a slightly different status, didn't you?

Admiral McCrea: That's right; we were second class midshipmen. We knew something about going to sea. We knew how to scrub our own clothes and hammocks, and all that sort of thing. We made out all right.

Our first class cruise was exceedingly interesting. We left the Naval Academy the first week of June 1914 in three ships. The Idaho was the one I was in. I think we should keep in mind how suddenly the war broke out in the summer of 1914.

Q: The drums of August.

Admiral McCrea: I am convinced the Navy Department never would have sent three battleships loaded with midshipmen to the Mediterranean if they had the slightest idea that war was going to be declared. Of course, Sarajevo happened the last week of June, and there we were.* Our problem was made a little bit more difficult by the fact that the Navy had sold the USS Idaho to Greece.

Q: She became the old Avaroust, didn't she?

---

*Archduke Franz Ferdinand of Austria-Hungary was assassinated at Sarajevo, Bosnia and Herzegovina (now Yugoslavia), by a Serbian on 28 June 1914, an act that precipitated World War I.

Admiral McCrea: No, she became something else, not the name you said; I think she was named for one of the Greek Islands. I have forgotten what it was.* Well, the <u>Idaho</u> was a very fine little ship; there's no question about that. The Navy Department sent the USS <u>Maine</u> to the Mediterranean to pick up the crew of the <u>Idaho</u> (which would be replaced by the Greek crew) and also us midshipmen. And there we were. We were there when the war broke on the fourth of August, in the harbor of Villefranche. Meanwhile, we had a very interesting time; we had gone up to Rome. All of the American midshipmen had an audience with the Pope, and we really saw lots of wonderful things.

Q: Did you do your duty and look up all the places that your father had told you to see?

Admiral McCrea: Yes, I did. I did the best I could. I stood there in the ruins of the Colosseum, looking in all directions and hoisting aboard everything I could think of. I wrote to my father about all that, but he died on the 21st day of July, and he never did get the letter that I wrote him. He was dead for six weeks before I ever found out anything about it. We had no mail; we had no anything. My mother sent a dispatch to the Navy Department, but it never drifted through to me, so I didn't know anything

---
*Her Greek name was <u>Kilkis</u>.

about my father's death for some seven weeks.

Q: Because of the outbreak of hostilities, I suppose?

Admiral McCrea: Sure. The other two ships that were in our squadron carried out the rest of their itinerary and were in England when war broke out. We were kept down in the Mediterranean, ostensibly to await the arrival of the Tennessee. The Tennessee was one of the big cruisers of the time, and she went to Europe loaded with gold to rescue all these stranded American tourists who were in Europe. There it was. It certainly was interesting. When the Greeks came there in Villefranche, we turned the Idaho over to them and then we went on board USS Maine.*

Q: That must have been an interesting ceremony.

Admiral McCrea: Yes, and I'll tell you about that ceremony too.

The ship was sold to the New York Shipbuilding Company by the United States Government. Someplace in one of my boxes I have the last log of the USS Idaho. I was assistant navigator, and William A. Glassford, who later got to be a flag officer and was an outstanding flag

---

*The USS Idaho (BB-24) was decommissioned at Villefranche, France, on 30 July 1914.

officer in the Navy, was the navigator.* I was his assistant, so I wrote the log in longhand as we wrote in those days. They didn't have typewriters to write the log as they do now. I'm trying to think of the fellow who represented the New York Shipbuilding Company. When we struck our flag, the captain turned to this chap and he said, "The ship is now yours."

And this chap said, "Well, now you know this is a wonderful occasion as far as I am concerned, and I came on board this ship prepared for it." He reached down and pulled up a briefcase and put it on the table in the captain's cabin and opened up this handbag. Out came four or five bottles of whiskey. And he said--of course by that time, the first of July in 1914, the Navy was dry, absolutely. "But here," he said, "this is my ship and I am inviting you naval officers [waving his hand at us and the Greeks] to have a glass with me."

I remember Bill Glassford--here I was standing there a midshipman, and midshipmen weren't supposed to drink, and Glassford said, "You'd better get a little sip, at any rate."

And that was that. It was an interesting experience. When they got through having their drinks, then the New York Shipbuilding fellow turned it over to the Greek captain and we were gone.

---
*Lieutenant William A. Glassford, Jr., USN.

J. L. McCrea #1 - 30

In the <u>Maine</u>, we went to Gibraltar. The war was on, of course, and the British didn't like us being there at all. We lost an anchor in Gibraltar. Well, we had to recover that anchor. I was a first-class midshipman, and I was a boat officer in this effort. We knew just about where the anchor was lying, and we knew that the chain was out pretty far. The links didn't drop all in one pile or anything like that.

Q: The currents are very strong there, aren't they?

Admiral McCrea: Yes. So I had this kedge anchor with a line attached to it and trailed--went back and forth across this area, hoping we would hook our chain with the kedge. Well, we hooked two or three chains that we thought were ours and pulled them up, and they weren't that at all. They had been there for God knows how many years, and with each one the British would send out a tug. And they would take the chain and heave around and finally they would recover some old-fashioned anchor with a wooden stock and all that sort of thing, and there it was.

Well, ultimately we got our own chain, and I hooked this damn thing. I suppose I was two or three days working on this effort, and each time we were hooked up to something like that, we had to stop everything and start heaving in by hand as much as you could. Well, then the

British tug would come alongside and take the chain away from you, take the bight of the chain away. So sure enough, we ultimately got our own chain; we got it back on board the USS Maine.

We were being provisioned by the British. They didn't have any provisions to spare, so we finally moved over to Tangiers, and there is where we stayed until the Tennessee arrived in European waters.

Q: You were being a drain on the British, I suppose.

Admiral McCrea: Yes, it was definitely a drain on their supplies.

One thing I did get to see, though, I saw a bullfight on a Sunday afternoon--one of the great bullfighters of all time was Belmonte.* He was the star performer, he was the Ty Cobb of bullfighters.**

We got down to Horta Horta in the Azores, and there we had to fuel. We got coal there to help us get back.

Q: By that time you didn't have to take part . . .

Admiral McCrea: We were supposed to be back in the United

---

*Spanish bullfighter Juan Belmonte (1892-1962). For a biography, see Henry Baerlein, Belmonte the Matador (New York: Harrison Smith & Robert Haas, Inc., 1934).
**Tyrus R. Cobb played baseball for the Detroit Tigers at that time. He had the highest lifetime batting average in baseball history.

J. L. McCrea #1 - 32

States. We didn't arrive back in the United States until about the 12th or 14th of September. And, of course, that was cutting into our leave period, which was supposed to be the month of September. Of course, a lot of these young midshipmen, and I suppose I helped them out in a way; we thought that we were being discriminated against as our leave was being cut short.

Q: Did you get back home then, to Michigan?

Admiral McCrea: Oh yes, I got back home to Michigan.

Q: And that's when you discovered that your father had died?

Admiral McCrea: Well, no, we got mail at Norfolk, and it was the first mail we had in almost two months. And I was going through my mother's letters, and I came across this letter and she said that everything seemed so lonesome. I knew from the tone of her letter that something had happened, and I went to the executive officer. We were on our way from Norfolk up to Annapolis. Commander Hugo Osterhaus said to me, "Directly we get to Annapolis, you go ashore in the first boat."* (I had told him I would like

---

*Lieutenant Commander Hugo W. Osterhaus, USN.

J. L. McCrea #1 - 33

to get in touch with my mother.) The midshipmen were not going to be disembarked until the following day, and he said, "The boat will wait in there until you get up and get a telegram off to your mother."

So I went ashore and got a telegram off to my mother, and I had an answer that my father died on the 21st of July. I went back to the ship and Hugo Osterhaus--I'll never forget that fellow; he was supposed to be a very tough, hard-bitten guy. And he said, "Look, young man, you get ready to leave the ship tomorrow morning. The moment the first boat goes ashore, I will have my mess boy look out for your bag and hammock and all that sort of stuff and see that it gets delivered to Bancroft Hall. You go on home just as fast as you can."

I have never forgotten the kindness of that fellow. I still have his last letter to me, which was written 25 or 30 years ago.

Q: He got to be quite a well-known naval officer.

Admiral McCrea: He had a son who was born that summer while he was away, and he later got to be a captain in the Navy and then he died a number of years ago. Of course, all that is a non sequitur; nevertheless, I'll never forget old Hugo Osterhaus's kindness to me, chasing me off the ship to get home as fast as I could.

J. L. McCrea #1 - 34

Well, that brings me up almost to . . .

Q: To the graduation and to your first tour of duty.

Admiral McCrea: Yes, all right. Well now, when I graduated--for my first class year the assignment of company officers had always been a problem to the Naval Academy, and they decided that for the first nine months of the academic year they would rotate the midshipmen officers, and I was given three stripes on that first rotation. The last three months of the year, there would be another assignment of midshipmen officers. It so happened that I was given the three stripes again; I had the Eighth Company.

Now as far as you remarked earlier about athletics, I liked athletics. I always aspired to be good at them, but I just never had the coordination of mind and muscle necessary for a good athlete for some reason or other. I was elected by my class to be the assistant manager for the football team, which was considered a good job. It meant that you would be the manager your first-class year. It just so happened that I always had trouble with the Frenchmen--they couldn't understand my French and I never understood theirs. And, as a matter of fact, that combination of circumstances damn near kept me from being a naval officer, because I spent more time trying to

J. L. McCrea #1 - 35

understand those Frenchmen, to no avail, and when I should be putting that time in another naval subject. It just so happened that the commandant disapproved of my being elected assistant manager of the football team, because I was "unsat" as they called it--unsatisfactory in French.

Q: And it would take you away from your French books.

Admiral McCrea: It was taking me away from the French books, so there it was; I finally got clear of the Frenchmen. I got a 2.6 or 2.17, something like that that helped me get out of their clutches. Well, by that time, of course, one of my great interests in athletics had been baseball, so I was elected assistant manager for baseball, and that stuck because I was clear. I was no longer unsatisfactory in the subject. So that's the way I wound up; I was the manager of the baseball team first-class year.

Q: What was the status of athletics at the academy in that time?

Admiral McCrea: Well, the status of athletics was most interesting. I somehow have got myself around to the point that I agree more or less with my father about athletics. But to the young, athletics seemed most important around a

J. L. McCrea #1 - 36

college campus. Sometimes it is a damn sight more important than even staying in the school is concerned. However, I liked it; I liked it and I still think it probably has a place. I just saw in this morning's paper, the morning Globe, that the Ivy Leagues are going to clean up their performances on the field. Did you see it this morning?

Q: I saw it in The New York Times, yes.

Admiral McCrea: Well, this morning's paper stated that they had to clean up what they have been doing with their recruiting of athletes and their bands and other fields with their athletics and all that sort of thing--that the parents and even the students are protesting the length to which collegiate athletics have gone.

Q: Somewhat pornographic, I think.

Admiral McCrea: That's right.

Well, being the manager of the baseball team, I fell in with one character that I could never forget; his name was Nick Altrock. I don't know if you remember Nick Altrock. Well, Nick Altrock was a great pitcher for the Chicago White Sox way back in the early 1900s. He was then working for Clark Griffith, who owned the Washington

Senators, and the Washington Senators were a poor club.

The big league clubs were just at that time starting to go south for their training season. Griffith, for the Washington Senators, could never get any farther south than Charlottesville, Virginia, or someplace like that. Nick Altrock was his pitchers' coach. We wanted to get Nick to coach our midshipmen pitchers. The deal worked out so that Nick came down to Annapolis, and he lived in Bancroft Hall.* And he brought down two or three pitchers with him, and they lived out in Carvel Hall, and he worked out with them every forenoon in the Naval Academy armory.** And then in the afternoon after classes were over, Nick worked out with the midshipmen.

Well, Nick was a great character, just one of the greatest of all time. I think I could have stood a lot better in my class if I could have kept Nick out of my room, or if I could have kept myself out of Nick's room, because he lived in Bancroft Hall. And he would sit there and fascinate me with the stories he would tell about his early days as a professional baseball player. He was a cobbler in Cincinnati; mind you, a cobbler, but he had this great talent being a left-handed pitcher, and he was one of

---
*Bancroft Hall is the Naval Academy dormitory.
**Carvel Hall was a hotel across King George Street from the Naval Academy.

J. L. McCrea #1 - 38

the great stars of all times--this cobbler.

He had one of the ugliest "physiogs" you ever saw in your life. One day, he said to me, "Listen, I have a doll over in Washington; I'd like her to see the Naval Academy. Oh, she's a nice girl. She's a hairdresser; she's my doll. Could I bring her over here some time?"

And I said, "Why sure, Nick, bring her over."

He brought her over and he introduced me to her and introduced the coach to her too--later Rear Admiral Theobald.* That summer of 1914, I was abroad and I picked up a copy of the Paris edition of the New York Herald, and down in a little corner of the paper was a small headline which originated in Washington, "Handsome Nick Altrock Takes a Bride." And it was a story about him marrying the doll from Washington.

After I left the Naval Academy and whenever I went back to Washington--and Nick was still there for years with Clark Griffith--I always looked up Nick and we would have a beer together and reminisce. He was a great person, that fellow.

And now for a non sequitur if there ever was one. I was in charge of division three in the New York. My turret captain was an enlisted man--a strapping, well-built person by the name of Gustave Adolph Schleuter. He was from Cincinnati. He and Nick were first cousins. What a

---
*Lieutenant Robert A. Theobald, USN.

happenchance!

Q: What was the system with the athletics and the athletic program at the academy in those days? Was the program largely supported by the football team?

Admiral McCrea: Pretty much so, yes. And, of course, they charged the midshipmen--they had some requirement. I have forgotten what the membership fee for the Athletic Association was--$10.00, $15.00, or $20.00.

Q: Tell me something about hazing in your time.

Admiral McCrea: Well, it never amounted to much as far as I could see. Some people, I thought, went to some extremes, but it never bothered me. The only thing that one had to worry about, I guess, was getting caught. One of the finest men that I ever knew in the Navy was dismissed; his name was Walter J. Tigan. He rowed on the plebe crew along with me, and he was dismissed because some discipline officer caught him standing a plebe on his head. That was the favorite thing; upperclassmen would bust into your room and say, "On your head, mister," or something like that, and up one went.

Plebes always walked down the middle of the corridor. A plebe never went in the corridor without being in full uniform. It wasn't too bad; I never thought too badly about it. But this fellow Tigan--he was later killed in France--and years later the letters that he wrote home from France were published in one of the women's magazines or something like that, like possibly the Ladies Home Journal.* They were wonderful letters.

I walked out to the gate with him when he was being kicked out that night, because we had been close friends and we lived in the same company. I felt so sorry about it all, because he would have made a topflight officer, no question about it. He came from Illinois.

Q: But the rules were strict.

Admiral McCrea: The rules were strict and enforced; that's all there was to it.

Q: Well, you came to graduation, and did you have a choice of your tour of duty?

Admiral McCrea: Yes. That is another thing that interested me. When graduation was approaching, one could put in for a particular ship. The classes were small in those days--there were only 179 in my class at graduation, and a number of them failed physically right at the end.

―――――――――
*Tigan died 19 July 1918.

Their eyes had gone bad on them or something like that. I have forgotten exactly how many were dropped right at the graduation. But groups of midshipmen would say, "Well, let's go to such and such a ship."

Well, I wanted to go to a new ship. A number of people, close friends of mine, would say, "You don't want to go to a New York ship; you ought to go to, say, a Norfolk ship"--which was the home port for them. The USS New York and the USS Texas were the two latest ships in the fleet, and I thought it would be a good thing to go to the very latest. Four or five of us who had been associated with baseball--the team captain (an outstanding catcher), one of its pitchers, the second baseman, and I, as the manager--we all knew each other well, and so we decided we would go to the New York. We put in for it, and we got it and away we went.

I was in the New York for four years, a little over four years, and in that time I had five captains. Four of those five captains got to be flag officers. Two of them went to the top--Charles F. Hughes and William Veazie Pratt, both were chiefs of Naval Operations.* Hugh Rodman, who as a rear admiral commanded our six battleships assigned to the British Grand Fleet, was made a four-star

---

*Admiral Charles F. Hughes, USN, was Chief of Naval Operations from November 1927 to September 1930; Admiral William V. Pratt, USN, was Chief of Naval Operations from September 1930 to June 1933.

admiral and given command of the Pacific Fleet.* I went with him as an aide when he went to the Pacific Fleet.

Well, service in the New York was interesting; it was just as interesting as it could be to go to this new ship and meet up with its older officers. I enjoyed it greatly.

Q: And your tour on board ship, your assignments were different all the time. Weren't you rotated?

Admiral McCrea: Yes, and, of course, our ship the New York--Admiral Rodman, when he left us--he was a captain. Then he went ashore to the General Board in Washington, and then he came back to us as a flag officer.** He was given command of what the British called the Sixth Battle Squadron of the Grand Fleet. He came to the New York and he used that as his flagship. We joined the Grand Fleet in the fall of 1917, and we were there until the surrender of the German Fleet and a little afterward.

It just so happened that there were three officers that stood all the deck watches at sea in the New York when we were in the North Sea, because whenever we went to sea, we always went prepared for action. And the three of us--

---
*Admiral Hugh Rodman, USN, was Commander in Chief Pacific Fleet, 1919-1922.
**Rodman served on the General Board in 1916-17. The board, comprised of a number of senior flag officers, existed to set strategy and policy for the Navy. Among other things, it was concerned with establishing characteristics for new warships.

J. L. McCrea #1 - 43

the three watch officers--stood watches and I was the junior one of the three. It just so happened--I suppose the golfers would call it the rub of the green--but it just so happened that the German Fleet surrendered on my watch, and I had not only the duty but the privilege of writing the log of the surrender of the German Fleet. I think I have a copy. Would you like it?

Q: Yes, I would indeed. Were you home-ported at Scapa?

Admiral McCrea: We based in Scapa and, of course, every once in a while we went down to Rosyth, which was right off Edinburgh. David Beatty took us down there once.*

Q: Tell me about some of your experiences during that time on the New York. It was also the time of the great flu epidemic, wasn't it?

Admiral McCrea: Yes, we had a hell of a time with that. We lost something around 14 or 15 people, including a couple of officers, with the flu. Some of the ships had much heavier concentrations--a much larger number of flu victims--but they didn't lose nearly as many as we did, and we had a comparatively small incidence of the epidemic, but it was bad.

---
*Vice Admiral David Beatty, Royal Navy.

Q: Did you contract it?

Admiral McCrea: Yes, but I got mine in May of 1918 for some reason or other, and the doctor said, "You must have Spanish influenza." Well, I was really sick, but much to my amazement, in the fall of 1918 when things really got bad, I didn't have a recurrence.

Q: You had probably acquired an immunity in May.

Admiral McCrea: The impact of the flu on the Grand Fleet was most pronounced. If the German High Seas Fleet had chosen to make a North Sea raid during September and October of 1918, the results could have been disastrous for the Grand Fleet. Some of the largest ships were virtually immobilized and had to have tugs provide steam to provide essential services. It was bad, bad, I can tell you.

Q: You were talking about Admiral Hustvedt*.

Admiral McCrea: Hustvedt was my commanding officer.

Q: Oh, he was?

---

*Rear Admiral Olaf M. Hustvedt, USN, was the subject of a Naval Institute oral history conducted by Dr. Mason. Admiral McCrea talks of him later in this transcript.

Admiral McCrea: Yes, as a flag officer, I carried his flag in the Iowa for some time.

Q: That was in the Pacific? He was with the fleet units in World War I.

Admiral McCrea: I am just trying to think what ship he was in. He was with Admiral Fechteler in the New York at one time, and Fechteler was detached and Rodman came on board when we were going to the North Sea.* Of course, Fechteler resented that greatly, but, unfortunately, Admiral Fechteler had been born in Prussia.

Q: He was the father of Bill Fechteler.**

Admiral McCrea: Yes, he was the father of Bill. I always liked the old man greatly. I have never known anybody who took more interest in the little things about the ship. I remember particularly in the summer of 1917, of course, before we went abroad. When the ship was at anchor anyplace, he would step through the door of his cabin about five minutes of 8:00 in the morning and take a good, deep

---
*Rear Admiral Augustus F. Fechteler, USN, Commander Battleship Division Six.
**Admiral William M. Fechteler, USN, was Chief of Naval Operations from 1951 to 1953.

breath of fresh air, then look aft, and he would stay there for morning colors. And when the band sounded off to play the "Star-Spangled Banner," the old man would stand there at salute while this was going on, and with the last note he would finish his salute, walk into the cabin, and have his breakfast. I remember him coming out there time and time again when I was a young watch officer to talk to the officer of the deck.

His wife was a very attractive person; they had these kids, two sons--both of them got to be naval officers--and three girls. At least one of the girls, maybe two, married naval officers. Mrs. Fechteler was the daughter of Judge Morrow, who was a United States District Judge in the California area. I have forgotten the name of that judicial circuit out there, the number of it, maybe the 12th. At any rate, she was most attractive. Old man Fechteler--Bill often told me, "There was discipline in my family. We sort of dreaded seeing him come back from at sea, because he would sit up there and preside at the table."

Q: Did you have anything to do with some of the other fleet units over there--American units?

Admiral McCrea: Oh yes, we had six battleships over there, and it was very interesting to be with them. We were all coal burners; that's one thing. The British used Welsh coal--the ones that were coal burners. Of course, they had a limited supply of oil. The New York and Texas could burn either oil or coal, but, of course, the operation was limited to beat everything.

Q: You had to be very concerned about submarines, didn't you?

Admiral McCrea: You know, you spoke about the New York, and I rushed back aways--our executive officer in the New York, when I joined her, was Leigh Palmer, and Leigh Palmer was my ideal of a naval officer.* He was brilliant, a gentleman from the word go, handsome, and just as thoughtful as could be about the ship and about the people in the ship.

One day, the executive officer sent for me, right after luncheon, and he said, "This afternoon we are going to have a distinguished visitor on board this ship, and your division officer is on leave. [This was just before Christmas.] I want you to be prepared to take Mr. Thomas A. Edison into your turret. He is working on a stainless steel--erosionless steel--and he wants to see the interior of guns that have been fired to see how they have been

---

*Commander Leigh C. Palmer, USN.

corroded."*

The <u>Texas</u> and ourselves were the only two 14-inchers in the fleet at the time. Well, Mr. Edison came on board, and I had prompted the turret's crew to be there. And we all crawled into the turret and opened a breech plug, and Mr. Edison sat on a stool. We opened the breech of the gun so he could see it all, and he broke out a microscope that he had in his pocket and he was looking all around everything to see, with particular reference to the breech plug itself. Mr. Edison was difficult to talk to because he was deaf.

After we got through with that, the executive officer said that he wanted to see the ship, so I took him all over the ship. Dr. Miller Reese Hutchinson was with him, and Hutchinson was this very important scientist in his employ. I have forgotten his exact relationship to Mr. Edison, but that was his name, Miller Reese Hutchinson. Well, we went down below deck and answered him as best as we could, talking into his ear trumpet. He spotted a Christmas box outside of the canteen there, and he said, "What's this?"

And I told him this box was right outside of the canteen, and the kids were encouraged to put their small change in there, because we always gave a Christmas party for orphans at the time. I remember he listened very

---

*Thomas A. Edison was a noted American inventor, credited with the development of the light bulb and phonograph, among many other things. He was involved in experimental scientific work for the Navy during World War I.

intently and then he turned to Mr. Hutchinson and he said, "Miller, put $10.00 in the box."

So after we had seen the ship, the executive had sent word that he would like to have tea in his cabin. I was included in the tea, and up we went. Well, we got up on deck just about the time--the ship was in the New York Navy Yard--and he was about to leave the ship. And somebody--I haven't the remotest idea now who it was--said, "Mr. Edison, what do you think about Henry Ford and what he is doing about getting the boys out of the trenches by Christmas?"

And Mr. Edison said, "What did you say?" He sort of shrieked it.

Q: Did he have one of those horns?

Admiral McCrea: He had something, but I've forgotten what it was. And Mr. Edison just looked off, and then he held up his hand and sort of waved it gently and said, "You know, Henry is crazy as hell."

Q: They were good friends.

Admiral McCrea: Wonderful friends; you see, they went on all these camping trips with Harvey Firestone and what was the name of the great Californian?*

Q: Luther Burbank.

Admiral McCrea: Yes, Luther Burbank.** Well, I have never forgotten Mr. Edison.

The years passed, and years passed. I find myself the executive officer of the USS Pennsylvania, which was the fleet flagship. I went there in 1938 and came out in September of 1940--just a couple of months short of two years. One day the Secretary of the Navy, Mr. Charles Edison, came on board the Pennsylvania.***

Q: He also was deaf, wasn't he?

Admiral McCrea: More or less, yes. He went to sea with us on a fleet problem seeking to familiarize himself with what the ship did. Well, as executive officer, I was the senior officer of the wardroom mess. So I got in touch with Mr.

---

*Harvey S. Firestone was an American industrialist who organized the Firestone Tire & Rubber Company in 1900. He served as the company's president, 1903-32, and chairman of the board, 1932-38.
**Luther Burbank was a noted horticulturist. He was credited with developing improved varieties of a number of fruits and vegetables.
***Charles Edison was Secretary of the Navy from 2 January 1940 to 24 June 1940. He had previously been Acting Secretary during the terminal illness of his predecessor, Claude A. Swanson.

J. L. McCrea #1 - 51

Edison's party and invited them to have dinner in the wardroom with us, which they accepted. Mr. Edison sat on my right, so I had the pleasure of telling Mr. Edison the story about his father saying that Henry was as crazy as hell. And he had a good laugh out of that.

Q: Now we are going to hear about your duty on the New Mexico, the battleship New Mexico, which occurred . . .

Admiral McCrea: Well, it was just by one of these things that come to you every so often in the Navy--you never know what is right around the corner. I had the forenoon watch one fine morning about the middle or the latter part of May, or it may have been in June--I'm still on the battleship New York--and we were at anchor in Hampton Roads, Virginia. The morning New York Times had carried the information that Admiral Rodman was being made a four-star admiral, and he was going to go and command the Pacific Fleet. A boat came alongside, and Admiral Rodman came up over the side, and I saluted smartly and said, "Congratulations, Admiral, on your fine new job."

His answer to me was, "Have you another pair of socks?"

"Yes, sir," said I.

"Well, where are they?"

J. L. McCrea #1 - 52

Q: Did you make the connection in your own mind at that point?

Admiral McCrea: No.

"Where are they?"

"Well, they may be in the laundry." I was just giving him a smart answer, see.

"Well," he said, "send for them, because I am going to be Commander in Chief of the Pacific Fleet, and you are going as my aide for personnel."

"Thank you, sir, but I'd like to think it over."

Well, that afternoon the executive officer of the New York sent for me and he said, "I just saw Admiral Rodman on deck, and he told me he had told you this morning that he wanted you to go with him as his aide for personnel to the Pacific Fleet when he went as Commander in Chief, and that you said you would like to think it over."

I said, "That's right, Commander Belknap."

He said, "Listen, you don't have to take my advice, but let me tell you something. After every war there is always a period of consolidation in the Navy and people mark time for the most part. My suggestion to you is that if you can do so, mark time on the staff of the Commander in Chief of the Pacific Fleet." I thanked him and withdrew.

J. L. McCrea #1 - 53

Q: Was that Reggie Belknap?

Admiral McCrea: No, it was Charles Belknap.*

So, in mid-summer of 1919 Admiral Rodman hoisted his flag as commander in chief in the New York Navy Yard on board New Mexico. New Mexico was the first electric drive battleship. We moved over there and in a couple of days started for the Pacific to assemble the fleet in those waters. I was there for two years with Admiral Rodman, and it was a delightful assignment.

Q: What else did New Mexico have in the way of innovations?

Admiral McCrea: Of course, all of the gunnery department was well up to date; it was a brand-new ship, but the innovation that attracted attention throughout the shipping world was the fact that she was an electric drive ship and the first.

Q: And she had 14-inch guns?

Admiral McCrea: And we had 14-inch guns.

Q: Tell me about your experiences during those two years.

*Commander Charles Belknap, Jr., USN. Belknap resigned his commission as an active naval officer in late 1919.

J. L. McCrea #1 - 54

You must have learned a lot.

Admiral McCrea: Well, we did on the Pacific Coast, when we got out there, what Admiral Rodman called a flower show-- going from port to port, showing the flag, and people were seeing the battleships on the West Coast for the first time in many, many years and nothing as modern as the <u>New Mexico</u>. It was a low point in the Navy, too, because it was with great difficulty that we got the ships assigned to the Pacific Fleet, from the Atlantic to the Pacific, because of personnel problems.

Q: It was hard to keep a complement.

Admiral McCrea: That's just the point.

We went up to Washington one day, and Admiral Rodman talked to the chief of personnel about the personnel problem, and they said they were just carrying out the orders of the Secretary. So the admiral then said to Mr. Daniels, "Mr. Secretary, we cannot take this fleet to the West Coast if all these orders, which are being issued to discharge people because the war is over, are carried out."*

And Mr. Daniels said, "I want them all discharged."

---
*Josephus Daniels was Secretary of the Navy from 5 March 1913 to 5 March 1921.

And Admiral Rodman said, "Very well. If we discharge everybody that is due to be discharged, the ships will never get to the West Coast. That's all there is to it."

Finally, Mr. Daniels stood up from behind his desk and looked out the window, then he turned around and said, "Rodman, get the ships to the West Coast and then discharge the men."

So that was what happened. We went to the West Coast and then right away we got an extension of that order, because Admiral Rodman said, "If we bring these ships out here and they are not seen because we haven't got men enough to man them, that's going to be a blow to the Navy that will take a long time to recover." Then he said, "We are merely carrying out, Mr. Secretary, the order that you have issued here that we are to show these ships on the West Coast. When we get through with doing that, we will secure the ships someplace and discharge the people, and that's all there is to it."

And that's the way it worked out.

Q: So demobilization after World War I was somewhat different from World War II?

Admiral McCrea: Yes, it was. At that time, by the end of World War II, people had gotten more or less used to the fact that ships were really sensitive things, and to lay up a ship was really a time-consuming and a most important job. And we were finally able to do it despite the fact that Mr. Drew Pearson and some of the rest of the columnists were raising a great hoorah that ships were just being kept in commission to give naval officers--both flag and command rank--a place to operate from. But it was done pretty successfully.

Q: With those limitations, how was Admiral Rodman able to carry on in the Pacific?

Admiral McCrea: Well, when we got through the parade up the West Coast, and this was topped off by President Woodrow Wilson coming to Seattle on behalf of the League of Nations, and being there when we were there, this shortly before his collapse in Colorado.*

The cruise having been concluded, the ships came back to Southern California for the most part. Some of the battleships tied up in the Bremerton Navy Yard. The more recent battleships stayed in the Long Beach area. The destroyers went to San Diego and were decommissioned and the men discharged in that area. Because the weather in

---

*Thomas Woodrow Wilson was President of the United States, 1913-1921. In the wake of World War I, the victorious nations developed a League of Nations, comparable to the later United Nations. Wilson drove himself to exhaustion in a cross-country campaign to sell the peace treaty and League of Nations to the people of the United States. His campaign was ultimately unsuccessful and his health ruined.

J. L. McCrea #1 - 57

Southern California was easier on the ships as far as upkeep was concerned, the Southern California area was ideal for this purpose.

Q: And that's where, in effect, they were put into mothballs?

Admiral McCrea: Yes. Many of those destroyers that we laid up in that area were the ones that we traded to the British--the four-stackers--when the British needed help in World War II. Before we got into the war, we exchanged those four-stackers for bases in the Atlantic.

Q: Had we had any experience in mothballing ships up to that point, or was this something new to us?

Admiral McCrea: As far as I am aware of it, we had no experience about it, but we learned an awful lot. For instance, one of the destroyers that was put out of commission had recently been built and then sent down to San Diego. I put her out of commission--the USS Babbitt, 128, and there she hangs up there; my first command was to put that ship out of commission. It took me about three months to do it, and we did a fine job of it. I must say so because a year and a half later the Board of Inspection and Survey inspected the Babbitt, and I and a number of officers attached to the ship were given letters of commendation which were true as to the condition of the ship, which would not have been, so they said, had not the initial work of putting the ship out of commission been well and faithfully done.

Q: That certainly was a different kind of command, wasn't it?

Admiral McCrea: That's right, it was a different kind of command. And this letter, which I got, came as a complete surprise, because it was a year and a half after the event.

Q: Will you tell me about Admiral Rodman as a naval officer?

Admiral McCrea: I should start off by saying that you are liable to get a prejudiced opinion of Admiral Rodman. I thought he was tops. He stood academically in the Naval Academy toward the bottom of his class, but he was an amazing person. He had a wonderful sense of humor; he always had command of things. He could make up his mind to do something and do it quickly.

Q: That's an essential characteristic for a successful naval officer.

Admiral McCrea: That's right. And he was always able and ready to ride with his decision. I remember that an officer on our staff served on the staff of another flag officer who was senior to Admiral Rodman, and this officer of my acquaintance said to me one day that his service with Rodman was a great experience as far as he was concerned, especially so since he had served on the staff of an officer who was considerably senior to Rodman. He said, "Over here [referring to the New York] you always were doing something and doing it right up to the hilt. You may have not been doing the right thing, but you were doing it. Whereas the staff with which I have been more recently attached, nobody is ever quite sure what they are going to do or when it is going to be done. Consequently, it's greatly different than serving with Rodman."

Well, Rodman was amazingly outspoken, and I should say right here and now that Admiral Rodman and Admiral King, for whom I have a high, high regard, were shipmates in their younger days.* Admiral King despised Rodman, and told me so on a number of occasions. When he did, I would always point out to Admiral King what I regarded as Admiral Rodman's strong points.

Q: You were reading off tape from Walter Whitehill's book on Admiral King and reading some estimate of King's opinion

---
*Admiral Ernest J. King, USN, was Chief of Naval Operations and Commander in Chief U.S. Fleet in World War II.

J. L. McCrea #1 - 60

of Rodman, which had personal overtones, but overtones which you do not agree with.* And you served under Rodman very intimately.

Admiral McCrea: That's right, I did. And I admired him in many, many respects. Some of the things that he did from time to time I could not agree with. Naval officers are human beings, and as such, sometimes will do things with which one might not wholly agree. On the other hand, the balance was largely in Rodman's favor, as far as I was concerned. And I was given to telling Admiral King so. He was big enough to respect my point of view.

Q: And for a young officer this was an exceptional opportunity to learn, wasn't it?

Admiral McCrea: Well, hopefully something might brush off sometime on young fellows as they come along. Lots of time one comes up against a situation and one might casually wonder for the moment, "Now how would Rodman, or Hughes, or Pratt have handled the particular problem?" I think it is good to have that sort of background to think about once in a while.

---

*Ernest J. King and Walter Muir Whitehill, <u>Fleet Admiral King: A Naval Record</u> (New York: Norton, 1952).

J. L. McCrea #1 - 61

Q: So it was somewhat different from what Commander Belknap had said, that it would be marking time. It was an instructive marking time, was it not?

Admiral McCrea: Yes. Well, I missed going to destroyers when most of my class were going as executive officers when I was with Rodman on the New Mexico. As a matter of fact, one officer, a flag officer later, for whom I had great respect, told me that he had asked that I be sent to his ship as executive officer but that he would have to arrange with Admiral Rodman for my release. My friend told me, "I told him I wouldn't ask Admiral Rodman for anything." So, consequently, he had to get another executive. I did serve later with this officer, however, in a battleship.

In 1922, I was told by the Bureau of Navigation that I had to make arrangements about going to shore duty. I didn't want to go to shore duty, but they pointed out that I had been at sea for quite some time--longer than was usual for one of my rank--and that I should take the curse off that by going to shore duty.

I was offered the job of being an inspector of machinery at an undesignated place or recruiting officer in Indianapolis. Neither of these prospects had any appeal to me, and I said that I would like very much to do something else. One of my friends in the Navy Department said that a class was being assembled of junior officers at the Naval

J. L. McCrea #1 - 62

War College, and that was a one-year assignment and might not that appeal to me. I jumped at the idea of going to the Naval War College for one year.

Q: Was this a special class of some sort?

Admiral McCrea: That was the first of the junior classes, and I don't know how much longer they ran it. They had it there in my time, and I went there for a year and enjoyed it greatly.

Q: What was the particular emphasis in that year?

Admiral McCrea: The class was set up so precipitously, without too intensive planning, don't you see, and we virtually did everything in company with the senior class. Of course, we did junior jobs around there, but nevertheless, we, for the most part, did exactly what the senior class was doing. There were one or two dissertations that we did not have to come up with. It was the first time--as a matter of fact, I think the only time--in my naval career that I didn't have something to do with personnel. One was on one's own completely, as far as the study went, your reading went, and your writing, and all that sort of thing. And you didn't have anybody to look out for.

Well, toward the end of that I decided that it was a good thing to go abroad the following summer, if possible. We had destroyers in European waters and also in the Asiatic waters. And I wrote to the detail officer and told him I would like very much to go as the executive officer of a destroyer in European waters. I had a very cordial letter back which said that it could be arranged and would be arranged; the name of the destroyer to which I would go could not be given at the moment, but that I could be assured that upon the completion of my course at the War College that's where I would go.

About a month before I completed the course at the War College, I got a hasty note from the detail officer saying, in effect, that a contemporary of mine had been given the job in Europe which he had in mind for me. Well, I couldn't quite understand that, but, nevertheless, I realized that was the sort of thing one ran into every once in a while in the service. I later found out that it was one of the young White House aides that wanted the job in Europe, so I was welcome in any other place. So in a light and offhanded moment I said, "Let me go to the Asiatic; I think that would be a good place to go," which I did. I went and enjoyed it greatly.

Q: A certain amount of romance attached to the Asiatic, wasn't there?

Admiral McCrea: Yes, and when I got out there, I found myself in command of the USS Bittern, which was the large fleet minelayer, and, of course, a minesweeper. Well, the Bittern looked much like a tugboat.

Q: Was she a four-stacker?

Admiral McCrea: No, a single stack was all she sported. She wasn't a tugboat. For the most part, she looked like a tugboat, but wasn't equipped to be a tugboat. She was a single-stack, single-screw ship, reciprocating engines, and the propeller was too small. The rudder was too small for a towboat, and there it was. At the end of the year the detail officer on the staff of the Commander in Chief of the Asiatic Fleet, with whom I had been shipmates in the New York, sent a signal one day and asked me to come by the flagship, which I was pleased to do, and he wanted to know where I wanted to go. I said, "Am I being kicked off the Bittern?"

He said, "No."

And I said, "What have you got to offer me?"

"The exec of a destroyer or a river gunboat."

I said, "Look, Commander, I'm the captain of the Bittern. I prefer being the captain unless you are kicking me off. I want to stay there."

"Well," he said, "Do you like towing targets? Do you like towing barges?"

I said, "You are begging the question. What I am saying is I'm the captain there and I like that."

So he said, "If that's the way you want it, we'll leave you there." In consequence, I had two years command duty on the Asiatic station.

Q: For your record, that's fine, isn't it?

Admiral McCrea: It was as far as I was concerned. One fine October morning I got a signal from the chief of staff that he wanted to see me. I went over to the flagship, the USS <u>Huron</u>. His name was Captain E. B. Fenner, and he said, "We want a ship to go to Palembang, and I am curious to know whether you would like to go down there or not."

And I said, "Yes, sir, I would."

And then he said, "By the way, where is Palembang?"

I said, "I haven't the remotest idea, Captain Fenner, where it is, but I am willing to go."

So he said, "Well, that's the spirit." He then told me that a group of astronomers and mathematicians were coming out from the Naval Observatory in Washington and were bringing out much equipment--telescopes and this, that, and the other thing. Palembang was about 40 miles up the Musi River in the middle of Sumatra, and this group

J. L. McCrea #1 - 66

from the Naval Observatory was going there to set up an observatory in the hills of Sumatra from which they were going to make observations of the total eclipse of the sun, which was due sometime in mid-January 1925. I was to get them down there by mid-October, because it would take some time to set up this operation.

The whole thing appealed to me no end, and away I went, and I had a wonderful time, a wonderful time down there.

Q: Did you learn something about astronomy at that point?

Admiral McCrea: I didn't learn anything about astronomy, but first off, when this captain came on board--the captain of the mathematical corps--he came down there, and I said, "Well now, Captain, have any arrangements been made, as far as you know, about us going down there and setting up an observatory in the middle of the Dutch East Indies?"

"Well, it was all right in 1901 when we were down there last time."

And I said, "This is a long ways away from that; this is 1925."

So I immediately sent a dispatch to the Commander in Chief saying: "My passengers reported on board, but as far as I am concerned, they have no authority to go down there and set up this observatory in the middle of a Dutch

J. L. McCrea #1 - 67

possession. And I want to know if I am being kept in the dark in any way about this. If no permission has been obtained, it seems to me it should be done."

Q: You mean no permission from the Dutch officials?

Admiral McCrea: Yes. So right away they came back, and they pleaded innocent too; they didn't know anything about it. Then it was suggested that I get in touch with the Governor General of the Dutch East Indies. In that event, I said, "I suppose I shall have to go to Batavia before I go to Palembang." This was agreed, and I went down and got in touch with our consul general--a chap by the name of Mr. Hoover.* And he got me in to see the Dutch authorities, and they assured me it would be perfectly all right for our people to land there, and go up into the hills and set up this operation. It was done.

I had many misgivings about their operation. The captain of mathematicians was no doubt capable of chasing DY and DX all over the lot, but he had only vague ideas about organization. He had brought with him a working party of about 20 enlisted men of various ratings. The senior of this group was a chief boatswain's mate. I called the CBM in and told him substantially as follows: "Don't be overwhelmed by the captain's four stripes. If I

---
*Charles L. Hoover, U.S. consul in Batavia, Java.

read things rightly, you are going to be pretty much on your own. Take charge and look out for your men. You are going to have to be more aggressive than you have ever had to be in your entire career. Your survival and that of this mission is largely in your hands."

Months later, after the mission had been completed, I saw the CBM in Manila. He told me that my appraisal of observatory groups was correct. He found that the high rankers had to depend on the enlisted more and more.

"I," said he, "was the executive vice president."

Q: Now, your intervention there is a prime example of the naval officer acting as a diplomatic representative.

Admiral McCrea: Yes. Well, down there in Batavia I ran into the Dutch Minister of marine, who was an enormous man. He must have been six feet, seven or eight tall, and he was a most interesting character. Our consul general, in the presence of this Minister of Marine, remarked about this fellow, and he turned to me and he said, "Captain, would you believe it, he is a vegetarian; he has been a vegetarian for years. "And," added the Minister of Marine, "a teetotaler for 28 years." Of course, that sort of terrified me for a moment. There he was, right on the hoof, and apparently very proud of the fact that he had been a teetotaler for 28 years.

Well, it all worked out wonderfully well. I got over to Palembang and I called on the representative of the Minister of Marine and the resident governor and the burgermeister. The calls were returned with the exception of the burgermeister. So I waited a couple of days, and I got my executive up and I told him, "I want you to put on your best bib and tucker and sidearms and sword and go ashore to the burgermeister's office and tell him that I expect to leave the ship for a couple of days to go up into the interior [which, of course, wasn't so at all] and that I would hate to miss his return call."

Q: Teaching him his manners?

Admiral McCrea: The burgermeister called a couple of hours later, and that was that.

Q: Were the Dutch interested in this scientific expedition?

Admiral McCrea: Sure they were. The burgermeister must have been interested in a way, don't you know, but hell, here I was the skipper of an American ship close to his city and there it was. Well, the first thing I knew I was invited to a party given by the burgermeister at a very nice club. I went and met his wife and two charming daughters, and one thing and another, and the music struck up, and I noticed that everybody got up. So I got up, and faced the music and one thing and another, and when we sat down this charming young lady said to me, "And what is the name of that piece of music?"

I said, "You've got me there; I don't quite know, but I suppose it is the Dutch national anthem."

And she said, "Well, that's amazing that you don't know your own national anthem. That was your national anthem."

Of course, it wasn't at all, and so I made inquiry as to where they had gotten this. The burgermeister wrote me a very nice note; they didn't have a copy of the "Star-Spangled Banner" in the town, but there was an American missionary that lived about four or five miles up in the hills, and she had a hymnbook that had a copy of the "Star-Spangled Banner" in it. So she gave the book to her runner, putting a marker in the book where our national anthem was. The runner on the way into town stumped his toe and fell down. The marker fell out, and he picked it up and stuffed it in the book. So, as far as I know, it might have been "Throw Out the Lifeline," or whatever kind of hymn it was, but it certainly wasn't the "Star-Spangled Banner."

Q: But it was intended that way?

Admiral McCrea: It was intended that way, and that's the way I thought, but I had a good laugh about it, and every time I see a Dutchman I tell him about it. It was one of my favorite stories I used to tell to my Dutch friend in Washington who was Dutch Ambassador and was also a member of the Pacific War Council. I also had the pleasure of telling the story to Queen Juliana.* Has she abdicated?

Q: Yes, Beatrix is now the Queen.**

Admiral McCrea: I was in Hyde Park with President Roosevelt in the summer of 1942, and Queen Wilhelmina and Juliana and Juliana's two daughters came down from, where is it in western Massachusetts, Lenox, wasn't it?***

Q: I thought they lived in Canada.

Admiral McCrea: Oh, no, they lived principally in the United States. They spent a little time in Canada. They had a home near Lenox, Massachusetts. And they came down to Hyde Park for a long weekend. That night the President remarked to me, "John, this is a little job for you. Her

---
*Juliana was Queen of the Netherlands from 1948 until her abdication on 29 April 1980.
**Beatrix became Queen of the Netherlands on 30 April 1980.
***Hyde Park was President Roosevelt's home in New York State. Wilhelmina was Queen of the Netherlands from 1890 to 1948.

Majesty tells me that the Royal Princess is carrying her third child and that her doctor prescribes that she walk every forenoon and every afternoon for an hour. Will you accompany her and see that she gets her exercise?"

Of course, I was glad to do it. During the time that we walked and talked about one thing and another, I told her the story about the national anthem, and I asked her if she had ever been down in the Dutch East Indies, and she said no, but that she hoped to one day.

Then the President told me, while we were in Hyde Park, that the Queen had said to him, about as follows: "Once this war is out of the way, there is going to be a different setup between us and our colonies. It must come about."

If you will recall, shortly after the end of the Second World War, Wilhelmina abdicated and the news stories at the time were to the effect that her abdication was brought about because of a disagreement between her and her ministers. I remember that particularly. No one ever said what the subject was about which they disagreed, but I often wondered maybe it was making the change in the relationship with the government of the colonies. That is just something to contemplate without ever arriving at a conclusion.

When I put the Babbitt out of commission in San Diego, it was given a very thorough inspection, and I was sure in my own mind that we had done a good job of putting that ship out of commission. My division commander had thought it best to put the ship out of commission by having one crew, for instance, go through all the destroyers of the division and lay up (I just pick this piece of machinery out at random) the steering engine. He thought that that would be the better way of doing it.

I took a good, quick look around and saw one of these jobs that had been done, and I didn't like the looks of it. I went to him--his name was Commander Nathan W. Post--and I said, "Commander Post, we will continue to give our contribution to your work parties, but when they get to the Babbitt, will you please tell them to move right on over to the next ship? I want to lay up my own ship; I want to lay it up myself. I'll keep an eye on it, and I will guarantee you that it will be done right."*

And I did.

Q: He didn't object?

Admiral McCrea: He didn't object. I thought he would object, but he didn't. I said, "We will furnish our contribution to your work party, but when it comes to the Babbitt, we lay the ship up ourselves."

---

*Commander Nathan W. Post, USN, Commander Destroyer Division 14 and commanding officer of the USS Badger (DD-126), another ship in the division. The Babbitt (DD-128) was decommissioned at San Diego on 15 June 1922.

We did, and we got a hell of a good report out of it. The senior member of that board that examined the Babbitt remarked about it, to the effect how well the ship was laid up. And that senior member is now Walter S. Anderson, vice admiral (retired), who lives at a nursing home in Maryland near the Bethesda Naval Hospital.*

Q: I know Walter.

Admiral McCrea: He was a division commander of destroyers, and he sent word to me that he would like me to come to his ship as his executive.

Q: That was the recommendation, your decommissioning the Babbitt.

Admiral McCrea: Yes. Well, I got in the boat and went over and I told him, "Commander Anderson, I have just received a letter from the Navy Department that I am going to be the executive officer of the USS Ramapo. She is a Pacific oil tanker; there she is out in the Pacific right now. I think I would like that job."

He said, "So you don't want to serve with me?"

I said, "Commander Anderson, it isn't that at all; I

---

*Commander Walter Stratton Anderson, USN. Anderson's oral history is in the Columbia University collection.

would be glad to serve with you, but I have had difficulty in keeping at sea, which I want to do. And I am fearful if I raise the point, once I have been told that I am going to the Ramapo, that they won't like it in the bureau, and I don't know where I'll wind up. At the moment I want to go to the Ramapo."

We left it that way. In a couple of days I got orders to go to the Zeilin. I went over to the Zeilin, and I told the captain of the ship my story about the Ramapo, and within six weeks I was off the Zeilin and going on to Pearl Harbor to pick up the Ramapo. So my experience in the Zeilin wasn't very long.

Q: As a footnote, tell me about the future history of the Babbitt. Was she recommissioned?

Admiral McCrea: Yes, but I don't know what happened to her.*

Q: On the Ramapo, as an exec on an oiler, that wasn't a very exciting assignment, was it? Was it Asiatic Station?

Admiral McCrea: No, but I'll tell you what. We went all over the Pacific; we never got farther west than Midway,

---

*The Babbitt was recommissioned in 1930 and remained in active service until 1946. The ship was used for escort of convoys during World War II.

J. L. McCrea #1 - 76

but we went down the coast: from Port Arthur, Texas, to Panama, to Puget Sound and places like that. One of the delights of serving in the Ramapo was my skipper. His name was George Franklin Neal, and he was a wonderful chap with a fine sense of humor.* We would leave, say, San Pedro with a cargo of oil, and he would say to me, "John, set the course and call me in ten days."

Q: Well, he had great confidence in his exec, didn't he?

Admiral McCrea: One thing I had to do, and that was after lunch every day at sea, I had to provide three chaps to play two rubbers of bridge with my captain.

Q: That was a heavy duty. This was in the days before there was any attempt at refueling at sea, wasn't it?

Admiral McCrea: Yes. I was out there in the Pacific when all this was done in the USS Pennsylvania some 15 years later. In 1940 we put on a fine show for the Secretary of the Navy to let him see us refuel the destroyers at sea. We did a good job of that, and when I was in Iowa, we were operating in the Pacific. Every morning at first light, two destroyers would come up, one on either side of us, to get fuel--to get topped off. It was necessary to top the

---
*Commander George F. Neal, USN.

destroyers off to keep them fueled to capacity.

This little dog that you see over there [pointing to a picture] was in the *Iowa* with me. He belonged to my daughter, and he went back to the ship one day with me, and he just stayed there. Whenever the destroyers would come alongside in the morning to get oil, Vicky was always on deck to see if they had a dog over there. And if so, he would bark and bark and bark all the morning long, almost to the point of exhaustion, at the dog on the destroyer. He didn't have anybody to bark at on board the *Iowa*; he was there by himself.

Q: He was a little bored.

Admiral McCrea: I suppose so.

That plaque was given to me last June in Des Moines. It was made by a son of one of the men in the *Iowa*. We had the reunion of the *Iowa*, and the son of one of the men who served in *Iowa* came up with the burned wood drawing of Vicky. It's a good likeness.

J. L. McCrea #2 - 78

Interview Number 2 with Vice Admiral John L. McCrea
U. S. Navy (Retired)

Place: Admiral McCrea's home in Chestnut Hill, Massachusetts

Date: Tuesday, 26 October 1982

Interviewer: Paul Stillwell

Q: I'd like to begin this second interview session by asking what associations you had with John F. Kennedy.

Admiral McCrea: We had luncheon infrequently, maybe once every couple months or so, and one day I found myself sitting at the luncheon table, and alongside of me sat John Kennedy. He was at that time running for the House of Representatives.*

Q: This was right after World War II then?

Admiral McCrea: Well, it was a little after World War II. I think it was probably about 1954 or 1955, someplace in through there, and he started to talk about the service. Of course, I had known about his effort in the service, and it was a very good one, too, and the Navy was very proud of what he had done down there in the South Pacific. Then he

---
*John F. Kennedy, a Democrat, served in the U.S. House of Representatives from 1947 to 1953. In 1952 he was elected to the U.S. Senate and took office in 1953. He was reelected to the Senate in 1958 and elected to the presidency in 1960.

came down with this remark: he said that he had long thought that the service academies were not getting as students the brains to which these various institutions were entitled. And he said that he had given some thought to it, and he thought it would be a fine thing to hold a competitive examination nationwide on a given date, and that the people for West Point and the Naval Academy and the Coast Guard would be selected on the basis of these examinations.

Then he said, "What do you think about it?"

"Well," I said, "Mr. Kennedy, I don't agree with you at all, and I'll tell you why. I think that the armed forces should be close to the people. The way it is now, all the congressmen have appointments, and the senators have appointments, the President has appointments, and things like that. And I think that is the way to get the cross-section of the country. Now, let me go a little bit further. When I was a midshipman at the Naval Academy, it was known that a great many of the people who stood at the top of their classes came from the states of Massachusetts and Michigan. Now I come from Michigan, but I was the exception that proved the rule, because I graduated halfway down my class. All kinds of people who starred--stood around the top of their class--came from Massachusetts and Michigan. And, based on these competitive examinations that you suggest, conceivably it could wind up that everybody who went to the Naval Academy had come from Massachusetts or Michigan, and I don't think that's what you want at all."

Well, he just laughed about that and let it go. Time went on, and he finally got to the presidency. By that time, of course, I was a vice president of John Hancock, and Smedberg was Chief of the Bureau of Personnel, and I had served with him with Admiral Stark, and I knew him well.* I wrote "Smeddy" a note and told him just exactly about my conversation with Kennedy. I said, "Just keep your eye out; if this fellow is serious about it as he apparently was when he talked to me, he might come up with something like that."

Well, in due course, I guess it was six months that elapsed, and Smedberg wrote me a note. He said, "I guess you probably sold your point to him, because nothing has come from the White House to suggest that we change the method of appointing people to the service academies."

When I was a vice president of John Hancock, we gave a dinner one night to all the--I can't give the exact number of pints set down there, but we had this dinner for 400 or 500 people who had given blood in this amount, and we were

---

*John Hancock Mutual Life Insurance Company, for which Admiral McCrea worked after retiring from the Navy in 1953; Vice Admiral William R. Smedberg III, USN, was Chief of Naval Personnel from 1960 to 1964. When Smedberg was a lieutenant commander in 1941, he and McCrea served as aides to Admiral Harold R. Stark, USN, Chief of Naval Operations.

looking for somebody to make a talk. Well, one of our vice presidents was Robert E. Lee, and he came from Charlestown, and he knew the Kennedys very well.* And he said he could get John Kennedy to make a talk; he was sure of that.

I said, "Listen, Bobby, I don't think that we should make this a political event at all. If you can get him to make a talk which would avoid politics [he was right at that moment running], if you can assure that he is not going to get into politics, why, okay."

Bobby said, "Well, that's easy."

Well, I introduced Kennedy and as I sat down, he said to me, "Thank you, Admiral, for that generous introduction." I had sketched what he had done in the PT boat and all that, and he made a very fine talk without any reference to politics whatsoever. So that was my only contact--oh, yes, I did see him later too; I went to Washington.

When Ted Kennedy was made a senator, John Hancock had in its possession a painting by some marine artist.** I have forgotten who it was now, but he was of enough prominence that I should remember, but I don't recall his name, and it was a marine scene. The people in the front office up there arranged to have this copy of this painting

---
*Charlestown is an area of Boston. Located there for many years was the Boston Naval Shipyard, which was closed in the early 1970s.
**Edward M. Kennedy, younger brother of John F. Kennedy, has been a U.S. senator from Massachusetts since 1963.

that John Hancock had used in their national advertising campaign with reference to New England, and I went down there and presented it to young Ted Kennedy.

Meanwhile, I dashed over to the White House, because my former aide was over there at the time, and I was in the outer office there talking to some of the girls whom I knew who had been there when I was naval aide to the President. And out of the President's office came John Kennedy, and so we greeted each other there, and that was the last time I saw him.

Q: Who was your former aide that was on duty there?

Admiral McCrea: John Crehan, and he was a nephew of Judge Crehan, who was a local chap here, and Crehan had been in the class of 1946, I think it was, at the Naval Academy.* I think he was the same class as Jimmy Carter, if Jimmy Carter was the class of '46--I don't know whether that is so or not.

Q: I think Carter was '47, but graduated in '46.

Admiral McCrea: I'll tell you, Crehan had resigned from the Navy, and he had worked for a chap out in Chicago,

---

*John F. Crehan was in the Naval Academy's class of 1946, which was graduated in June 1945. He resigned from the Navy as a lieutenant (junior grade) in 1949.

whose name escapes me at the moment. Crehan came back as a reserve officer on active duty, and he was down at Newport. He came in to call on me one day, just after I got here, and he was wondering whether or not there was spot for him up here in this naval district, because it was closer to Boston and his family connections--his mother and sisters and all of them were living out here in Dorchester. The young man that I had inherited as a flag lieutenant was ordered to sea, so I took on Crehan.

Q: Well, Admiral, when Dr. Mason was here last year, he carried your career up to the point where you were in command of the Bittern, a minesweeper out on the Asiatic Station, so I think that would be a good point to resume this time. You mentioned to me during a previous visit that you encountered Admiral Kimmel during the course of that time you were commanding the ship.*

Admiral McCrea: Well, I better go back a little bit farther with Admiral Kimmel. The first time I ever fell in with him was in the North Sea, and it was right after my ship, the New York, had gotten up to the North Sea as one of our Sixth Battle Squadron, and we served, of course, as

---

*In the early 1920s, Commander Husband E. Kimmel, USN, served as commander of two destroyer divisions in the Asiatic Fleet. When the Japanese struck Pearl Harbor in December 1941, Admiral Kimmel was Commander in Chief Pacific Fleet.

I have pointed out earlier, with the Grand Fleet.* Kimmel was an ordnance expert, and he came over to pay a visit to us shortly after we arrived in the North Sea. He wanted to compare our gunnery and our gunnery practices with those of the British, so that's what happened. The next time I fell in with him was on Asiatic Station and he was out there as a commander and had command of a division of destroyers. His wife did not accompany him out there. I played golf with him many times, and he was an amazing golfer; he was left-handed and cross-handed at that. I wasn't very good, but we always had a nice match and we generally wound up having a glass of beer at the Army-Navy Club, which was just across the street from the 18th hole, 18th green.

One day when we were having our beer, he remarked again that Mrs. Kimmel was back in the United States, and he said, "For long enough, I have felt that we might one day be engaged in a naval war in the Pacific. I had never been out here. I didn't have the feel of the Asiatic Station, and I thought that I should get it. Mrs. Kimmel objected to coming out and away. She felt she should stay back in the United States to be near the boys that were in school, and we decided that as long as that's what I wanted to do--serve out here--that that's the plan we would carry

---

*The New York was one of the American warships that served with the British Grand Fleet during World War I.

out."

She, Mrs. Kimmel, of course, had a naval background; her father was an admiral in the Engineering Corps.

Q: Admiral Kinkaid.*

Admiral McCrea: His sister, young Tom Kinkaid's sister. Well, that struck me as most unusual at that time, about this man. He was so interested in the service, and he felt strongly that he should get the atmosphere of the Asiatic Station. And I thought it was a splendid thing for him to do, and I still think it was a splendid thing for him to do. Well, I followed his career pretty much. I remember he was executive officer of the <u>Arkansas</u>, and I used to see him around Long Beach--that was in earlier years when we first went to the Pacific, when I was with Admiral Rodman.**

Well, Stark sent me out to the Orient in November of 1940, and I went out there to take out the changes in war plans to the Commander in Chief of the U.S. Fleet, and also out to the Asiatic to take the changes in war plans out there, WPL-44, as I recall the number. While I was out there, a dispatch came through that Admiral Kimmel would

---

*Rear Admiral Thomas Wright Kinkaid, USN, was the father of Thomas Cassin Kinkaid, who achieved fame in World War II, and of Dorothy Kinkaid Kimmel.
**Admiral Hugh Rodman, USN, became Commander in Chief Pacific Fleet in 1919; McCrea was a member of his staff.

relieve Admiral Richardson some time in February of 1941, and right on the heels of that came another dispatch for me to be sure to contact Admiral Kimmel on my way back.* This came from Admiral Stark, and little Admiral Hart standing there pulled his neck inside his high collar and he said, "If Stark didn't think you had that much sense, he shouldn't have sent you out here in the first place."** Well, that was just a laugh, because that was just the way it went.

When I came back I fell in, of course, with Admiral Kimmel. And Admiral Richardson had a conference at which were all his staff and Kimmel. Then I accompanied Admiral Kimmel back to his flagship. We started to pace the deck, and as became one of my rank, I fell in on his left. He grabbed me by the arm and said, "I know you have manners enough to fall at my left, but that's my bad ear. Get around on my starboard side; my right ear is very good, and we'll get along much better."

My whole contact with Kimmel, I have a high regard for him. I don't know of anyone who worked harder at being a good naval officer than he did, and it was most unfortunate that the attack on Pearl Harbor came as it did. I have

---

*Admiral James O. Richardson, USN, Commander in Chief U.S. Fleet in 1940-1941.
**Admiral Thomas C. Hart, USN, was then Commander in Chief Asiatic Fleet. Admiral McCrea describes this trip in detail in "War Plans Under My Mattress," pages 98-105 of Air Raid: Pearl Harbor! Recollections of a Day of Infamy (Annapolis: Naval Institute Press, 1981).

long thought that he was destined that way; that's all there was to it. If we had had Horatio Nelson and Napoleon Bonaparte out there, I still think Pearl Harbor would have happened. The country wasn't ready for it at all, and I don't know how you could accuse anybody of not getting more war-conscious. When I was executive officer of the _Pennsylvania_, I was very war-conscious, because I had been in the _New York_ when we had gone over to join the British. And no sooner were we there than we recognized so many things about our ship that, if we had been more war-conscious, we would have caught up with. And I was constantly after these people aboard ship about thinking in terms of war.

In May of 1940, we went ashore one morning to attend a critique of the war game that had been played on the way out there to Pearl. And when we came back aboard ship, we were met at the gangway by George Dyer--now vice admiral retired--who was flag secretary to Admiral Richardson at the time, and he had this dispatch saying the fleet was to remain in the Hawaiian waters.* Well, all the goodbyes had been said. Everything was all ready to go for home, and to get an order to stay out there indefinitely interfered with a hell of a lot of personal plans. That afternoon late, two young officers were out in the passageway right outside my cabin, and I heard one talking

---
*Lieutenant Commander George C. Dyer, USN. Dyer's oral history is in the Naval Institute collection.

J. L. McCrea #2 - 88

to the other, and this chap said, "I don't think the people back there in the Navy Department know what they are doing." And he said it in a tone of voice loud enough so I could hear it inside my cabin.

I went to the door and I called these two young fellows in, and I said, "Now you two young fellows are not part of the ship's company. You belong to the commander in chief, but I don't think very much of you standing out here with the captain's orderly and the chief of staff's orderly and the admiral's orderly all within earshot of what you people are saying, and I think there is something missing in your officer qualities when you do that."

That night I sat there thinking about a lot of things, and the next day I called a conference of all the officers in the ship, closed the wardroom doors, and I started out like this: "The orders to stay out here, as of yesterday, come as no surprise to anyone who has thought in terms of eventualities." And I said, "More than ever it behooves us to get this ship ready for war. Every time you go through the ship now, in addition to looking out for little odds and ends and cleanliness and a few other things, is there something that you see that should be done in the event of hostilities?"

Well, that was briefly the way I attacked the problem. I told them that they had to bring themselves to the point where they would think in terms of war.

About an hour after the conference, I was sent for, and my captain said, "I hear you had a conference in the wardroom."

Q: Was this Captain Cutts?*

Admiral McCrea: Yes, and I said, "Yes, I did."

"What did you say?"

I told him what I had said, and he said, "John, I think you are taking too serious a view of this; we will be home by the first of June."

Well, the first of June came and went six times before we got home.

Q: That's right.

Admiral McCrea: I don't know whether Cutts ever forgave me for that; nevertheless, that's what happened, and I saw considerable of him after I left the Pennsylvania. As a matter of fact, I visited him when he was on his deathbed at the naval hospital in Chelsea.** I went over there and saw him a couple of times.

It was hard for people to think in terms of

---
*Captain Elwin F. Cutts, USN, commanding officer of the Pennsylvania.
**Cutts, who retired as a captain in 1946, died at Chelsea, Massachusetts, in 1965.

eventualities; that's all there was to it. And that's the way we live; I guess we just can't help it apparently.

Q: You said Kimmel came over to see a comparison of the British and American gunnery. What were the differences?

Admiral McCrea: Well, there were many differences. The reason that we were over there at all was because all the ships that were there could make their contract speed, which was 21½ knots. The British had been working the very life out of their ships, and for the most part their top speed, excepting for the Queen Elizabeth class, was down around 17 to 18 knots, and so we were given the job of being one of the fast wings of the Grand Fleet. The other fast wing was the Queen Elizabeth class of ships. That's the way it worked out.

The British are a great race of people, despite what Joe Kennedy thought about them.* It is hard for me to put my finger on it exactly, but they are just a great race, that's all. And with all their foibles and one thing and another, they have turned out some remarkable people in all walks of life. It doesn't make any difference whether

---

*Joseph P. Kennedy, Sr., was U.S. ambassador to the United Kingdom at the beginning of World War II. He was removed from that post by President Franklin D. Roosevelt, in part because the President didn't believe Ambassador Kennedy had sufficient confidence in Britain's ability to wage war successfully against Germany.

it is literature or music or in the military or what; they are just a great race of people.

Q: In what sense were the American ships not prepared when they went over for World War I with the Grand Fleet?

Admiral McCrea: I can't tell you exactly what went on in other ships, but I was quickly aware in the New York. When we got up there, many of the watertight doors didn't fit properly, because they had been opened and they had been hooked open and had been that way for years. All sorts of little odds and ends, all sorts of things that needed correction.

Q: She was a relatively new ship at that point, wasn't she?

Admiral McCrea: Well, the New York was commissioned in 1914, and she was a relatively new ship.

Here is another thing too. There was a young fellow by the name of Thomas Hallaran--Thomas Fellowes Gordon so and so Hallaran--he had about five names.* He was an amateur boxer and a good one and a rugger player, and he was quite a fellow, and he was a contemporary of mine. One night over a drink many years ago, he said, "You know,

---
*Acting Sub-lieutenant Charles Francis George Thomas Hallaran, RN.

McCrea, when you and I get to be commanders in chief of our respective fleets, and there is war between our countries, you know what I am going to do? I am just going to sit on my duff and let you fellows run yourselves to death, because you will, because that's the way you're given to. And when you have run yourselves to death, then I am going to come out and have a major ship engagement and win the war."

At the time, of course, we just laughed and it was something to laugh about; that's all there was to it. Well, when we broke off relations--when we were ordered out there to stay in Pearl Harbor, we immediately started running our aircraft lickety-split, all over the lot, up and down, up and down, and up and down. By the time when Pearl Harbor hit a year and a half later, the critics who come along here now complain about a lack of air patrol and all that sort of stuff--well, it was true, it was true. We had almost run ourselves out of the muscles.

Q: Kimmel worked the ships pretty hard during that period also.

Admiral McCrea: Well, sure. Everybody worked hard, see; everybody worked hard. It was, of course, an unfortunate thing to have happen, but it happened and some of the critics rally around and try to pin it on President Roosevelt and a whole lot of things. I can't believe that, because he wasn't that kind of man. I have also read recently, and not long ago, that Kimmel said that Stark perjured himself. I don't think that Stark was that kind of a man.

I don't know whether I told you about Kimmel coming on board the Iowa, did I?

Q: No, you didn't.

Admiral McCrea: Well, after Pearl Harbor, of course Kimmel was relieved, and he wrote a letter to Admiral Stark in longhand from the hotel in San Francisco, and if I recall rightly it was the Stewart Hotel, but I may be wrong in that respect. But it was written in longhand, and it ran something like this: "My detachment came as no surprise to me, because I was an unsuccessful commander." That was the theme of his letter.

In due course, Admiral Kimmel was retired, and he went to work for an engineering firm in New York headed up by a former classmate of his at the Naval Academy.* After we got Iowa in commission and we were down the bay at anchor off the narrows--and I knew Admiral Kimmel was in New

---

*Admiral Kimmel retired from active duty 1 March 1942. The battleship Iowa (BB-61), commanded by McCrea, went into commission 22 February 1943 at New York Navy Yard.

York--it occurred to me that he might like to see the ship. I called the executive officer in. He was going ashore that afternoon, and I couldn't go, and I said, "I wish you would go ashore and run down Admiral Kimmel. He is with the Harris Engineering firm, and invite him to lunch a couple of days hence [and I gave him the day] and tell him that there will be no one present excepting you, the executive officer, the gunnery officer, and myself."

The next morning when the executive officer came back, he said that Admiral Kimmel accepted, and so we had the boat in there to pick him up. He came over, and we had lunch, and we took him around the ship, and he went in the turrets and things like that. He was in civilian clothes; nobody knew him, and he left the ship about 4:30 that afternoon. At the gangway as he turned to leave the ship, he turned and he stuck out his hand and he said, "John, this is the nicest thing that has happened to me in a long, long while, and I am grateful to you for doing it."

I felt so damn sorry for the fellow, because I don't know of anybody who worked harder at trying to be a good naval officer. The cards were stacked against him; that's all there was to it.

Q: Was he being shunned by other naval officers at that point?

Admiral McCrea: No, not to my knowledge at all. I think everybody had a high regard for Kimmel. Kimmel, I am not sure what his origin or nationality was; I think it was German, but am not too sure. He was opinionated, but, by God, you have to be opinionated in a job like that. You have to call the shots as you see them. He got along well with Stark, I thought, and there was a great deal of personal correspondence that passed between Stark and Kimmel and also Hart. They wrote to Admiral Stark, of course, about odds and ends. And Stark would give me the letter, and I would go shopping around in all the department getting answers to the questions that they had raised. Then I would draft a letter and incorporate everything that I had picked up in answer to their questions.* Stark, of course, would edit the letter, and it was his letter completely, but I did a great deal of the spadework digging up things for these fellows, which he didn't have time to do. I was very fond of Stark too.

Q: What was the substance of your conversation with Kimmel over the lunch on board the *Iowa*?

Admiral McCrea: Oh, we talked about the ship. Of course, the *Iowa* was the very latest and the biggest, and that was it. We didn't discuss Pearl Harbor or anything like that,

---
*The department McCrea refers to was the Navy Department, Washington, D.C.

J. L. McCrea #2 - 96

nothing. I just wanted him to see the ship, and that's what he wanted to do. The nearest reference to Pearl Harbor was when he left the ship and he said, "This is the nicest thing that has happened to me in a long, long while."

Q: He probably welcomed the chance to get his mind on something else.

Admiral McCrea: Sure. I was very fond of him, very fond of him.

Q: You said he came over there in World War I to compare gunnery. What was the finding of that comparison?

Admiral McCrea: Well, there were so many things that we and the British went separate ways about. I, as a young officer--of course, my opinion didn't amount to too much--but I thought that our ship construction was a lot better than theirs. For this reason--if a shell hit the roof of the turret of a British ship, there was nothing to stop that shell going right straight through to the bottom; that was all there was to it. Whereas, our turrets were greatly subdivided, and all that sort of thing. I thought in that respect we were much better, ship for ship. I recall a turret officer calling down in this turret, and he said, "Arbuthnot, Arbuthnot."

"Well," I said, "gosh, have you got some more Arbuthnots around here?"

And he said, "Oh, we are always raising Arbuthnots." He just talked--he had a little coxswain's megaphone, and he talked to Arbuthnot clear down in the bowels of the ship. Well, you couldn't do that in our ship; you couldn't do that. I'll never forget going aboard Lion, which was David Beatty's flagship at Jutland.* I had number three turret on the New York at that time, and the turret that I was in was the turret in the Lion that was normally assigned to the Marines, which would be the corresponding one to my number three turret--they called it the X turret, I think. I crawled in there and I got down below and I was looking around, and the first thing I saw was a plaque where it said, "In this turret on 30 May 1916, Major So and so and 58 of His Majesty's Marines gave their life for King and Country."** I'll never forget that. My gracious, I realized that I was in the war zone. But the ship had been refitted, and there it was.

---

*Vice Admiral David Beatty, RN, commanded the First Battle Cruiser Squadron in the Battle of Jutland. The Lion was one of a number of battle cruisers sunk or damaged at Jutland.
**But for the action of Major F. W. Harvey, Royal Marines, turret officer who flooded powder magazines, the Lion would probably have exploded.

Q: What about pure shooting ability? Did you get a chance to compare that with the British?

Admiral McCrea: We did well; we shot well; we really shot well, I thought. The British conducted their gunnery exercises, and we did it just the way they did. They would send the King Orry, I think it was, this ship that towed the battle targets. And you were told to go to sea, and on such and such a day, between latitude so and so and longitude so and so, you would sight the King Orry that was taking the place of an enemy ship. And you opened fire on there, and the observers on the King Orry plotted all the spots of shells, and you could analyze the whole thing after it was all over. The British were very--I thought they did a wonderful job on it.

Q: Did you use an offset to avoid hitting the ship?

Admiral McCrea: Yes. Well, the King Orry towed the battle raft, and it had 500 or 600 yards of towline. As far as offset goes, we used to shoot at each other out in the Pacific with offsets. When I was out there, the Iowa was shooting at 45,000 and 50,000 yards, don't you see, and all you could see would be the tops of the target that you were shooting at--it was all offset.

J. L. McCrea #2 - 99

Q: How good a shooting ship was the Iowa?

Admiral McCrea: Excellent, I thought. It had a hell of a good gunnery officer.

Q: Was that Commander Pinney, Frank Pinney?*

Admiral McCrea: No, Frank was the assistant gunnery officer. Lynne Quiggle was the gunnery officer.** He got to be a flag officer and he, unfortunately, suffered a health problem that bore down on him, and he committed suicide; he went over the side at sea. I think that his problem was a circulatory thing, completely circulatory. His extremities failed to get a blood supply, which distressed him to the point where he went overboard.

Q: You mentioned to me earlier that someone had asked you what momentous thought you were thinking about when you signed the log for the surrender of the German Fleet.

Admiral McCrea: I told you that, I guess. Well, it doesn't amount to much at any rate. This old gal in Boston was asking me about it. She said, "This document that you have shown me has considerable history attached to it. What was going through your mind when you were writing this log?

---
*Lieutenant Commander Frank L. Pinney, Jr., USN.
**Commander Lynne C. Quiggle, USN, who died in 1958.

I said, "Well, madam, I couldn't tell you, because I know I would shock you."

And she said, "Oh, no, you couldn't shock me."

And I said, "Oh, yes, I could."

So then she said, "All right."

Then I explained to her how I had gone on watch at ten minutes before 8:00 in the morning. It was a very raw day, and the days can get raw in the North Sea in November, I assure you, and we were out there to meet the German Fleet coming back. I said, "My relief didn't get up to relieve me until about 12:30, because he had to get his lunch, and in the Navy you don't quit the deck until you have written and signed your log."

And she said, "That's what I am interested in; what were you thinking about?"

So I said, "I can tell you frankly, madam, that right at the moment I was writing that log, I thought what a wonderful thing it would be to get to the head."

She looked rather quizzically at me for a moment and said, "Well, I understand exactly what you are talking about. You know, we have a yacht, and we refer to it as the head."

Q: Moving on again to your time in command of the _Bittern_, your biography says that you rescued a Chinese merchant ship. Would you like to cover that, please?

Admiral McCrea: Well, I happened to come across a letter about that. It says: "I would like to take this opportunity, the first I have had since my arrival at Shanghai, to convey to yourself, your officers and men my sincerest thanks for your recent generous conduct towards myself and my unfortunate vessel. I feel sure that your prompt action materially assisted in averting a more serious turn of events and on behalf of the passengers and the crew, whose fears were undoubtedly allayed by your ready assistance, and the company, I desire to again express my gratitude.
"With my best respects, sir, I remain
Yours sincerely,
F. M. Stokes, Master, SS *Irene*."

Q: This was July 27, 1925.

Admiral McCrea: Yes. And I wrote to Captain Stokes: "Receipt of your kind letter of the 27th is hereby acknowledged.

"Accidents of the sort that befell the SS *Irene* are to be deplored, yet when they do occur the unfortunate results are partially compensated for by the fact that such feeble assistance as can be given by sailormen outside the stricken vessel tends to strengthen the bond of brotherhood that exists amongst seafaring people the world over. Whatever assistance or service the Bittern may have been to you in your trouble you made most easy for us by the thoughtful consideration which you displayed during the trying event to my officers and men who came closely in contact with you. We were all very happy that the Irene escaped with as little damage and that she was able to proceed so comfortably to Shanghai.

"In order that my crew may know of your thoughtfulness in remembering them, I have taken the liberty of publishing your letter in its entirety for their information. They deeply appreciate your remembering them.

"Sincerely,

John L. McCrea, Lieutenant, USN."

Q: What had you done?

Admiral McCrea: We went out there and I was going to pass our towline over there, because we were equipped to tow target rafts. We got in position to do this thing, but the tide was rising, and suddenly the fellow sent word over there that he was afloat. So I pulled up my anchor and got out of his way, don't you see. He came backing down and went past us close aboard and we got him out. He was all right.

Q: What had he done? Had he run aground?

Admiral McCrea: Yes. Oh, it was very thick.

Q: That was near Chefoo, was it not?

Admiral McCrea: Yes, right at Chefoo.* This is another one: "On behalf of the directors of our company, I wish to express our sincere thanks for the invaluable and courageous help rendered by the USS <u>Blackhawk</u>, the USS <u>Pillsbury</u> and the <u>Bittern</u> to our steamer <u>Irene</u> when she ran ashore in a dense fog on West Coutas Island on July 17. All passengers from the damaged ship were taken off by boat from these vessels and the <u>Bittern</u> sent on board our <u>Irene</u> armed men to watch during the night.
"May I ask you to kindly convey our heartfelt gratitude and appreciation to Captains Wickham and John L. McCrea and all other officers and men who most kindly assisted.
"Yours faithfully,
for the China Merchants Shipping Company."
Signed So-and-So.

---
*Chefoo is a port at the end of the Shantung Peninsula in China.

Q: The China Merchants Steam Navigation Company--what a name.

Admiral McCrea: From the Commander in Chief:

"The Commander in Chief takes pleasure, great pleasure in commending you on exceptional official performance of duty on the night of 17-18 July when you proceeded with the vessel under your command, to the rescue of the Chinese steamer Irene aground on a rocky island off the entrance to the harbor of Chefoo, China. The judgment shown in promptly placing an armed guard on board the Irene to preserve order among the more than 300 coolie class passengers, thereby preventing a riot beyond the capacity of the ship's officers to quell, and the excellent seamanship displayed in taking off the passengers without the loss of a single passenger or their luggage or baggage on a dark and foggy night are worthy of the best traditions of the Naval Service.

"A copy of this letter is forwarded to the Bureau requesting that it be filed with your office record."

Q: This is from the Commander in Chief of the Asiatic Fleet.

Admiral McCrea: Yes.

Q: That's a very nice commendation.

Admiral McCrea: Sure.

Q: I take it that was a very satisfying command for you, because you told me earlier you had turned down a chance to leave that ship.

Admiral McCrea: Oh, sure. I would like very much to have gone up the river, but I turned it down, because they were only going to give me the job of being exec, and I said, "Well, am I being fired off the Bittern?"

And he said, "Oh, no, you are not being fired, but your rank would make you exec of a river gunboat."

And I said, "Unless you are going to get rid of me, I would rather be where I am, because I am the captain there. I run the damn thing."

So he understood.

Q: Where did you go when your tour in the Bittern finally did come to an end?

Admiral McCrea: I went back to Washington, because I had been at sea for ten years, lacking a year at the War

College. I was a young bachelor. I had been at the War College--that was my year out--in '23 and '24 at the War College at Newport. And I enjoyed that greatly.

My father had always been partial to the law, and a letter came along from the Navy Department asking for volunteers for the law course. The law course was known to be a tough thing; you had to work like hell and some people had broken up under it. And so I put in for the law just for the hell of it. Whenever they were short of officers, they could always fold up and drag the line officers out of the JAG office because standing on the sidelines were all sorts of lawyers they could employ.* So that was one of the reasons, the principal reason, I guess, that I wanted to take law. Then I got interested in that and I enjoyed it.

Q: What were the advantages to the Navy in having line officers who were lawyers?

Admiral McCrea: Just to look out for the legal end of things.

Q: Today, of course, they have law specialists who do nothing but that.

---

*JAG--the Judge Advocate General heads the Navy's legal office.

Admiral McCrea: That's right, and I don't know that that is too good for the Navy. It seems to me that people who can carry a little knowledge of what they are talking about--for instance, I suppose some of those lawyers around the JAG office now have never been in a ship.

Q: So you think there is an advantage to the operational experience?

Admiral McCrea: Yes, but it's all--they are probably getting better law and all that sort of thing the way it is now.

Q: Where did you take your law course? At George Washington?*

Admiral McCrea: At George Washington. And then I went back to the Navy Department on duty after I had been at sea quite some time, and I made a mistake in going up and calling on one of my old law profs, a chap for whom I had great respect and at whose feet I had sat. He said, "Why don't you come back and take your master's work, because your work on the bachelor's side would qualify you for admittance to law school?"

I said, "Mr. Collier, I am a naval officer, and I don't think I would want to take it."

---

*George Washington University, Washington, D.C.

J. L. McCrea #2 - 108

Well, my family was on the West Coast. My house was rented in town, and I couldn't get in it until September. My family was out with her family on the West Coast. So by the time she got back there in September, I was well on my way in the master's course. The reason I did it was that I was always a fairly early riser, and one of the courses that I would have to take had its session at 7:30 in the morning. And so I just signed up for that, and by the time my family got there a few weeks later, I was on my way for the master's, and I got that when I was 43.

Q: So that would have been during the 1930s?

Admiral McCrea: Yes.

Q: How difficult a course was it? You said some people broke up under it.

Admiral McCrea: Well, yes, because you had to work in the JAG office, and you had to carry on the job in the JAG office as well as go to law school. When I took my master's work in law, I did that all at night, and I paid for it myself. The postgraduate the Navy paid for. So that's how that worked out.

Q: What sorts of cases were you involved in when you

served in the JAG office?

Admiral McCrea: I was on the disciplinary side and it was all--no trouble with that. A number of people went into the patent. We had patents there, and we had ship construction. We had all sorts of thing, but I stayed on the disciplinary side of it.

Q: Did this involve reviewing records of courts-martial?

Admiral McCrea: Yes, and I have never had anything to do with courts-martial.

Q: Do you remember any particular cases that you were involved in when you were reviewing the courts-martial?

Admiral McCrea: No. I enjoyed working with the courts of inquiry more than the courts-martial, because when you are dealing with courts-martial, you are dealing with sad things, and I didn't like it. Courts of inquiry and things like that appealed to me, and I enjoyed that.

Q: Well, usually courts of inquiry involve sad things also, don't they?

Admiral McCrea: Yes, but then, on the other hand, so many

J. L. McCrea #2 - 110

of the problems that you run onto in general courts-martial involve personal conduct.

Q: Whereas courts of inquiry would deal more with professional matters.

Admiral McCrea: Yes, completely.

Q: We were talking about your law school time.

Admiral McCrea: At the end of my time at the law school, when it was in sight, of course, I started preparing for the District of Columbia bar exams. The District of Columbia bar is a very strict bar. I suppose that it and New York State bar are probably the two toughest bars in the country. I knew that I would never be in a better position to take a bar exam than after I'd finished law school--directly after. So I went to quiz courses at night, and I took the bar exams in the District of Columbia. And the day following the completion of the bar exams, I shoved off and went to Panama, and I was away from the District of Columbia for three years.

The bar exams were held in the Georgetown Law School, and sitting across the aisle from me was a gray-haired black. Before we started the exams, he took a look at me, and I took a look at him, and he said, "How many times is

J. L. McCrea #2 - 111

this for you?"

I said, "This is my first time." Well, since he'd asked me how many times it was for me, I thought it was perfectly all right for me to say, "How many times for you?"

So he said, "This is my fourth time, and it's my last time unless I pass, because I'll never get another chance." And he said, "You got a kind of late start, didn't you?"

"Well," I said, "I'm a naval officer."

So he said, "What do you want to take the law for?"

And I said, "Just for the hell of it."

And I did, but I will never forget this guy. I have often wondered what happened to him, whether he ever passed or not. I was down in Panama in the Special Service Squadron.* I was down there for two years. I was on the staff of the Commander of the Special Service Squadron, senior member of the staff, and I enjoyed the duty a great deal. I was greatly distressed when we gave up the Panama Canal two or three years ago--greatly distressed.

Q: How soon did you get the results on your bar exam?

Admiral McCrea: Two months or six weeks. The United States District Judge for the Canal Zone--one night I told

---

*The Special Service Squadron, commanded by a rear admiral and comprised of a number of relatively small warships, operated from 1920 to 1940 to look out for U.S. interests in Central and South America.

him about my bout with the law, and he said, "I would like you to be a member of my bar. We could admit you on motion."

I said, "You couldn't, Judge, because I am not a member of any bar, and you couldn't admit me on a motion."

And he said, "Well, I'll appoint a committee to examine you."

So I said, "That's fine."

So he did. So I called up the chairman of the committee once and he said, "The important things about the Canal Zone are the Acts of Congress, the Treaties and Acts of Congress that have to do with the Canal Zone and the Republic of Panama, and you have to know those."

So I said I didn't know too much about them, but I would read up on them. My family had gone to the West Coast to visit and so I did, and I called up one day and went over and they asked me a few questions. And then the chairman said, "I think I can say, without leaving the room, that you will qualify to be a member of the bar."

And I said, "Well, I am just wondering if the examining board wouldn't like to walk across the street [which was the Republic of Panama] and we can have a drink over there."

Prohibition was in the Canal Zone, and they all said, "Yes." So we went across the street and had a drink. But I used that time to get to be a member of the Canal Zone

Bar, to accredit me for admission to the Bar of the Supreme Court of the United States. You have to have three years. I am no more of a lawyer than that window washer out there is right now."*

Q: What was the mission of the Special Service Squadron?

Admiral McCrea: Well, the principal thing at the time was Nicaragua--that was a hot time down there, and Sandino was rushing all over.** The whole Central American problem beggars description and beggars solutions, as far as I am concerned. They don't know what the answer to it is. The only thing I am sure of is that democracy, as we understand it, isn't exportable; that's all. I knew an old Italian down there, Mr. Pellacio, who was in his 80s. Mr. Pellacio had come to Nicaragua as a boy of eight with his father, and he stayed on, of course--his father was a trader and one thing and another--and one day I said to Mr. Pellacio, "Mr. Pellacio, why is it you have always got revolutions going on down here and seem not to be able to stop them?"

And the old man looked at me and he said, "My dear McCrea, when the party in power uses at least 90% of the governmental revenue to perpetuate itself in office, the

---

*The windows of Admiral McCrea's home were being washed during the interview.
**Augusto Sandino was a Nicaraguan guerrilla proclaimed an outlaw by the U.S. Government. He waged guerrilla warfare against the U.S. Marines in Nicaragua from 1927 to 1932.

only solution is violent revolution." I have never forgotten that. His Italian view was that that was the only solution--violent revolution; and they seem to keep it going.

Q: Did you help to look out for the interests of the United Fruit Company down there?

Admiral McCrea: Yes, and the United Fruit Company, in my judgment, did a splendid job all through Central and South America. And here is how they did it. They built schools for the employees and their children. They gave them medical services and did all sorts of things. I thought they did a hell of a good job. I am sure they did.

Q: The flagship then was the Rochester, wasn't it?

Admiral McCrea: The Rochester--that's the one I was in.

Q: What was your duty on the staff?

Admiral McCrea: I was the senior member of the staff and everything went through me. We had, of course, the flag lieutenant, and we had our Marine and all the communications, and we worked hand-in-glove with the

J. L. McCrea #2 - 115

Marines up in Nicaragua, and we used to go up there.

Q: Who was the commander of the squadron then?

Admiral McCrea: Admiral Campbell, Edward H. Campbell.*
He wanted me to go down there on his staff, and I wanted to
have command of a destroyer, but I didn't have seniority
enough to get command of a destroyer. He told me that if I
would work my way into that bracket where I would have
enough seniority to have command of a destroyer, he would
release me any time I could get command. So that was the
way I went. But he left me before I left, because he was
taken up and given command of the Thirteenth Naval
District--that is up at Puget Sound area. That's the way
it wound up.

Q: Are there any incidents that stand out in your mind
from that time in the Rochester?

Admiral McCrea: Yes. There was a local attorney by the
name of Natalio Ermine, and Natalio Ermine was head and
shoulders educational-wise ahead of most of them. Whenever
Natalio Ermine would get a drink under his belt, he would
start saying, "Well, of course, John, you people just beat

---
*Rear Admiral Edward H. Campbell, USN, Commander of the
Special Service Squadron.

us to it. We would have built the canal." And he kept after that thought. One time when he was in my house, I gave him a drink, and away he went again that the Panamanians would have built the canal.

And I said, "Listen, Natalio Ermine, you couldn't have done any such damn thing; and the French couldn't do anything about it. Where the hell were you going to get the E Pluribus Unum bucks to finance this operation down here?"

"Well, we would have worked it out."

"Well, you couldn't have done it at all and, Natalio, I have to do this to you in my own house, but you never could have done it. You must know you couldn't have done it. What you are saying is just wishful thinking."

Well, the fellow that really disappointed me, years later, was my friend Dwight Eisenhower.* When Dwight Eisenhower gave the Panamanians permission to hoist the Panamanian flag over our schoolhouses in the Canal Zone, that just burned me up. I knew Eisenhower well; he served down there a couple of years, a year or so, and he must have known better, but he did it. This thing can't get political, but the senior member of the Senate now on the Republican side--his vote and the vote of Mr. Brooke from this area got us out of the Canal Zone.** That disturbs

---
*Dwight D. Eisenhower was President of the United States from 1953 to 1961.
**Senator Edward Brooke (Republican, Massachusetts).

me.

This country, in my judgment, owes a duty to the maritime countries of the world about that canal, to keep that thing open, to keep it working. Thus far, it has been doing fairly well, but there is no assurance. I mean that no one yet has come up with a solution to offset the rascality that Castro can get into in connection with Central America, and the press has been filled with reports about his operations down there.* The maritime countries of the world could be safely assured that we would keep the canal open, and we would do a good job of it.

Q: Was Panama the headquarters for the Special Service Squadron?

Admiral McCrea: Yes.

Q: Where was your base?

Admiral McCrea: Right there in the Canal Zone. I think the most ships we had down there when I was there was six, and we worked closely on both sides of the canal, on both sides of Central America. One time we had a very bad earthquake down in Nicaragua, and a great many people were

---
*Fidel Castro has been Premier of Cuba since 1959.

killed.* About a thousand, I guess, were killed when the prison shook down. It was bad, but we helped these people greatly.

Q: In what sense did you provide help?

Admiral McCrea: By setting an example to them as to how they could run their government. Last night on the TV there was something about Salvador. I went all up in through those countries, and I don't know the answer to it, any of it. A sympathetic dictatorship--that's a bad word to use, I know--can do more for those countries. Every one of those countries--their base is ignorance--thousands and thousands of people that couldn't write their own names. We try to call them democracies, and they are not democracies; they're just anything but, when you get down to it.

You know, years ago I ran onto something. Owen Wister, the novelist, wrote a book, and he called it <u>Theodore Roosevelt: A Friendship</u>.** They were classmates at Harvard, and Wister said to Theodore Roosevelt once,

---

*On 4 March 1931, Nicaragua's capital city of Managua was virtually destroyed by a violent earthquake and resulting fire. The disaster killed approximately 2,000 people and injured another 7,000.
**Owen Wister, <u>Roosevelt, The Story of a Friendship</u> (New York: Macmillan, 1930). Wister is best known as the author of <u>The Virginian</u>, perhaps the most popular of all western novels.

"What sort of a prognosis have you for our form of government that we now enjoy?"

Theodore Roosevelt was alleged by Wister to have said, "Oh, give it a hundred years." They were, I think, in the class of '81 at Harvard, but I wouldn't be as pessimistic about it as he was at the time when he said, "Give it a hundred years." He probably did it with a shrug of the shoulders and very lightheartedly. I think we've got a chance to do a lot better job than a hundred years, but every once in a while it gets shaken.

Q: What was Trood Bidwell's duty on board the Rochester?"*

Admiral McCrea: He was executive officer and a damn good one. He was a good naval officer, that fellow. We got to be good friends.

Q: What qualities made him a good officer?

Admiral McCrea: He could make a decision and ride with it, and he was a no-fooling guy. I enjoyed serving with those fellows; I would rather have a no-fooling guy than one of these wishy-washy somebodies.

---

*Commander A. Trood Bidwell, USN.

Q: Was he a good seaman?

Admiral McCrea: Yes, he was a good seaman and he was all right, that fellow. A good officer; he cracked up, you know.

Q: I didn't know that.

Admiral McCrea: Yes, he cracked up right after the start of the war, and he had to be relieved. He went ashore, and he never went back to sea--right after Pearl Harbor.

Q: So there was a good working relationship between the staff and the Rochester itself?

Admiral McCrea: Oh, yes. Bidwell was the detail officer in Washington when I went to work for Stark.* I had a letter from one of Bidwell's subordinates saying that they were going to change my orders. They had me originally going to JAG office and changed my orders and were going to send me to the Chief of Naval Operations, so I got a note from Bidwell: "We had to change your orders, and you are going to go with Admiral Stark. Before you report in, I wish you would come and see me. I think I would like to

---

*McCrea reported for duty in Admiral Stark's office in 1940; Bidwell was then a captain serving in the Bureau of Navigation.

talk to you."

I said okay to that, of course, and when I got to Washington, the first thing I did, I went down to see Bidwell.

"Well," he said, "I told you we had to change your orders, and you are going to go to the Chief of Naval Operations. I think I should tell you that Stark doesn't want you. He has nothing against you at all, but he says that he doesn't know you. I told him that I knew you and that I was sure that you and he would get on together well. But I thought that I should tell you that you are not particularly wanted by Stark."

So that was the way it worked out. I went down there and was given an office down the corridor. And in due course I was moved up to Stark's front office, and one thing and another, and I did all sorts of things for him. Then Kelly Turner took an interest in me, and he was the fellow who insisted that I go with the change of the war plans out to the Pacific that time, and it turned out to be a most interesting duty.* And directly Pearl Harbor came across--he and Stark and King sent me to the White House to be naval aide to FDR and all sorts of things opened up.** If Bidwell hadn't succeeded in selling me to Stark, I might never have been there.

---
*Captain Richmond Kelly Turner, USN, was director of war plans.
**Admiral Ernest J. King, USN, was Commander in Chief U.S. Fleet.

J. L. McCrea #2 - 122

Q: What was his problem later? Do you think the shock of Pearl Harbor was the cause of it?

Admiral McCrea: I haven't any idea. He had left and was in a ship down in the Special Service Squadron, and this was when he really broke up, I think. Bidwell was a very smart officer; he stood very high in his class.

I remember he wanted to know if I knew Kelly Turner, and I said, "I have never laid eyes on him."

And he said, "You watch out for him; that fellow has more brains than you can shake a stick at."

And I said, "Well, that's good; we need fellows like that."

The first thing I knew, Turner and I got to be good friends. There was a hell of a good officer. I said that I thought he drank too much, and that's right. He did, but I didn't go as far as Bill Mott did to Toland. I think Bill Mott told Toland that he was a complete alcoholic and a few other things.* I always thought that he was very much like U. S. Grant; he could drink, but it never

---

*See John Toland, Infamy: Pearl Harbor and Its Aftermath (Garden City, New York: Doubleday & Co., Inc., 1982), p. 177, for a description of Admiral Turner's drinking both during and after World War II. Toland's source was Rear Admiral William C. Mott, USN (Ret.), who had served with McCrea in the White House and was later on Admiral Turner's staff in the Pacific.

bothered him.*

Q: Lincoln said about Grant, "Find out what brand he drinks. I'll get some for all my generals."**

Admiral McCrea: Yes. Well, this fellow Turner--God, he was a little bit on the ruthless side. One of his officers told me when he took command of the Astoria that he called all heads of departments in and introduced himself to them and told them what he thought about things.*** He pointed to the gunnery officer and said, "You're the gunnery officer? Just remember I know more gunnery than you do." Next, "You're the chief engineer? Just remember that I know more engineering than you do." And that's the way they started in doing business--but what a guy.

Q: You went from the Special Service Squadron to the Trever; you had finally gotten senior enough.

Admiral McCrea: Oh, yes, I got to the Trever, and I enjoyed that. I will dismiss the Trever with saying that about a week after I got there, I got a report of an inspection of the Trever by the squadron commander, and the

---

*Ulysses S. Grant was a Union general during the Civil War, later President of the United States from 1869 to 1877.
**Abraham Lincoln was President from 1861 to 1865.
***As a captain, Turner commanded the heavy cruiser Astoria (CA-34) from 1938 to 1940.

J. L. McCrea #2 - 124

last sentence in the inspection report, as I recall it, said something about: "The *Trever* is not considered to be an effective unit of the fleet."

I pondered that for a few minutes, and after lunch I had all the officers sit there, and I went in and got this report, and I read the thing to them, and came down there to the *Trever* was not an effective unit of the fleet. And I said to the mess, "I am not content to serve on a ship like that, and I don't think you fellows are. Now get going and put this ship up where she belongs." Well, we did.

Q: What did you have to do to make that change?

Admiral McCrea: Just make that growl--that was all. I told them, "Remember always that enlisted men take their cues from their officers, so I expect you fellows to be in proper uniform." The first inspection that I made of that ship on a Saturday morning, I said, "I came up here prepared to criticize this morning anything I saw that didn't measure up to my ideas of what we should do in this ship. But looking at you gentlemen standing here, there isn't any one of you that, in my judgment, is ready for captain's inspection--the state of your uniform, your sword knots, and a few other things. If you want to see somebody that's ready for inspection, look at me."*

Now that's a hell of a thing to say, but I said, "Look at me. Next Saturday I expect to see you fellows turned out the way you should be." And that was the way it went. We moved from the bottom right up close to the top, and a year later, just as I was leaving the ship, we were designated to be inspected by the Commander Battle Force.

Q: Do you think they just hadn't had sufficient good leadership before?

Admiral McCrea: Yes, that's the only thing I can attribute it to.

Q: What specific areas was the ship weak in?

Admiral McCrea: Everything--gunnery, engineering, torpedoes.

Q: Where was she operating primarily?

Admiral McCrea: San Diego.

Q: What did you use as a basis for your changes?

---

*The sword knot is a gold-colored tassel attached to the hilt of a sword for decoration on formal occasions.

Admiral McCrea: The influence of your earlier service, you see. For instance, in the New York I had five captains. Four of those captains made flag rank. Two of them were Chiefs of Naval Operations--Charles F. Hughes and William Veazie Pratt. And Admiral Hugh Rodman was the Commander in Chief of the Pacific Fleet. Now, unconsciously, I think you absorb a few things serving with people, positive characters like that. They were all positive characters. The first one was Thomas Slidell Rodgers, and he was one of the original Rodgers clan that went right back, and he was relieved by Hugh Rodman, who was the captain of the ship. Then Rodman came back there when we went to the North Sea. Rodman was relieved by Charles F. Hughes, a great sailor, and then it was Edward L. Beach, who was the father of the young fellow who writes from time to time.

Q: Ned Beach.

Admiral McCrea: Yes. And he unfortunately had been on board the old Memphis when she was hit with this hurricane down in the Pacific and they lost the ship.* Then William Veazie Pratt succeeded Beach. But those three four-star fellows--you are not aware that you are absorbing

---

*Captain Edward L. Beach, USN, was in command of the armored cruiser Memphis when she was struck by a tidal wave and broached at Santo Domingo on 29 August 1916. His son, Captain Edward L. Beach, USN (Ret.), is a noted novelist, best known for the submarine story Run Silent, Run Deep.

J. L. McCrea #2 - 127

anything at the time, but you are just going along, and you see how fellows got to the top--how they made out.

Q: So this kind of influence was in your background when you came to the Trever?

Admiral McCrea: You don't really realize it either.

Q: You were very fortunate to have served with such capable people that set a high standard.

Admiral McCrea: That's right. I say I was lucky as hell in going to the New York. In addition to those captains, we had Leigh Palmer, who was my first executive officer, and I have never known a finer naval officer than that fellow, and why he resigned from the Navy--he just saw no future in it I guess.* He resigned and was the head of the General Petroleum Corporation and a few things, but brilliant man, brilliant. One of the things that I picked up from that fellow was to listen, and when he sent for you about anything and you talked to him, he couldn't have paid any closer attention to you than if you had been the President of the United States. That's the kind of a guy he was. He was a wonderful person to be with, and I have

---

*Palmer resigned his commission in September 1920 when he was a captain.

always tried to be a good listener. I'll admit to being a talker.

Here: "At the 1931 annual inspection of the Trever, it was found to be a non-effective unit of the fleet and to be inefficient in administration and gunnery and torpedoes. The Trever under the present commanding officer, who took command subsequent to this inspection, has shown unusual improvement. At present the Trever is considered to be an effective unit of the fleet and is standing sixth out of thirty vessels of this flotilla in gunnery. Special credit is due the officers enumerated for this marked improvement."

Q: That's a letter in 1932 from ComDesRon Four, 13 June 1932.*

Admiral McCrea: It's funny how things go along. I was most fortunate, I know. I was fortunate in coming in contact with King too.

Q: When did that come about?

Admiral McCrea: It came about in an unusual way in that he despised Rodman, and he knew that I had served with Rodman. Every time he took a crack at Admiral Rodman, I would pipe

---
*ComDesRon Four--Commander Destroyer Squadron Four.

right up and say, "Admiral King, Admiral Rodman had certain traits of personal character that I think you would admire." And I would let him have it, and that was the way it worked out.

I was up in command of the North Pacific Task Force when President Roosevelt died, and 12 days later I got ordered out of there to go back to Washington.* Well, I never knew why I was ordered back to Washington, but Sam Rosenman, who was FDR's legal advisor, you remember, and he also worked with Bob Sherwood on Roosevelt's speeches, which were always Roosevelt's in the end, because he edited them all vigorously.**

Sam Rosenman told me that King brought me back to Washington to go to the White House to be naval aide to Mr. Truman, but he said that Truman had other ideas, and he got this fellow, Vardaman, who was a shoe manufacturer out in St. Louis or Kansas City whom he knew well, and he was in the Naval Reserve.*** And so I guess he thought that just dressing the guy up in a naval uniform made him know something about the Navy; that was it. King never told me that, but Sam Rosenman told me.

---
*Franklin D. Roosevelt died 12 April 1945.
**Samuel I. Rosenman; Playwright Robert E. Sherwood, author of Roosevelt and Hopkins: An Intimate History (New York: Harper & Brothers, 1948).
***Captain James K. Vardaman, USNR, soon promoted to commodore. Vardaman did not last long in the role, according to Margaret Truman's memoir of her father, because Vardaman caught a case of "Potomac fever."

J. L. McCrea #2 - 130

Q: What was the basis for King's dislike of Rodman?

Admiral McCrea: He said that Rodman was shallow and that he was this, that, and the other thing. Of course, King could very easily say that Rodman was shallow, because Rodman stood around the bottom of his class and King stood around the top of his.*

Q: After you left the Trever, then you went back for your postgraduate work in law?

Admiral McCrea: Yes, I went back there, and I wanted to get out of there. I'd had considerable staff duty, you see, and I wanted to get away and get back to sea as soon as possible. I knew the Astoria was going to go into commission, and so I fiddled around and finally got the detail officer to send me there as a navigator.

Q: That was a choice assignment. How did you manage to swing that?

Admiral McCrea: I just went around and camped on the guy's doorstep until he gave in. I wound up going as executive of the fleet flagship, and I was a junior executive in the

---

*Rodman finished 61st of the 62 graduates in the Naval Academy class of 1880; King stood fourth of the 67 graduates in the class of 1901.

battleships by four Naval Academy classes.

Q: Where was the Astoria being put into commission?

Admiral McCrea: She was in the Puget Sound Navy Yard, and I went up there for that.

When I was in the Astoria, one day I got a letter from the Navy Department that said they were looking for somebody of my seniority to go to Guam, and what would my reaction be to that? Well, I promptly let them know what it was--I didn't want to go to Guam, and I told them that I had been out of the Naval Academy so many years. And I lined up that I had been out of the continental limits of the United States for something like five or six years and that there were scads of people of my seniority who had never served five minutes outside the continental limits of the United States.

Well, the answer to that was a nice letter saying that they acknowledged the fact that I didn't want to go to Guam. Then the next thing I got said, "Regret that exigencies of service require that you be attached to so-and-so to go to Guam."

Well, I wrote off, and Admiral Andrews, the Chief of Personnel at that time, wrote me a nice letter in which he said that he sympathized with me in not wanting to go to

Guam, but nevertheless that was the way it was.* And he said, "If you go out there and do the kind of job that I am sure you can do, we will see that you get a good job when you get back in the fleet."

I thought that was all right, but I knew what it was. It was just a letter to send me off to lick my hurts, you see. Besides, I knew that he would be long gone by the time I'd get around again. I kept the letter, and I kept after them, and finally they ordered me as executive to the Pennsylvania. Then I got scared when I got my orders to go. They said detached in November, and I got them around the sixth, seventh, or eighth of November, and I was fearful that somebody would intercede when they found out that, as junior as I was, I was going to fleet flag. So I got panicky, and I went to the JAG and I said, "Listen, I would like to get detached right now in early November."

And they said, "We were going to detach you later on."

"I know it, but I would like to get detached right now, because I want to get out of this town, and when I start my orders it is going to be harder for them to cancel my orders than it would be if I was to stay here."

I went out and I sat for ten days in a hotel in Seattle that I knew. And on the day that I reported in to the Pennsylvania, the selections had been announced the day before. The guy I was relieving, who was a hell of a

---
*Rear Admiral Adolphus Andrews, USN, Chief of the Bureau of Navigation.

popular guy in this ship, had not been selected for captain.* Of course, there was great gloom in the ship and here a brand-new guy shows up. I always thought that the Pennsylvania was one of the greatest jobs that I had.

Q: What made it a great job?

Admiral McCrea: Well, you were running the ship, by gracious. The wonderful thing about being an exec of a ship, you can stick your nose into everybody's business and you can find out what's going on, whereas, the captain of the ship can't; that's all there is to it. The exec can legitimately stick his nose into everything and find out what's going on and straighten it out if it needs straightening, and that's why it was a wonderful job.

Q: Going back to the Astoria, what were some of your experiences in that ship?

Admiral McCrea: On her shakedown cruise we went down through the mid-Pacific. We stopped in Hawaii, of course, Palmyra, Christmas Island, across the line down into American Samoa, and we ultimately got down to Sydney. I

---

*McCrea's predecessor as executive officer of the Pennsylvania (BB-38) was Commander Robert M. Hinckley, USN. He was later selected for captain and promoted with a date of rank in September 1939.

had never been down in that country, and it was a wonderful experience. We came back up via Noumea. I got a good glimpse of the south Pacific and Australia.

Q: That was quite a shakedown cruise, wasn't it?

Admiral McCrea: Yes, quite a shakedown cruise.

Q: Wasn't that a pretty good test for a navigator? I don't know that those waters were that well charted, were they?

Admiral McCrea: Oh, yes, they are pretty well charted.

Q: Who was the commanding officer?

Admiral McCrea: Captain Root--Edmund S. Root. He had been on the Island of Guam, and I used to talk to him about Guam. Then all of a sudden I find myself going out there.

Q: What did your duties entail when you were in Guam?

Admiral McCrea: I was executive officer of the naval station, and I was the aide for civil administration. We ran the island of Guam in a rather high-handed way. I would say it was high-handed, but it was a damned efficient way.

Q: Wasn't that a case of exporting democracy then?

Admiral McCrea: After a fashion--no, because they didn't have much democracy there.

Q: Do you think the fact that you had had the legal training played a part in getting you that job in Guam?

Admiral McCrea: The Navy Department said so, but I didn't think that at all, because we had a Marine major who was a legal specialist who came out there.

Q: What were some of the problems involved in administering a country of that sort?

Admiral McCrea: When I got back to Washington that time, in no time at all, I was in the Office of Chief of Naval Operations, and then when the surrender came and Nimitz came in there and brought all his people with him, and I still hung on to that Central Division.* And Conolly was my boss, and in no time at all Conolly got ordered to London and he went to Nimitz and said that he wanted me to relieve him.**

---

*Admiral Chester W. Nimitz, USN, was Chief of Naval Operations from 1945 to 1947.
**Vice Admiral Richard L. Conolly, USN, was Deputy Chief of Naval Operations (Administration) until September 1946, when he became Commander U.S. Naval Forces Europe.

Now here is something that I will show you; I just got it here from my family. This is 10 April 1942, which is after I had been at the White House--you can read that.

Q: "From: Admiral Harold R. Stark, U.S. Navy.

"To: Chief of the Bureau of Navigation

"Subject: Captain John L. McCrea, U.S. Navy; Special Report

"Paragraph 1. My reports of fitness on Captain McCrea show my very high opinion of him when he was performing extremely valuable service in operations.

"Paragraph 2. My recommendation for him for Naval Aide to the President, particularly at a time like this, shows my high regard and opinion of him perhaps better than anything else could. My confidence in him for this extremely important assignment has been fully justified. I have had opportunity to observe closely the work he is doing for the White House. He has brought to that work an exceptionally high order of intelligence, thoroughness, judgment and initiative in making it easy for the President to keep abreast of practically everything of interest in the Naval situation from day to day. Because of his energy and thoroughness in this billet he relieved me of much detail in keeping the President informed.

"Paragraph 3. I cannot too strongly commend Captain McCrea for his excellence of performance of duty while serving directly under the Chief of Naval Operations involving such diversified duties as a trip to the Far East, contacting the Commander in Chief Asiatic Fleet and Commander in Chief Pacific Fleet, on the subject of war plans, his follow-up work in all departments in the Navy Department and for his splendid liaison work between the department and the White House.

Signed,

H. R. Stark"

Well, he certainly speaks highly of you.

Admiral McCrea: Yes, he painted it with a broad brush. Here I copied these out of my fitness report, see this-- marks of FDR.

Q: This is the period from 16 January 1942 to 31 March 1942:

"Captain McCrea has given me every satisfaction as naval aide. He has shown tact and ability in conference work with foreign naval and staff missions and also marked speed and efficiency in keeping and getting current Naval information to the Commander in Chief."

Then for the period from 1 April 1942 to 3 February 1943:

"I am sorry to lose his services as Naval Aide. His duties especially in time of war are varied and difficult. He has shown real ability in his staff work for me in the position of Secretary of the Pacific War Council, and his handling of the recent trip to North Africa and in his coordination of war information. I have greatly enjoyed having him with me."

Could you tell me, please, how you came to become the naval aide to President Roosevelt?

Admiral McCrea: How did I come to be that? Well, yes, I relieved Captain Beardall and it happened this way: Russell Willson was the Superintendent of the Naval Academy, and King wanted him on his staff in Washington.* All right, that was going to leave the Naval Academy vacant and Beardall had his eye on it, and he suggested it, and he got it. So they had to have somebody to relieve Beardall and McCrea was the guy. Stark and King sent me over there.

Q: Do you think this was because Stark had had the opportunity to observe you closely and knew of your abilities?

Admiral McCrea: He said so, and I had been with him. This letter dated the 10th April '42, and I had gone there in September of 1940.

---
*Rear Admiral Russell Willson, USN, was Superintendent of the Naval Academy from February 1941 to January 1942. Captain John R. Beardall, USN. As a rear admiral, Beardall served as Superintendent of the Naval Academy from January 1942 to August 1945, essentially the duration of U.S. participation in World War II.

Q: That mentions liaison work; was that before you actually became the naval aide?

Admiral McCrea: Yes. I was always trying to prepare Stark for his interviews with the President, don't you see, and he told me from time to time what the President had on his mind, and that's the way it worked out.

Q: Didn't you initially have some reluctance about going to the White House?

Admiral McCrea: Yes, of course I had reluctance about it. It was an expensive job in the first place, and when I was--it came on me--nobody told me a thing about it. Randall Jacobs stuck his head in the front door of my office one day and said, "How fast can you move?"*

And I said, "I can move fast if it's in command of that cruiser that I have been promised."

And he said, "Well, it isn't in command of a cruiser, but it's an important job." And with that, he backed out and slammed the door and that was it. And I sat there and wondered what the hell it was, and in about ten minutes he came back and handed me this thing.

---

*Rear Admiral Randall Jacobs, USN, Chief of Naval Personnel.

One day in early June, I guess it was, 1942, the President called me in and said he was expecting the Prime Minister, Mr. Churchill, to arrive in this country later that week and that he wanted me to meet him and give him a message from him, the President, to the Prime Minister. Well, Mr. Churchill arrived and the plane put down in the Potomac, and he finally got to the landing, and there was Halifax, the British Ambassador, and Cordell Hull and this little bit of a walk that we had to walk out on going out to the plane.* And Mr. Hull turned to me and in a squeaky voice of an old man, said, "Captain, I was informed that the President said that you were to greet the Prime Minister on his behalf and give him a message from the President."

I said, "Yes, Mr. Secretary, those are my instructions."

He said, "Well, you had better get out there then."

And I said, "Well, I was going to get there, but in my getting I didn't want to push His Majesty's Ambassador overboard and the Secretary of State. I'll get there."

I went out there and I met Mr. Churchill and told him exactly what the President had said--that he had to go to Hyde Park, and he wanted Mr. Churchill to join him at Hyde Park the next day.

---

*Edward Frederick Lindley Wood, Third Viscount Halifax, British Ambassador to the United States; Cordell Hull, U.S. Secretary of State.

J. L. McCrea #2 - 141

Well, I thought about that a lot. I came to the conclusion long, long ago, that it was a move by the President to get the PM to Hyde Park, which, if he had waited and met Mr. Churchill in Washington and he tried to induce Mr. Churchill to go to Hyde Park, that Mr. Churchill might have been clever enough to see a way of not going. But with the President at Hyde Park, it was a case of the mountain going to Mohammed--that's what it amounted to. Mr. Churchill stood there when I told him exactly what I was supposed to, and I said that he could go up by train tonight, or by air the next morning.

He said, "I shan't make a decision in this matter until I have had my bath."

Well, I turned to young Thompson--Mr. Churchill had two Thompsons on his staff, Thompson a commander in the Navy and Thompson a Scotland Yard man--his bodyguard.* And I turned to young Thompson, the Navy fellow, and I said, "Now listen, fellow, I've got a special train sitting down here with a couple of cars to take the PM up tonight if he wants to go. I would like to get a decision from him as soon as I can, because these 12 people, the train crew, cost money. You call me as soon as you can get a decision

---
*Commander Charles R. Thompson, RN, was the naval aide; Detective-Inspector W.H. Thompson was the bodyguard. See Gerald Pawle, The War and Colonel Warden (New York: Alfred A. Knopf, 1963) based on the recollections of Commander C. R. Thompson, CMG, OBE, RN (Ret.), Personal Assistant to the Prime Minister, 1940-1945. "Colonel Warden" was Churchill's cover name.

from the Prime Minister. Call me at my office in the White House."

I went up and sat in the office, and about ten minutes after 8:00 that night, the telephone rang. It was young Thompson. And the PM said he would like to go up the next morning at about 11:00 o'clock by air.

And I said, "I'll be out at 10:30 to pick up the party and take them down."

So I went out the next morning and in the car here sits the PM; Halifax; Oliver Lyttelton, the Minister of Supply; and here sits McCrea on the jump seat in front of Lyttelton. And the PM was conversing at great length about everything. Then all of a sudden he hit Halifax a slap on the knee and he said, "Halifax, the more I go about, the more convinced I am that a couple of generations ago there were many bitches abroad."

Silence. Oliver Lyttelton whispered in my off ear, "I wonder who he has in mind. Wouldn't it be wise for him to tell us who he is thinking about?"

Well, there was no answer to that, but that's what happened. So it remains as far as I am concerned to this day, a mystery as to who the hell he was thinking about.

Q: An interesting way of putting it.

Admiral McCrea: Yes--many bitches aboard.

Well, they came back from Hyde Park, ultimately, and the PM had dinner with the President and Harry Hopkins, up in the President's study.* And the President told me that he wanted me to take Mr. Churchill to Baltimore to get his plane. The reason was, at the end of the flight--these Pan American Clippers that were flying could land in the Potomac all right, but when it came to taking off with a full load of gas, they had to be some place where they could maneuver. And the Potomac wasn't big enough for them to maneuver, but they could up at Baltimore. So he took off up there.

Well, we got on board the plane that night, and here sat his doctor, his physician, Sir Charles something. I have forgotten what his last name was right now, but Sir Charles wrote a book about him.** The PM said, "Charles, you've been on my mind lately. You are supposed to be looking out for me, and I am doing pretty well by myself, but I am wondering who is looking out for you. Charles, I think that I'll just give you an examination." And he went over and started tapping the doctor on his chest and put his ear down and everything, and he said, "Charles, my

---
*Harry L. Hopkins held a variety of posts in the Roosevelt Administration, beginning in 1933. From 1942 to 1945, he was a special assistant to President Roosevelt. He was one of FDR's most trusted advisors.
**Sir Charles McMoran Wilson (Lord Moran). See his Churchill: Taken from the Diaries of Lord Moran: The Struggle for Survival, 1940-1945 (Boston: Houghton Mifflin Co., 1966).

J. L. McCrea #2 - 144

considered opinion is if you last out this trip, you will get home all right."

So that was that.

On the way over we went along, and here was a road sign--Valley Forge Beer--and Mr. Churchill said, "How clever, how deucedly clever, history and relaxation at once."

Well, there was a British naval officer that we knew up there and he was the skipper of the Lion with Sir David Beatty at Jutland, and Sir David Beatty thought so much of him he took him with him when he went to be the Commander in Chief. He was an exceedingly brilliant chap. His name was Alfred Ernle Montacute Chatfield, and this says that he was the first Baron Chatfield.* Chatfield was an exceedingly capable naval officer and a gunnery expert. Riding all the way from Washington to Baltimore, you have to talk about something, and I spoke about Chatfield, how he had been the First Sea Lord.** And I said, "I suppose with his age and one thing and another that he is now unemployed." The British refer to naval officers like that as unemployed, not retired.

And Mr. Churchill said, "Unemployed--not a bit of it. When he feels he has nothing better to do he races up and down the country making speeches against my government."

---
*Captain A. E. M. Chatfield, RN.
**In the rank of admiral of the fleet, Chatfield served as First Sea Lord and Chief of Naval Staff in the mid-1930s.

And that was Mr. Chatfield.

Well, we'll hurry on. I was interested to see him and, of course, the moment I saw him at the Casablanca Conference--his villa was just a little ways away from ours, the President's--and I had the Marines guard it unnoticed, and when they saw Mr. Churchill coming down the street, they were to let me know so I could be there to welcome him at the door.* He was in and out of the house two or three times a day for dinner or lunches--anything that was going on--so I would meet him. One day I didn't stay to all the conferences and things that they had, but the President had a look that he used to give me when he wanted me to stay. When I got the look, I just made myself as comfortable as I could and let go. One day I got the look, and Mr. Churchill fell to talking about the Russians. He went right after them and finally he said, "Mr. President, it is my considered opinion, sir, that the Kremlin has been in the past, and is now, populated with wicked men."

And how he bore down on the wicked men. The President was quiet for a second and then with a twinkle (with which he was very good) said, "Winston, do you realize that you are talking about one of our allies?"

---

*Held in North Africa, 14-23 January 1943, the Casablanca Conference was the first summit meeting of the leaders of the Allied nations after they had seized the initiative in World War II.

And the PM said, "Mr. President, I have considered that as well."

Q: How much did you get to sit in on these conferences that were conducted?

Admiral McCrea: At the Casablanca Conference, none. I didn't go because the military was in complete control. They were all there--King, and Marshall, and Arnold and all of those fellows.* I didn't go to any of them, but I was there for many of their talks in private. That's the way it goes.

Q: What were some of the other things that the President had you do for him?

Admiral McCrea: Well, I can't begin to tell you everything, but there was always something that I was doing for him. You remember the Battle of Savo Island?

Q: In August 1942.

Admiral McCrea: Yes. The Australians lost the Canberra

---
*General George C. Marshall, USA, was Chief of Staff of the Army; Lieutenant General Henry H. Arnold, USA, Commanding General, Army Air Forces. Both were promoted to five-star rank before the end of the war.

J. L. McCrea #2 - 147

down there. One day I was taking over a bunch of names to him. He always insisted on seeing the names of ships that were going to be assigned by the department, and he was looking over this list. He finally looked up, and he said, "You remember the Australians losing the Canberra?"

And I said, "Yes, Mr. President, I very well do."

And he said, "What do you think of the idea of us naming one of our ships the Canberra?"

I said, "Mr. President, I think that would be wonderful, only, of course, we would have to get permission from the Australians, sound them out."

And he said, "Well, that's where you come in. You get hold of Sir Owen Dixon." He was the Australian ambassador to the United States at that time. "See what he thinks about it."

So I got on the telephone, and I told Owen Dixon I would like to come out and see him, that I had a message that I wanted to deliver to him. And he asked if he couldn't come to see me. I said, "No, not at all, Mr. Ambassador, I'll be on my way right now."

So away I went, out there to see him. And I told him the story that the President was turning over in his mind--the idea of naming one of our new heavy cruisers the Canberra--and how he was wondering if this would meet with the approval of Sir Owen Dixon's government. Well, I saw, I thought, one tear in his eye, and he thought it was the most wonderful thing. He said, "Of course, I will have to consult with my government."

In a day or two he called me up, and he said that he had a message for me, couldn't he come to see me. I said, "No, I'll come and see you."

I went out there--I had previously told the President about it, of course, and that I was going to go out and see him. So after that, he said that the government would be very pleased. I returned and told the President, and he said, "You are not finished with this yet. Now, will you go out and see Sir Owen Dixon and tell him that, with his approval, I would like to designate Lady Dixon as the sponsor for the Canberra."*

Well, I went out there, and if I saw one tear before, I saw two tears this time. And the ambassador said, "I can't imagine anybody being so thoughtful."

And that's the way it turned out; she christened the heavy cruiser Canberra. The Navy Department, though, didn't like the idea, because they took the name--one of the plans for the Pittsburgh--and changed it into Canberra, and the engineering people said, "My God, there are 50-some-odd-thousand blueprints that have got to be changed."

So I said, "I wouldn't think that would be insurmountable; all you have to do is scratch out Pittsburgh and write or paste Canberra."

---

*Lady Alice C. Dixon.

Well, that is the way it worked out. Now, years and years passed. I was retired from the Navy and was with John Hancock as a vice president down there, and one day our president at lunch remarked about the very interesting international legal seminar that was going on over at Harvard. And he said that that morning he had heard a talk given by the Chief Justice of the Supreme Court of Australia. I pricked up my ears right away, and I said, "Judge Elliott, is Sir Owen Dixon here?"

And he said, "Yes. Do you know Sir Owen Dixon?"

I said, "Yes."

So when I got down to my office, I called up the Harvard Law School where they were holding this thing and said I wondered how I could get in touch with Sir Owen Dixon. Well, the word came back that he would call me back in about 20 minutes. He did, and I told him I would like very much to come over and see him. I told him who I was, and he remembered me right away.

He said, "I have something better. Why don't you and Mrs. McCrea join Lady Dixon and me at 5:00 o'clock this afternoon for tea?"

They had quartered him in some fancy house over there at Harvard. I have forgotten what the name of it was now. So that's the way it worked out. And when Estelle (my wife who has passed on, of course, some time ago) and I went over there promptly at 5:00 o'clock, he hadn't shown up.

He was about 10 or 15 minutes late getting in there. But Lady Dixon sat there, and she was all filled with Australia and about the Canberra and everything. And she said, "Often people will say to me, 'Lady Dixon, how about your family?'"

And she said, "My reply is always this: 'Two sons, two daughters and a heavy cruiser.'"

Q: That's beautiful.

Admiral McCrea: Well, about that time, Sir Owen Dixon popped in and we had quite a to-do.

The years passed, and Martha and I decided to go down to Australia.* I wanted her to see it, and we went on the Mariposa down to Australia, by Bora Bora and Fiji and New Zealand, everything.** And when I got down there, I made inquiry about Sir Owen Dixon. I was told by one of the people in authority down there that he was in bad shape mentally, so I never did try to get to see him.

But getting back to FDR, he was the fellow who thought about that, and I think it was a fine touch.

Now, comes the next one. When the Juneau was lost, our light cruiser out there, there were five boys on there--brothers--by the name of Sullivan, and they came

---
*Martha was the name of Admiral McCrea's second wife.
**The Mariposa was an American passenger ship.

from Iowa.* The Navy got around to assigning the names for ships, and I took the list by him, and he was going down it. "Sullivan," he said, "and who is this?"

I said, "Mr. President, the name Sullivan is for the five boys who were lost in the Juneau."

He said, "Listen, haven't they any imagination down there? Why did they put Sullivan; why didn't they put The Sullivans?"

I promptly went back and said, "We can arrange that, Mr. President."

I went back and they changed the name to The Sullivans. All right, the father and mother came on and I met them. He interjected himself into this thing and changed the name from Sullivan to The Sullivans, which was most appropriate, as far as I was concerned.

Again, the years passed. I was up here as the commandant, and The Sullivans was in the navy yard down there, and I was invited to Thanksgiving dinner on board The Sullivans.** And who should be there as well but John

---

*The USS Juneau (CL-52) was torpedoed and sunk in a battle against the Japanese off Guadalcanal the night of 12-13 November 1942. Her magazines exploded, with the result that she sank so rapidly only ten members of her crew survived.

**This is a reference to Admiral McCrea's tour of duty as Commandant of the First Naval District.

McCormack--later the Speaker of the House.* They had a shipside podium, and they had the crew on the ship, and John McCormack made a talk, and then I was introduced as the commandant to make a talk. So then I told them the story about how the ship got named. Of course, none of those fellows knew that--how it got named that way--but that's how it got named. Of course, it added something to the ship.

Q: Was President Roosevelt instrumental in naming the carrier Shangri-La?

Admiral McCrea: Not to my knowledge, but President Roosevelt always liked to go to Hyde Park because he despised Washington summers. Of course, he always had some business up there, too, with the estate and one thing and another. So, in March or early April of 1942, he had Ross McIntire and Steve Early and myself in there one night, and he said, "I can't go to Hyde Park as much as I would like to, as I have in the past.** I wish there was someplace that I could go to around here where the weather wouldn't be as oppressive as it is usually in Washington. Hoover had some place up here in the Maryland mountains or something."

---
*Representative John W. McCormack, Democrat-Massachusetts.
**Rear Admiral Ross T. McIntire, Medical Corps, USN, the presidential physician; Stephen Early, presidential press secretary.

And we said, "Yes."

He said, "Now, you fellows get out and look this thing over and see what you can come up with."

It just so happened that he grabbed me--we were going up on Tuesday and I can remember just as well as can be, it was on Tuesday, and he sent me over into Virginia. So Steve and Ross McIntire went up, and they went down on the Rapidan up there and took a look at it, and they decided that wasn't for the President. It was down in a gully, and he liked to be up in the air where he could see things. So they finally came up, and they came across this little camp that had been up there. I have forgotten the exact details of the thing, but the city of Baltimore had had something to do with it.

At any rate, the Army was looking for a place to train these roughnecks who charge in--commandos--and they wanted someplace to train, and so they decided that they could get this little camp. Well, Steve and Ross McIntire took a look at that and said, "With a little bit of changing around here, we could get this fixed up for the President with a swimming pool over there." So it was rigged up, and Ben Moreell was called in--the Chief of Yards and Docks.[*] They went up there, and here was a little cottage that had been occupied by the administrator, and they thought with a

---

[*]Rear Admiral Ben Moreell, CEC, USN, Chief of the Bureau of Yards and Docks.

little bit of modification that they could fix it up. So they finally wound up with a cottage--a main bedroom for the President and three other bedrooms and a couple of baths and one thing and another, and a porch that looked out across the Maryland countryside. It was a beautiful view from up there on the porch.

Of course, his infirmity was such that he couldn't get around much, and this would be a fine place for him to sit around and monkey with his papers. Finally, one day, the opening date was decided upon, and I had stripped the people from the presidential yacht, the Potomac, the caretakers and the stewards and one thing and another, and got them up there. I had Jack Kevers, who was a former chief boatswain, and he was now a lieutenant in the Navy, so he was the local caretaker.*

Well, the President every so often said, "Now, you're the proprietor of this camp." He had never seen it, and always he was saying to me, "John, do it on the cheap, do it on the cheap."

I knew he liked a three-quarter size bed, so I went to the survey section of the Washington Navy Yard, and up there I found a three-quarter size brass bed, and it was the only three-quarter size bed up there. So I walked off with it. I told him about it, and he said, "John, don't you know that brass beds are in now?"

---

*Lieutenant John H. Kevers, USN.

And I said, "No, I didn't know anything like that."

He said, "All I want to be sure is that it has a good, comfortable set of springs and mattress."

And I said, "Well, we'll look out for that too, Mr. President."

And he kept saying every so often that I was the proprietor of it. Then all of a sudden he said one day, "What are you going to name it?"

I said, "Mr. President, I haven't given any thought to what to name it."

He said, "What would you say if we call it Shangri-La?"

Of course, he had read the story, and from that time on it was Shangri-La.* I had a little sign fixed up over the front door like this: "Shangri-La."

So it went along as Shangri-La for quite some time. I don't know what Truman called it, but don't think he changed it.

Eisenhower promptly changed it from Shangri-La to Camp David, which always irked me somewhat. I told you that Eisenhower irked me on two or three occasions, and he did that. That was his contribution, calling it Camp David, which I think we could have done well without.

---

*The term came from the 1933 novel <u>Lost Horizon</u> by James Hilton, who wrote of a desirable remote paradise in Tibet. The term has entered the language with a meaning of a remote, beautiful place where life approaches perfection.

One of the things that I came across when I was furnishing this place up there--incidentally, I took the dining table off the Potomac and the chairs that went with it, and took them up there for him.* We took everything out of the Potomac that we could and also out of the survey section. It went on the cheap. Some writer a few years ago, I think it was some gal that wrote this thing up, said that it cost $60,000 to fix this thing up. I don't think it cost anything like that at all.

But here I came across this fresco which had been on the front page of, I think, The Saturday Evening Post, or it may have been Esquire. But here are two or three little boys and this fellow rapping on the door. And this lady is at the door, and they said, "Mrs. So-and-so, Johnny has just written a nasty word on the sidewalk." And you looked down at the sidewalk, and there was "Roosevelt" written there. We hung that right outside his door so that first thing in the morning he would see it as he came through the door. And he would stop and laugh at that thing. He just got a hell of a kick out of it.

Now we go along a little bit further. Came the 18th of April 1942, and Tokyo was bombed by planes from an American carrier, the Hornet. The planes dropped their

---

*The USS Potomac, which had previously been a Coast Guard vessel, was the presidential yacht during the period before World War II. The addition of increased equipment in the superstructure made her topheavy and essentially unseaworthy, so she was little used during the war.

bombs on the way over to China where they were going. He was at Hyde Park, and I was in Washington. I always called him two or three times a day, so I called him and I said, "Mr. President, Tokyo was bombed yesterday by planes, and there is great excitement in Tokyo, and they all wonder where the plane came from."

He said, "Really? Really?"

Of course, he knew that the thing was going to be bombed that day, because that was a target date, and he was well aware of it, but he acted as though it was brand-new news to him, which it wasn't at all. And I remarked that they wondered where they came from. That afternoon, shortly after noon, I was in my office down there, and the chief operator said the President wanted to talk to me. He said, "Are the Japs still interested in knowing where those planes came from?"

"Well," I said, "I suppose they are, Mr. President."

He said, "Well, I've got the answer for them. Tell them they came from Shangri-La. Tell Ernie King, unless he has some good objection to it, I think it would be good to let off a press release that those planes that bombed Tokyo came from Shangri-La." That's what was done. This was his quick wit and his thought--tell them they came from Shangri-La. That about ends the thing with Shangri-La.

It was interesting to be around a guy who was quick witted.

Q: Were there other cases where you saw that quick wit?

Admiral McCrea: Oh, yes, all the while.

Do you remember the book The Robe?

Q: By Lloyd Douglas? I read that one in high school.

Admiral McCrea: Yes, that would be about your time. I am trying to find my copy of it that I have around here someplace. Up at Hyde Park I would be in one corner of the library, and he'd be off in the other, and he would be either playing double solitaire or sitting there thinking. And one day he slapped this book shut, and he said, "Have you read this book The Robe?

"No," I said, "I haven't, Mr. President."

And he said, "I think it's one of the best books I have ever read."

And I wrote that in the fly leaf of the copy that I had that that's what he said, and it is around here someplace.

Q: I was interested in that story you told me once before about how Samuel Elliot Morison came to be historian for the Navy in World War II.*

Admiral McCrea: Yes. I guess I told you the whole story about how this fellow who wrote the article for The Globe, how Morison had to work his way into the White House to see President Roosevelt, to sell himself to President Roosevelt, to be the historian, don't you see?** So I wrote a story to the fellow who had written the article and told him exactly how it happened. I got a call from Mr. Winship, the editor of The Globe, and he wanted to take that letter that I had written to this guy, the author, and change it into a letter to the editor.*** I said, "If you will do me the favor of looking it over closely. Naval officers have trouble writing simple declarative sentences. I don't know how many rules of grammar that I would be breaking in that thing. If you can fix it so that it won't reflect too much discredit on me, why, okay."

So he did, and he didn't do too much to it. I told him just exactly how it was, that the President asked me if I had read this thing, and I told him that I had and said, "As a matter of fact, I just finished it last night; it's a Book of the Month Club book and is exceedingly interesting."

---
*Morison was a Harvard history professor who eventually produced an unofficial 15-volume work titled History of United States Naval Operations in World War II.
**The Boston Globe is a daily newspaper.
***Laurence L. Winship, managing editor of the Boston Globe.

And he said, "What did you think of it?"

I said, "I thought that the enterprise the author exhibited in sailing over the routes of Columbus was perfectly wonderful, and it really made the book."*

And FDR said, "I think somebody has told me that Morison is a Naval Reserve officer. I'm going to get in touch with Frank Knox and tell him to send him over here.** I'd like to talk to him. The story of the Navy in the First World War was written years after the war was over and was all written from reports in there. I think it would be interesting to have the history of what the Navy does this time written contemporaneously with the action. I think this fellow Morison might be able to do it."

So the first thing I knew, Marvin McIntyre called up one morning and said, "Listen, skipper [I'd known him since 1920], don't these naval officers know that they can't come barging over here to the White House to see the President any time the notion hits them?"***

And I said, "Of course, they do."

He said, "I think you had better have the word passed."

I said, "Well, better yet, you tell me who it is who

---

*Samuel Eliot Morison, <u>Admiral of the Ocean Sea: A Life of Christopher Columbus</u> (Boston: Little, Brown and Company, 1942).
**Frank Knox was Secretary of the Navy from 1940 to 1944.
***As official secretary to President Roosevelt, Marvin H. McIntyre handled appointments.

is trying to get in over there, and we will see that he is set right."

So he said, "Janet, what's the name of that naval officer who wants to see the President?"

And I could hear Janet in the background mumbling way back there someplace, and then he said, "His name is Samuel Elliot Morison, Lieutenant Commander, USNR."

I said, "My friend, you had better let him in, because I think he is the President's nominee for writing the naval history of this world war."

"All right."

So I wrote all this--that Sam went over there at the behest of the President, not his own idea. Then it turned out that some monkey in the history department over at Harvard wrote and answered all this stuff. He said what Morison did is not the history of the Navy in the Second World War, not the official history of the Navy, because Mr. Forrestal said it wasn't the official history.*

Well, I wrote to Mr. Winship, and I said, "Until something better comes along, people are going to take Sam Morison as being the authority; that's all there is to it." That's the story that I guess I told you.

Q: It has certainly proven to be the case--nothing better has come along.

---
*James V. Forrestal, Secretary of the Navy at the end of World War II.

Admiral McCrea: And it won't come along; it won't come. I don't know what you know about it, but Sam just went out and recruited all these young Ph.D.s in history--for instance, George Elsey, the fellow I picked out of the ONI in the Navy Department and took to the White House in my map room over there.* And that's another thing I want to tell you about. I want to tell you about that map room, and I am perfectly willing to go on record about that.

When I reported over there, I found two charts in the old cabinet room and a pair of parallel rulers and a pair of dividers sitting over there on this table. That was the only naval information that the President had, the only bit of it. Well, President Roosevelt remarked to me that he wanted to get some information and he said, "Winston had the traveling map room with him."

That appealed to me right offhand as an idea. So I got a room set aside over at the White House for me. We had these four walls, and it was bigger than our living room out there and maybe the whole side of the house. It was near the Diplomatic Reception Room, down below on the ground floor. It just so happened that one of our young reserve officers, Bob Montgomery, the movie actor, had gone to France as an ambulance driver or some other damn thing,

---

*Ensign George M. Elsey, USNR; ONI--Office of Naval Intelligence.

and he wound up in Great Britain.* And he got into the reserve in some way or other, and he was assigned to duty in the map room over in the Admiralty.

I found out that he was working in our ONI section, and immediately got ahold of this guy and we got him over there, and he helped us immeasurably in coming up with something that the British had done. And in that way we avoided a lot of the mistakes that we might very well have tumbled into. He suggested this and that and the other thing, and his help was invaluable. I was awfully fond of Bob, and some Hollywood writer turned on him and said that he was living in style in Washington at the Mayflower Hotel and a few other things. He was living at the Mayflower Hotel, but he had his own money and was paying for it himself, but he was doing a good job for us.

Well, then one day he called me on the telephone, and he said, "Captain, I'm up against it over here. These newspeople are after me all the while, and they are publishing things on the West Coast about me and my family. What I am calling about now is that the newspeople at the White House want me to come out and have my picture taken with Diana Hopkins feeding the pigeons on the White House

---

*Lieutenant (junior grade) Robert Montgomery, USNR. By the end of the war, he rose to the rank of commander. He starred in a 1945 movie titled They Were Expendable, which depicted the activities of the U.S. Navy's PT boats around the Philippines at the beginning of World War II.

lawn."*

I said, "Bob, look, they can take all the pictures that they want of Diana Hopkins feeding the pigeons, but you are not to be in it."

He said, "I thought that that was what your answer would be."

Then, a few days afterward, I got hold of him and said--oh, yes, somebody else came at me around the White House and I won't name who it was--and they said did I realize that one of my helpers was a Republican and was against all Democrats and all their works and all that sort of thing. "Now I'll listen," I said. "Tell me."

"Well, Bob Montgomery is a Republican."

And I said, "He is damn good, and he has been a lot of help to me, but that's all."

After thinking these things over one day, I called Bob in and I said, "Listen, there is only room for one person at 1600 Pennsylvania Avenue, and that's the President of the United States. And you are getting so damn much publicity, and there's nothing you can do to stop it and nothing I can do to stop it, much as I would like to."

And he said, "Well, I thought that I would like to go to sea."

I said, "You tell me, where do you want to go?"

He said, "I would like to go to the PT boats."

---

*Diana Hopkins was the nine-year-old daughter of Harry Hopkins, special assistant to President Roosevelt.

And I said, "Now listen, wait a moment. I want to think this over because at 39 or 40, you are a bit too old to go to the PT boats. What do you think?"

"Well," he said, "I would like to give it a try. I'm in pretty good shape."

And he was in good shape. He went and he came back-- and he did very well. He just passed on here a few weeks ago.*

Q: I saw that in the newspaper.

Admiral McCrea: I had a high regard for him. So many times I have the idea, well, I'll write to so-and-so and bring up old times and something. I thought about Bob Montgomery this last year and I didn't do it, and now I feel badly that I didn't do it. Because he was a great deal of help to me, I'll tell you.

Now this situation room--this map room, I call it--Pa Watson came over there one day right after we really got going and he said, "Well, where is the Army around here?"**

I said, "You are the military aide to the President. This is the office of the naval aide to the President."

---

*Montgomery, who was born 21 May 1904, died 27 September 1981.
**Brigadier General Edwin M. Watson, AUS.

And he said, "Well, can't you use the Army around here?"

I said, "Yes, but one thing, General Watson. This is my operation, and if you want to send some Army people over here, they can come over here. But they are going to work for me and they are going to work for my number one fellow here, who is junior to most of your fellows." (The Army promotions were much more rapid.) "I'm going to run this thing, and my fellow Mott is going to be my number one here."*

And that's the way we worked it out, and it worked out wonderfully.

About mid-August of 1942, one Sunday afternoon, I was down there, and Admiral Leahy came barging around there and he said, "You know, McCrea, I think there is probably more information in this room about the progress of the war than any other place in Washington."**

I said, "Well, that's just where it should be then, because we are giving to the President everything that we can get, and we are improving on it all the while."

We did, too, and we did a good job. Now that thing has grown and is no longer the map room, but it is called the situation room. Of course, I ran the thing night and day, too, and it is night and day all the while down there.

---
*Lieutenant (junior grade) William C. Mott, USNR.
**Admiral William D. Leahy, USN (Ret.), chief of staff to Roosevelt in Roosevelt's role of Commander in Chief of the Army and Navy.

J. L. McCrea #2 - 167

The copy book says that "Big oaks from little acorns grow," and that's exactly what happened in the case of this situation room. Because I started with nothing but two charts and a pair of rulers and a pair of dividers and that was all. We did it all.

Q: What were some of the things that Montgomery brought over from the British that helped?

Admiral McCrea: It was the organization and what you did, the information that you wanted to keep. He knew what they had. We improved on some of it, I suppose, but we were saved, I am convinced, from a lot of unnecessary projecting around wondering whether something would be of service or not. We had Bob to tell us that the British did thus and so, and it was very helpful. We had everything there. I had the only complete file of the messages that passed between President Roosevelt and Mr. Truman and Chiang Kai-shek and Stalin, and the whole damn outfit--the only complete file.* Everything that went out went out Navy communications, and what came back came back through the Army communications, and we had it there under lock and key, night and day.

---

*Harry S Truman succeeded Roosevelt as President in 1945. Chiang Kai-shek was supreme commander of allied air and land forces in the Chinese theater during World War II. Stalin was dictator in the Soviet Union and a major player in establishing Allied strategy during the war.

Q: Did you give the President a daily briefing on the progress of the war?

Admiral McCrea: No. He got his briefing out of dispatches, just exactly where I got it. I got them every morning, and Admiral King made arrangements for me to get them every morning, weekends, day in and day out, and I went to Secretary Knox's conference. He had a conference every morning at 8:15, and I went and listened to that. I got in there about 7:00 o'clock in the morning and went over the dispatches. Then I went to Knox's conference, then I jumped into my car, went right over to the White House, and went up to catch the President reading the paper in bed or shaving. And I would sit and read the dispatches he ought to hear. I didn't give him unnecessary things, and then at night when I came over, when he was getting his sinuses packed, I would read the day's dispatches to him. That's the way it worked out. He was satisfied with the information, and I gave him everything I could get my clutches on.

Q: Did Admiral King give him briefings also?

Admiral McCrea: Once in a while King would go over there, once in a long while. I remember when King came over and told him that they were setting up the plan to bombard

Tokyo--King came over and told him that. I was talking with Admiral King, and we had gotten a dispatch from Mr. Churchill hoping that the Navy in the Far East could do something in the way of aggressive employment out there. And the President said, "Get in touch with Ernie King."

I got in touch with Admiral King and told him we had gotten this dispatch. And Admiral King said he would like very much to come by and see the President the next morning, if that would be agreeable. So he did, and he told the President what they had in mind. That's the only time I knew of that he ever came there to brief him about any upcoming operation.

Q: What was the President's reaction when he got the news about those cruisers being lost at Savo Island?*

Admiral McCrea: He was heartsick about it, as all of us were. I got it on Sunday morning, and he was up there at Shangri-La. I called him and said, "Mr. President, I have some information that I don't want to trust on the telephone, and I'd like to come up and see you if I may."

He said, "Sure," and so my driver just drove me up

---

*In the early morning hours of 9 August 1942, Japanese ships attacked and sank four heavy cruisers: the USS Astoria (CA-34), USS Quincy (CA-44), USS Vincennes (CA-39), and HMAS Canberra. For a detailed account, see Richard F. Newcomb, Savo: The Incredible Naval Debacle off Guadalcanal (New York: Holt, Rinehart and Winston, 1961).

there. It's about 60 miles up there. I went up there, and Sam Rosenman and his wife were there that weekend, and Mrs. Roosevelt. And when I came through the door, they all scattered. And I sat there and I told the President the whole story and showed him the dispatches. He was heartsick about it. There wasn't anything he could do about it. The Astoria was lost there.

Q: The Astoria, the Quincy, the Vincennes, and the Canberra. Admiral Ghormley was the commander down there then.* What was the chain of events that sent Ghormley from London to the South Pacific?

Admiral McCrea: Well, I'll tell you about that. Ghormley went from London to the South Pacific. Now Ghormley had worked closely with Admiral Stark, and from there he had gone to England. Stark was being sent over there to replace Ghormley, and President Roosevelt said to me, "What's going to happen to Ghormley?"

I said, "I haven't the remotest idea, Mr. President."

And he said, "Well, find out."

I said, "Well, he is a vice admiral temporarily now, and I suppose he will lose his rank and go as rear admiral, to his permanent rank."

---

*Vice Admiral Robert L. Ghormley, USN, was Special Naval Observer in London until April 1942, then in June 1942 became Commander South Pacific Area with headquarters at Noumea, New Caledonia.

And the President said, "Well, tell Ernie King for me that I think it rather unfair because we have to find a place for Stark that Ghormley is to lose his rank as vice admiral."

The net result was that Ghormley was sent to the South Pacific where somebody of his rank was needed. Ghormley didn't bring about his own downfall, but you could well forecast it. He was pointing out shortages; in every dispatch that came down there, he wanted this and he wanted that. Well, this and that didn't exist, and there wasn't any way you could do it. King, as you may recall, used to say, "Do the best you can with what you have."

He was always talking that way, and, of course, it was the proper way to talk. King didn't have anything up his sleeve that he could send down there; he was doing the best he could.

Interview Number 3 with Vice Admiral John L. McCrea,
U.S. Navy (Retired)

Place: Admiral McCrea's home in Chestnut Hill, Massachusetts

Date: Wednesday, 27 October 1982

Interviewer: Paul Stillwell

Q: Admiral, what do you remember about your service on the island of Guam in the 1930s?

Admiral McCrea: When I got this letter from the Navy Department wanting to know my reaction on being ordered to Guam, I was very much annoyed, because duty on Guam had been associated with people who had not measured up to their abilities. And invariably, when orders were published in newspapers, as they were in those days--every day, The New York Times carried orders to naval officers, and if you'd see somebody ordered to Guam, the reaction was, "I wonder what he's done."

I had spent nearly six years outside the continental limits of the United States, and I thought I was getting a bad shake to be considered for going to the island of Guam when any number of people of my seniority had never spent five minutes outside the continental limits of the United States, and I thought that they had first call on those fellows.

Well, I just dismissed it; didn't think too much about

it. Then, all of a sudden, out of the blue one day came this dispatch: "Regret exigencies of service. Require that you be ordered to Guam. You will depart San Francisco early in March, USS Chaumont. Report to the medical officer for examination as to physical fitness for duty on the island of Guam."*

A few days after I got my orders to go to Guam, I ran into Admiral Hart at the annual ball that was given by the Los Angeles Chamber of Commerce for Navy personnel who were attached to the Pacific Fleet.** It was always quite a bash. Admiral Hart was there, and when the music stopped, it just so happened that I was near him, and he said, "You don't want to go to Guam, do you?"

I said, "Of course not, Admiral, but I don't know any way of getting out of it."

He said, "Well, I haven't any suggestions. Just go ahead if you have to and do as good a job as you can."

I swallowed my pride, and off I went to Guam. I had previously had, as one of my skippers, Captain E. S. Root-- class of 1905 at the Naval Academy--and I had talked from time to time with him about Guam, because I had visited Guam twice: once en route to the China Station in 1924, and then I came back to Guam towing a submarine that needed

---
*USS Chaumont (AP-5) was a Navy transport that operated throughout the Pacific.
**Rear Admiral Thomas C. Hart, USN, Commander Cruisers Scouting Force/Commander Cruiser Division Five.

help.* I stayed at Government House for two or three days, and then I went back to the Manila area.** So I had somewhat of an interest in Guam. When I received my orders to go to Guam, Root said to me, "There's one thing I want to suggest to you. No matter how urgently you think something should be done in Guam, just choke down that thought for at least three or four months and think it over; think out all the angles."

When I arrived on the island of Guam, I was promptly met with the situation that the island had no source of fresh water, excepting a few springs around the island and the rainfall. They had reservoirs adjacent to all the schoolhouses, because the schoolhouses had relatively large roofs, and they would catch the rain. A lot of rain had fallen on Guam, but it just disappeared. That was all there was to it.

Both Governor McCandlish and I got to thinking about if we wanted to do something for the island, it was to get

---

*Captain Edmund S. Root, USN, had previously been commanding officer of the USS Astoria (CA-34), the heavy cruiser in which McCrea was serving at the time he had received orders in early 1936 to report as executive officer of the U.S. naval station on Guam. Before commanding the Astoria, Captain Root had held the dual post of Governor of Guam and commandant of the naval station. After Guam had come under U.S. control in 1898, the Navy was in charge of both military and civil aspects of the island's life.

**Government House was the residence of the governor-commandant of the island and also housed the executive offices of Guam's naval government and naval station.

fresh water, if possible.* A year or so before that, I had found out that there was a groundwater geologist who had come out to Hawaii and had made a lot of surveys out there. And he had come up with a lot of fresh water on the island of Maui--that there was a great deal of rain that fell on the island of Oahu, but it disappeared into the ground. And this fellow knew something, of course, about what he was doing. It turned out, which was news to me, that there was a definite relationship between the density of salt water and fresh water and that, in contact with each other, certain things happened.

The way this chap worked it out, he would take a sounding and find out the difference in the height of the fresh water and the salt water. And for the difference of about a foot, I guess, it turned out that there was about 20 feet or thereabouts of fresh water floating on top of the salt water. So if you went down and skimmed this fresh water and didn't get contact with the salt water, you were in pretty good shape.

Well, we wanted to get this groundwater geologist out to Guam to give us the benefit of what he had found in the Hawaiian Islands. We found out we couldn't get him, because the appropriation that covered his salary very definitely limited him to the continental United States, the Canal Zone, and the Hawaiian Islands. So what we did,

---

*Captain Benjamin V. McCandlish, USN, Governor of Guam and commandant of the U.S. naval station on Guam.

we got this fellow and his wife, and she was a water geologist too. He took a leave of absence, and the government of Guam paid his way out to Guam and set up his wife and him in a little suite over the officers' club. He would go out and do all his notebook work and hand it to her at the end of the day, and she processed it, and there we went.

Meanwhile, Governor McCandlish and I had thought that we could do something ourselves, and we had sent off to the United States and gotten a well-drilling machine--we got it out there. When the well-drilling machine came out there, what were we to do with it? We had a little newspaper out there, and I put a note in the newspaper that anybody who had any well-drilling experience on the island to please get in contact with the governor's office. Sure enough, a first class machinist's mate who was on duty in the little Navy yard out there came in to see me. His name was Myers--I'll never forget old Myers--he came in to see me, and he said, "I don't know anything about drilling water wells, but I worked on a drilling rig with an uncle of mine in the oil fields out in Wyoming. And I do know something about drilling."

I said, "Do you think that you could take ahold of this well-drilling machine?"

Meanwhile, we had gone out and taken a look at it, and

he said, "Yes, I'd like to give it a try."

Well, he did. We moved the well-drilling machine up in the Barrigada Heights where the need for fresh water was really urgent and let him start drilling. I guess he had been drilling for three or four weeks when my friend, the groundwater geologist, showed up, and I took him up there to meet Myers and to show him what we were doing on our own. Our geologist (his name escapes me at the moment, might be Watkins) told me, "I don't think you are going to get any fresh water here, but this fellow knows what he is doing. I looked at his records, and he is keeping the sort of records that are invaluable for drilling. So just let him go ahead, and I will go ahead and start making my survey of the island."

One Saturday afternoon I came in from playing golf, and my wife said, "Myers has been on the telephone this afternoon, and he has been looking for you."

I got in touch with Myers within a few minutes, and he said, "Commander, we have struck fresh water. I stopped drilling right away."

I said, "That's exactly right, Myers. You should have stopped."

So I got hold of the groundwater geologist, and we went up there and took a look around. And, sure enough, he agreed that the fellow had found fresh water. He ran levels down to the shoreline, and he found that we had about four or five feet of difference between the fresh water level and the salt water level. That meant that we had around 100 feet of fresh water down there someplace. Of course, that was greatly interesting and greatly exciting. We went ahead and developed along those lines. When I left there about a year later, I had the satisfaction of knowing that we had 16 producing wells on the island of Guam.

When I went out to the Orient then, with the war plans, in December of 1940, I stopped at Guam, of course, and the governor put me up at Government House, and he took me out to a reservoir that was being built on the southern end of Guam. I had the pleasure of seeing all these lengths of pipe that were alongside the road from this reservoir some six miles away, and the pipes were being laid on the road to pipe fresh water into the city of Agaña. Now that was in December of 1940.

December 1941 came and Pearl Harbor, and the Japs arrived on Guam, but when the Japanese left Guam--much to the amazement of many, because the Japanese believed in the scorched-earth policy--the Japanese did not do anything about destroying our fresh water system. This, of course, was providential in many ways. I have often thought maybe that the Japanese thought that their withdrawal was just temporary and that they would be back and that they could use the fresh water system again.

Well, there it was, and that's the story about what we did on the island of Guam about getting fresh water. It was greatly helpful to these people. Mind you, they had been living out of storage tanks and what rainwater they could catch from the roofs of the little houses and things like that. And here we had these 16 producing wells scattered around on the island of Guam when I left out there.

Q: You mentioned yesterday that you also helped out with a labor contract while you were there.

Admiral McCrea: That's right. Pan American wanted people to work on Midway.* They wanted machinists, and they wanted people to be waiters for hotels that they had, because in those days Pan Am's going across the Pacific-- daylight jumps--and they would spend the night in the hotel, get an early breakfast, and go to the next jump. The only overnight runs were the runs between San Francisco and Honolulu and then from Guam to Manila. From Hawaii to Midway and from Midway to Wake--those were all daylight runs, and then from Wake to Guam was a daylight run. Well, Pan Am absorbed a lot of our local labor force in Guam, but when it came to putting people on those islands out there,

---

*In the mid-1930s, Pan American World Airways established a string of island maintenance facilities and hotels. These were needed to operate a fleet of planes known as Clippers in transpacific passenger service to the Orient.

it would be a very unusual type of person who could go out there. The Guamanians had lived their whole lives on this small island, so they didn't feel too badly about getting these good jobs. I got in touch with Pan Am, and I didn't know what they were going to come up with. But I talked it all out with them; we drew up a labor contract saying that anybody that they employed on the island of Guam, to serve on Midway or Wake, could make a visit of ten days, or thereabouts, every three months back to his home on the island of Guam, if he so wished. They agreed to that, and we signed up and all that sort of stuff.

I was looking out for the interests of these Guamanians, and that's the only time I ever had anything to do with the law--the labor contract that we signed--and it worked out fine. When Kelly Turner came around and said I was to make this trip out to the Orient with the war plans, incognito, I told him, "You are talking to the worst person in the world. If you want somebody to go incognito, on every one of these islands there are young Guamanians out there who know me and all that sort of thing. They have seen me around Guam."

And that's the way it worked out. But it was most interesting. Then I was on the island of Guam when they started the passenger trips across the Pacific. For a number of weeks they ran just these trips across the

Pacific to break in their crews--with no passengers whatsoever. They did carry mail, however. I remember that. For 50 cents we could send an airmail letter to the United States from the island of Guam, which seemed a little bit exorbitant in the days of two-cent mail.

Then the first passengers started coming through, and on the very first trip that carried paying passengers, out came people from Hawaii, the Dillinghams, who were looking for development. They knew that there was bound to be development, so they sent their engineers out. Two people in the first passenger flight of some note were Gilbert Grosvenor and his wife. Mrs. Gilbert Grosvenor was the daughter of Alexander Graham Bell, and the Grosvenors' son, Melville Grosvenor--who just died a few weeks ago, within the last three months--he was class of 1923 at the Naval Academy.* By that time, when his parents came out there on this first trip of the passengers across there, he had left the Navy and was with the National Geographic. Mr. Grosvenor was exceedingly interested in everything that we were doing there.

Another thing we did out there when the passengers started coming across the Pacific--Guam was a closed port; very few people ever got there--looking for a change of

---

*Melville Bell Grosvenor resigned from the Navy as an ensign in 1924 and spent the rest of his life with the National Geographic Society, including service as president of the society and editor-in-chief of National Geographic magazine. He died 22 April 1982.

scenery, we told the manager of the Pan American operation out there to pick out about a dozen passengers out of these lists at the time they came through there, because they stayed there overnight, and we would invite them to dinner at Government House. The governor and his wife and I and my wife represented the Navy and the rest of these people (the table would take only about 16 people or something like that), and we got these pioneers, as it were, crossing the Pacific. And it was a break for them to have dinner not in the little hotel out there, and they saw the Navy in operation, and we created, I am sure, a lot of good will in that direction.

Among other things, Gilbert Grosvenor and his wife were on their way to visit their son-in-law and his wife who were attached to our embassy in Tokyo. Gilbert Grosvenor wrote a thank-you note back to us, but the thank-you note got in the wrong envelope. And what arrived on the island of Guam was instructions that he was writing to the caretaker of his home up in Canada, telling him how he wanted the house opened by such-and-such a date and all that sort of thing.

So here was the plane going east, and, of course, the things went once a week. And I could see by the dates in the letter that to send the letter out to Tokyo, he would never get it back in time. So I just packed it up and I sent it to the editor of the National Geographic and told him, "You'll know what to do with this letter." I promptly got a letter back from the executive editor of the National Geographic in which he enclosed 50 cents worth of stamps, because that was the amount of stamps I had to put on the letter to him, and he thanked me very much.

When I ultimately got back to Washington, I was there about a week when Mrs. Grosvenor called up and invited me to come to dinner at her house. They were going to have the Canadian ambassador there and all that sort of stuff--a white-tie deal--so I saw considerable of the Grosvenors just because they had been out there on the island of Guam.

The board of directors of Pan American made a trip through there--about eight or ten. Right off the top of my head, I can remember Mr. McAdoo, who had been our Secretary of the Treasury during the First World War; Tom Beck, the publisher of Collier's magazine; and then Roy Howard of the Scripps-Howard people; then Jimmy Stahlman, who was the publisher of the Nashville Banner; and there was a chap by the name of McDonnell who had been a first classman at the Naval Academy when I was a plebe there, and I just knew him by sight, and he was a director.*

We saw a lot of interesting people on Guam, and it so

---

*William G. McAdoo, U.S. Secretary of the Treasury, 1913-18; Thomas H. Beck; Roy W. Howard, head of the Scripps-Howard chain of newspapers; James G. Stahlman; Edward O. McDonnell, who was graduated from the Naval Academy in 1912, won the Medal of Honor at Veracruz, Mexico, in 1914, and later was one of the U.S. Navy's first aviators. After World War I, he became a reserve officer, then served on active duty in World War II.

happened that the plane that had the directors had engine trouble, and they had to stick around there for three or four days. And so they were sitting on my porch, and I was sitting on the governor's porch and talking to these people, and you got to see a lot of them.

One of the passengers going east was an attractive lady, and the manager of Pan Am called me up this morning, and he said, "Sully [referring to Rod Sullivan, who was the captain of the plane] tells me that he has in his passenger list General MacArthur's girlfriend. Looking over the list, I just want to know whether you want her included in this list.*

I said, "Now wait a second. Sullivan is an ex-bluejacket, and I know him pretty well. [Because I had met all these pilots, and they would come in town when they were coming through and would talk with me.] A girlfriend, according to Navy jargon, has a lot of connotations, and I would just like to know further about this gal. Will you call me back?"

He said yes, he would. He called me back in about 20 minutes or half an hour and said, "My wife sighted her. She is most attractive, and I got hold of Sully, and Sully says that the rumor around Manila is that she is going to

---

*Captain R. O. D. Sullivan; Major General Douglas MacArthur, USA (Ret.), had previously been U.S. Army Chief of Staff. In the late 1930s he was running the Philippine Army.

J. L. McCrea #3 - 185

marry General MacArthur. I think she should go on our list to have dinner at Government House tonight."

And I said, "That's wonderful. You extend the invitation." And I gave him the people we wanted to have come in there.

Governor McCandlish and his wife were in Japan on a month's vacation, and I was the acting governor, and, of course, I had the full run of the governor's quarters and all that sort of thing. And so Jean Faircloth, later to be Mrs. Douglas MacArthur, sat on my left--I was at the head of the table, and she sat on my left--and the wife of the local medical officer, a captain in the Navy, sat on my right.* During the course of dinner, Miss Faircloth announced to me that she and General MacArthur, indeed, were going to marry.

General MacArthur at that moment was on board a merchant vessel bringing his mother's body back to the United States. She had died in Manila, and he accompanied her remains on this President liner going back to the United States. Miss Faircloth told me they were going to go down to Murfreesboro, Tennessee, her hometown, and she and the general were going to be married. Well, they didn't get to Murfreesboro for the wedding, and I was told later they were married by a JP in New York City.

---
*Jean Marie Faircloth and General Douglas MacArthur were married in New York on 30 April 1937 by Deputy City Clerk Philip A. Hines.

At any rate, when I was with John Hancock, I went to all the companies that John Hancock had interest in, both as stockholders and debt and all that sort of thing.* General MacArthur, of course, he got retired and one thing and another, and he got to be chairman of the board of Sperry Rand Corporation. And John Hancock had thousands of shares of Sperry Rand, so Mrs. MacArthur used to attend all of these meetings that I always went to. I used always to go and sit with her and talk to her about her experiences in the Philippines and how she liked New York and all that sort of thing. So my association with the island of Guam was most interesting.

Mr. McAdoo was a son-in-law of President Wilson, and his wife died, and he remarried. She was on this trip along with the directors when they went across the Pacific.** He had written a book about his experiences as a businessman. He was the fellow who supervised the building of the tunnels between Manhattan and Jersey and all that sort of thing. I remarked to him once, sitting on the porch, about his interests as a businessman, and I said, "You had, of course, a lot to do in the business life, and I am just wondering how you selected your people to work for you, because you couldn't do it all yourself."

---
*After his retirement from the Navy, Admiral McCrea was a vice president with the John Hancock Mutual Life Insurance Company.
**McAdoo married President Woodrow Wilson's daughter Eleanor in 1914. They were divorced 20 years later when he was a U.S. senator from California.

And he said, "Well, you haven't read my book, have you?"*

And I said, "No, Senator, I haven't read your book. I didn't know that you had written a book."

And he said, "I'll send you one."

He sent it to me, and I think it's around here right now on that bookshelf someplace. Then he told me about selecting people to work for him. He said, "I take my time selecting people to work for me. When I once decide that I am going to take them on to work for me, I let them alone completely. I keep my eye on what they are doing, but only in rare cases will I interfere. That is the way that I administer all my business activities. I suggest it to you. If you ever want somebody to work for you, be most careful about your selection, and once you give them the job, keep your hands off."

And that's right, too, you see.

Q: That's if you get a good person.

Admiral McCrea: Well, he and the rest of the passengers on there--the rest of the directors, especially Roy Howard--didn't think too much of McAdoo, but everybody had a great time. When the plane was stuck there in Guam for four or

---
*Crowded Years: The Reminiscences of William G. McAdoo (Boston and York: Houghton Mifflin Company, 1931).

five days, they were in and out of our houses, and we had them for cocktails.

It was very interesting, and I went out there so reluctantly. It turned out to be one of the most interesting jobs I ever had, and it paved the way for me to get to be the executive officer of the Pennsylvania. Because Admiral Andrews wrote me, as I told you yesterday, and said that they were sorry to have to send me out there, and if I did a good job, they would see that I had a good job in the fleet when I got back. And I held them to it, despite the fact that Andrews was gone by the time I got back. That left me the Pennsylvania, and from then on a lot of things happened.

Q: What was your impression of the future Mrs. MacArthur from that time?

Admiral McCrea: Most attractive, most attractive. General MacArthur had the reputation of being somewhat of a ladies man and everything, but she was a most attractive girl.

Q: Was she interesting in conversation?

Admiral McCrea: Oh, yes, exceedingly interesting in conversation. So much so that I really looked forward to seeing her at the Sperry Rand meetings, and I would go and sit and talk to her. It was always interesting to see her. They had one child, a boy, who I don't think measured up to the general's standards.* I think he was a musician of some sort. He didn't go to West Point; I'm sure of that.

Q: How much help did the Navy provide to Juan Trippe and Pan American in going across the Pacific?**

Admiral McCrea: Well, we did a great deal for them, as I told you. We dug up people for them to send out to these islands, to Midway and to Wake. And they got their mechanics, and they got the stewards, and they got the cooks, and they got the messboys to work these hotels and all that sort of thing. We were most helpful to them in every way. One thing that they rather growled at was that we required them, when they picked up gasoline with us, to pay the tax on the island of Guam. They said, "Well, listen, why should we have to pay a tax?"

"You are a foreign corporation doing business on the island of Guam, that's all, and you have to obey the laws of Guam."

They paid the tax; everybody else did; that's all there was to it.

---
*Arthur MacArthur IV.
**Juan T. Trippe was founder and head of Pan American World Airways.

Q: How much contact did you have with Trippe personally?

Admiral McCrea: Of course, I saw him out there, and then I saw him at different times later on. I went out there after the war to Japan when MacArthur was out there. That's another story.

Admiral Standley, who had been our ambassador to Russia, had been my destroyer commander when I had command of the <u>Trever</u>.* And his son-in-law rented my house in Washington, and Admiral and Mrs. Standley lived in my house in Washington there for quite some time. I was very fond of him. I was second in command of the Pacific Fleet, and Standley passed through Hawaii along with the rest of the directors, going to a meeting of the Pan American directors in Tokyo.** And I told him this story about meeting Mrs. MacArthur on the island of Guam, and I said, "I think you will find her most attractive, Admiral." Which he ultimately told me that he did.

A few months after they had gone out there, I was sent out by my commander in chief, Admiral Ramsey, to see General MacArthur.*** The Navy Department had sent word

---

*Admiral William H. Standley, USN (Ret.), was U.S. ambassador to the Soviet Union in 1942-1943. In the early 1930s, as a rear admiral, he was Commander Destroyer Squadrons Battle Fleet. From 1933 to 1937, Admiral Standley was Chief of Naval Operations.
**In 1948-49, Vice Admiral McCrea was Deputy Commander in Chief Pacific Fleet.
***Admiral DeWitt C. Ramsey was Commander in Chief Pacific Fleet, 1948-49.

that they wanted Ramsey to go out there and see him, but Ramsey absolutely bucked out. He had been out there in May, and this was in the fall--around September or October--and he didn't want to go back out there. I said, "Why don't you want to go out there, Admiral?"

"Well," he said, "General MacArthur pushed me around. I don't think that he could push you around the way he pushed me around, and I want you to go. Will you go?"

I said, "If I get orders to go out there, I'll do it, of course."

Well, Denfeld and Ramsey were classmates at the Naval Academy, and Ramsey told Denfeld that he didn't want to go out there and to send me instead.* That's the way it worked out, and that's the way I got out there to see MacArthur. The day I arrived out there, I was met, of course, by MacArthur's aide, and he said that the General and Mrs. MacArthur wanted me and my flag lieutenant to come to lunch. And I said, "Of course, we'll go."

And he said, "I'll pick you up at the general's headquarters and we'll go out there."

So he did, and promptly at 1:00 o'clock the door opened. Our embassy out there in Japan is a beautiful place. We built this thing ourselves, and it is a lovely place. The door opened, and here at the far end of the

---

*Admiral Louis E. Denfeld, USN, Chief of Naval Operations from 1947 to 1949. He and Admiral Ramsey had both been graduated from the Naval Academy in the class of 1912.

drawing room stood the General and Mrs. MacArthur. As I stepped through the door, she started shaking her finger at me. She said, "What I know about you. What I know about you."

And I thought to myself, "My God, Admiral Standley must have told her all about the yarn that I told him at Pearl on his way out here about meeting her on Guam."

Then she turned and she said, "General [she pronounced the word "general" as though it had an "I" in it] this is Admiral McCrea, and I met him on the island of Guam when he was a commander, and he had me looked over most carefully before he issued an invitation to have dinner with him at Government House."

And the general said, "Well, I don't blame him at all. You know, darling, in the service we have to be very careful who we invite to government quarters."

We had a good laugh about it, and that was the end of the thing. We had a great time at luncheon, and promptly at 3:00 o'clock, she said, "General, it's time for your siesta." That gave me a chance to buck out, and away we went. That's the way it worked out. MacArthur kept funny office hours. He used to go to his office about 5:00 o'clock in the afternoon, and no one knew when he was going to leave. A couple of his officers told me, "Our personal lives we just can't count on, because we must stay here. We want to stay here as long as he is here."

Of course, from the far Pacific when he came back--when Mr. Truman called him back--then he went with Sperry Rand, and, of course, my contacts with them kept up there.* It was an interesting sidelight. MacArthur, of course--I had seen him in the Philippines in 1940 when I went through there with the war plans. He liked an audience, and it didn't make any difference whether the audience was one or more. He'd have a thought, and he'd jump out of his chair and march up and down and stop every so often and shake his cigar for emphasis at you. And there I sat in Manila and listened to him tell all about the war. He took a dim view of what was going on in the war. I told Hart--I think it's in this book someplace, I'm not too sure--about my seeing MacArthur and his ideas on the war.** Admiral Hart said, "Thus far, Douglas has generally been wrong about what's going on in the war in Europe."

In one of our talks out there in Tokyo, MacArthur referred to Formosa, and he said, "I am sure that we must have a base of operations out here. I think that the United States is bound to remain an Asiatic power. We have, of course, bases in the Philippines; geographically they are not located properly for our best interests. We

---
*In 1951, exasperated by what he considered MacArthur's insubordination regarding the conduct of the Korean War, President Harry S. Truman stripped the general of his commands and had him brought back to the United States.
**Admiral Thomas C. Hart, USN, who was then Commander in Chief, U.S. Asiatic Fleet.

must have a base on Formosa." There was no Taiwan or anything else; it was Formosa. Then he said this, and I am quoting him exactly: "By negotiation if possible, by force of arms if necessary." I've never forgotten that.

Well, the years passed, and I was back in Washington. Mr. Truman was then the President. He was giving a luncheon for Bill Hassett, the guy who wrote this book down here about FDR.* Hassett was either retiring that day, or it was in honor of his 70th birthday or something. And I found myself, rather than Bill, sitting on the President's right. And I spoke to General Vaughan, his military aide, who was putting out the place cards, and said, "Listen, Bill Hassett is the guest of honor. Shouldn't he be sitting on the President's right?"**

And he said, "You in this room are next senior to the President, and I have shown [him] my proposed seating arrangement, and he has approved it. You are going to sit on the President's right."

I said, "Okay."

Well, while we were in the midst of our luncheon, along came the noon newspapers, and one was dropped right in front of the President and four or five on the table.

---

*William D. Hassett, who later turned his diary into the book Off the Record with F.D.R., 1942-1945 (New Brunswick, New Jersey: Rutgers University Press, 1958). The book contains a number of references to McCrea.
**Major General Harry H. Vaughan, military aide to the President. Vaughan was a reserve officer on active duty.

And here in bold headlines was the fact that Truman had ordered MacArthur to withdraw a letter which he had written to Joe Martin, and Martin was going to read this letter to an American Legion convention that was going to meet in Chicago.* And when the President found out about it, he told him to withdraw the letter. Well, seeing MacArthur's name, I told the President this yarn that I have just told you about needing a base on Formosa. And the President said, "General MacArthur, no doubt, is a very fine military man. He has one weakness, and it's a consuming one. He cannot bring himself to recognize that the President of the United States is his senior."

Well, there it was, and when he came back there, he was dumped, and that was that.

Q: That was the reason he was dumped.

Admiral McCrea: Sure it was the reason he was dumped, I guess.

I sit here once in a while and think about the past, and I think about some of these things that I experienced. And it was most interesting, that is all, most interesting.

---

*Representative Joseph W. Martin (Republican-Massachusetts), minority leader in the House of Representatives, to whom MacArthur wrote with his complaints about the President's leadership in the Korean War.

Q: You mentioned Standley. What was he like as a commander when you were in the Trever?

Admiral McCrea: I'll tell you what he was like; he was damn good. One day the patrol officer picked up one of my men at a dance hall the night before and sent him back to the ship for creating a disturbance and a few other things. I looked this thing over. I listened to the man, and the man said that he was dancing with this girl, and he said that somebody cut in on him, and he bowed and stepped backward, and he accidentally stepped on the foot of a girl. And she immediately grabbed her foot and started yelling and all that sort of stuff. He said, "I was apologizing in every direction, and that was it. I didn't create any disturbance; she was the one who created the disturbance."

I sent my executive ashore, and he dug up the patrol officer, and I got him out to the ship, and he repeated essentially what this bluejacket had said. It was just an accident, and that was all there was to it. So I just dismissed the charges against him, and I wrote across it, "After careful investigation, I have dismissed the charges against this man of creating a disturbance."

I went off to sea and came back, and the first thing I knew, I got an order to report to Admiral Standley, commander of the destroyer squadrons. I went over there and went to his chief of staff, Captain Stott.* And we went in to see the admiral, and he said, "I have this thing, and I would like to know why you dismissed these charges."

And I told him what I had done--investigated the thing--and I said, "After careful consideration, I could see that this fellow had not created the disturbance that this patrol officer said that he had. And the patrol officer appeared at mast and admitted as much."

He just looked up at Stott and said, "Let's not bring McCrea back here anytime again to defend his position in matters of this sort." And I thanked him and walked off.

By that time, his son-in-law, I guess, was living in my house in Washington and all that sort of stuff.

Q: What kind of a leader was he at sea?

Admiral McCrea: Good. And President Roosevelt was very fond of him, and he thought he had done well in Russia. He did well in Russia.

Q: You mentioned that Kimmel worked his ships hard to train them and get them ready.** How did he compare with

---
*Captain Arthur C. Stott, USN, chief of staff to Commander Destroyer Squadrons Battle Fleet. The incident occurred when McCrea, then a lieutenant commander, was commanding officer of the USS Trever (DD-339).
**Commander Husband E. Kimmel, USN, was a destroyer division commander in the Asiatic Fleet in the early 1920s.

Standley in training?

Admiral McCrea: I was never under Kimmel as far as any training went, so I don't know. But I can assure you, as I told you yesterday, I knew of no one of Kimmel's time who worked harder at being a good naval officer. Incidentally, I didn't remark to you yesterday about his sons. Both of them got in the Navy, and one was lost in one of our submarines.* He was one of the two boys, of course, that kept Mrs. Kimmel in the United States rather than having her go out there to the Philippines when he was out there. I had a high regard for Kimmel. That's all I can tell you.

Q: Did Standley ever use the Trever as his flagship?

Admiral McCrea: No, no, he didn't. I used to see him ashore. Of course, we had Prohibition in those days when I was out there in the Trever, and he said that he liked a drink, and anybody that offered him a drink, he was liable to take it. But he said, "You've got to remember that we are breaking the law [and this, that, and the other thing], and be most careful about what you do."

I was very fond of Standley. He made a good Chief of Naval Operations too.

---

*In the summer of 1944, Lieutenant Commander Manning M. Kimmel, USN, was lost while in command of the submarine Robalo (SS-273). His brother, Thomas K. Kimmel, was also a submariner and eventually retired as a captain.

Q: Do you remember anything else about him?

Admiral McCrea: Not particularly, at this moment.

Q: If we could, I would like to go back to Naval Academy time and have you tell the story you did yesterday at lunch about your service in the choir at Annapolis.

Admiral McCrea: Well, when I entered the Naval Academy it was just nip and tuck, in that on the 29th of May 1911 I would be 20 years of age and be ineligible to enter the Naval Academy because of age. I had one crack at the examinations--the entrance examinations--and I took them in April. And when my name was posted on the gate that I was a successful candidate, I got in touch with the commandant's office and told them--the academic year was going to start sometime the first week of June--and I told them that I would be 20 years old and I wanted to get sworn in early. It so happened that I did; I got sworn in on the 10th of May. when I got back from seeing my family up in Michigan and entered about the sixth of June, across the corridor from me lived a midshipman of the class of 1913 by the name of Alfred Hyde Donahue, known to everybody up and down the corridors as "Mike." Mike Donahue had had typhoid fever, and he had not recovered enough in time--in the spring of that year--to let him go on the midshipmen's cruise, and he spent that summer on duty as a midshipman resident in Bancroft Hall. He lived across the corridor from me, so he started advising me how to get on in the Navy, and he said, "One of the best things to do in the Naval Academy is to have some sort of a racket."

Well, I didn't know what he was talking about, and he said, "One of the most interesting rackets around here is the Naval Academy choir. I don't know whether you can sing or not."

I said, "Hell's bells, I used to sing solos as a boy soprano in my hometown choir."

And he said, "Well, you are a natural for the choir then. You just put in for the choir, because if you do that, you don't have to go on the Thursday afternoon hikes."

So I did. I put in for the choir, and I went through the Naval Academy without ever standing a Sunday morning inspection, because the choir always went off early. Right after breakfast, you would go over and rehearse some of the anthems and the Te Deums and a few other things that we were going to sing in the choir, and it was just that much fun. I enjoyed it.

Q: But then you had a little too much fun and got into mischief.

Admiral McCrea: Well, in avoiding the Thursday afternoon walks, we would have choir practice instead. Some of the people who had solos and a few things like that to do would be engaged around the organ, and so these midshipmen got out in the middle of the chapel, and for acoustical purposes there was not an awning but a spread that went across the base of the cupola of the chapel building. And somebody discovered that taking a prayer book or a hymnbook and standing out in the middle where the people sat, with a little effort on the hip they could throw this thing up and it would hit the awning. Every time the awning was hit with a hymnbook or prayer book or whatever it was, there would be laughter about it that the fellow was able to do it.

All of a sudden, we looked up and here was the Naval Academy chaplain looking in the door--old Commander Cassard.* He was horror-stricken. He turned on his heel, and away he went. We knew that trouble was coming. We got back in the choir loft, and by the time the chaplain got back there with the commandant, whose quarters were just a few yards away, we were up there singing "Praise God from Whom All Blessings Flow," and putting in all the

---
*Commander William G. Cassard, Chaplain Corps, USN.

swipes and everything, and the commandant came in there, and he said, "Young gentlemen, come out of the choir loft." We all got out of the choir loft, and then he said, "Now come outside, because what I am about to say to you young men I should not say in the house of God."

So we went outside, and he laced into us and gave us hell. It was just an incident and, of course, all Navy chaplains were known as--well, ours, we called him the Apostle Paul, because his name was Paul Cassard. But that's just an incident which we shouldn't have gotten into.

Q: But didn't your singing fall off a little after that?

Admiral McCrea: Oh, yes, he stopped us from having this choir practice on Thursday. The midshipmen measured up to that all right, because the performance of the choir fell off remarkably. There was some comment about it, and somebody remarked, "Well, what can you expect? They don't have any rehearsals any more, so therefore they couldn't be kept up to standard."

Of course, we got back on the old program right away then.

Q: He capitulated.

Admiral McCrea: Yes, he capitulated. Crazy kids will do most anything, I suppose.

Q: To go back to your time with President Roosevelt, you told me yesterday that he was very considerate to your daughters. Would you repeat that one, please?

Admiral McCrea: Somebody gave him a few little Falas, little iron castings of his Dog Fala, and he sent one to my daughter. He was very considerate about people. When my daughter Meredith was 16, I had her to dinner along with her mother and her sister, and the President was leaving for Hyde Park that night. And I always made it my business to be there when he left, if I didn't go with him, and also to be there when he returned. Grace Tully said to me, "Has Meredith ever met the President?"*

And I said, "No."

And she said, "Well, she must meet the President."

And I said, "Now come on, Grace, he's busy. I put her in Ross McIntire's office, and she will sit there and wait until the President goes."**

Well, the President came down in his chair and the first thing I knew, here was Grace Tully with my little

---

*Grace Tully was President Franklin D. Roosevelt's personal secretary.
**Rear Admiral Ross T. McIntire, Medical Corps, USN, Chief of the Bureau of Medicine and Surgery and physician to the White House.

blonde daughter, and Grace said, "Mr. President, this is the captain's daughter. This is her 16th birthday."

And the President reached up and pulled her down and bussed her on the cheek, and he said, "Now you are sweet 16, and you can't say that you haven't been kissed." And that was the way it went. He was most considerate of my family, and Mrs. Roosevelt was too. After I had left there and gone to sea, they were constantly doing things for my family in Washington. Any function at all at the White House, Estelle was invariably included, and they would send a White House car out for her. You don't forget little things like that--people who are kind, and they hadn't any reason to be at all. None whatsoever.

Q: You mentioned that you had helped him on a speech he had to make once. If you'd give me that story again, please.

Admiral McCrea: I had a White House phone at my bedside, and one night about 11:30 or so the telephone rang, and the operator said that the President wanted to speak to me.

He said, "John, you know I am going on the air tonight, and everyone here says my talk lacks color. Sam Rosenman and Bob Sherwood said to me that they wonder if you could come up with some story with drama and pathos in it. And he pronounced the word <u>drama</u>, DRAY-ma. "Drayma and pathos."

"Well," I said, "Mr. President, I'll do the best that I can, but what's the deadline on this?"

And he turned from the telephone, and I could hear him say, "What's the deadline?" And he came back, and he said, "About 9:00 o'clock tomorrow morning."

I said, "I'll do the best I can."

Briefly put, I called General Marshall--I didn't have anybody else to go call--and I also called General Holcomb, the Marine, and told him what I was up against.* And when I got down in the Navy Department the next day, I saw Admiral Glassford, who had just come back from out there, and I told him what I was up to.** And he had a story to tell about a medical doctor out there and what he had done in helping people. Well, Glassford said he could do something for me about 4:00 o'clock that afternoon, and I said, "I want it in 45 minutes. I've got to have something." Which he did; he dictated it.

At any rate, this thing all went that night.*** And

---

*General George C. Marshall, USA, Chief of Staff, U.S. Army; Lieutenant General Thomas Holcomb, USMC, Commandant of the Marine Corps.
**Rear Admiral William C. Glassford, USN, who had held a number of positions in the Far East at the beginning of the war, including taking over from Hart.
***In his "fireside chat" of 28 April 1942 on the radio, Roosevelt talked of Lieutenant Commander Corydon M. Wassell, Medical Corps, USNR, who had aided wounded American sailors in Java as the Dutch East Indies were falling in early 1942.

when they went on the air, three out of the four yarns that I considered had "drayma and pathos" to them were used on the air. From then on, every time they wrote a piece, I was always designated to come up with something, if I could find it, which I did--the best I could.

I am trying to think of the name of that director--Cecil B. DeMille--sitting out in Hollywood, heard the President's talk and he recognized something that he could make into a picture, which he did, and it was an exceedingly successful movie.* It went all over the country, and this doctor was dragged back, and he went all around the country talking to labor groups at factories and gatherings. That little item, that little thing, that little start, had tremendous repercussions.

Q: How much contact did Roosevelt have with Admiral Hart after he returned from the Far East?

Admiral McCrea: None that I know of. The last time I was down to see Mrs. Hart, she broke out this decoration, which he wasn't going to go to get, and showed it to me. A beautiful thing, of course.

---

*In the spring of 1944, Paramount released a movie directed by Cecil B. DeMille, titled The Story of Dr. Wassell, starring Gary Cooper as the doctor. A review published in The New York Times on 7 June indicated that the usual Hollywood touches had been added to the story to dramatize it for the audience.

Q: You told me that story just before we turned on the tape this morning, so if you could please run through that one again about Hart going to get the decoration.

Admiral McCrea: Well, I was a friend of the Dutch ambassador, Alex Loudon, and I saw a good deal of him, and I thought highly of him.* He called me--this is 1942, of course--and the Queen had come to Washington, and the Dutch had made the decision to decorate Admiral Hart. Admiral Hart was relieved of his command. His command had really disintegrated because of the war--the ships that were lost and all that sort of thing. And the Dutch had a few ships, and they were using them, and they called it the ABDA Command. There were American, British, and Dutch ships-- ABDA. When the Queen was going to be in Washington, the Dutch wanted to decorate Admiral Hart. He felt that the Dutch had been instrumental in getting him relieved, which wasn't exactly so. And still it was, a little bit, because his command had virtually gone to nothing, and the Dutch wanted a piece of what was going on--that was all there was to it. It seems--and I think the President and Mr. Churchill decided that it wasn't an unreasonable request, and that's what they did.

The Dutch were going to take the sting out of it by

---

*Dr. Alexander Loudon, Netherlands Ambassador to the United States.

decorating Admiral Hart. Well, Alex Loudon called me one night about 6:00 o'clock, and he said he had been in touch with Admiral Hart. Admiral Hart had called to say that he would not be in attendance the next day at the investiture when the Queen was going to give him this decoration. Loudon said to me that it would be disastrous to have anything like this happen, and I said, right off the top of my head, "Alex, I am inclined to agree with you. I'll do what I can, and I'll let you know."

I promptly got in touch with the President. I went over and told him the whole story. He said, "John, you get ahold of Admiral Hart and do what you can to get him to recant what he has told the ambassador and to show up at the investiture tomorrow and accept this decoration. If you are completely unable to do this on your own, you can tell him that I would regard it as a personal favor if he would go and receive this decoration at the hands of the Queen."

I went back, and I rang up Admiral Hart. I started off my conversation with the admiral, and I said, "I want to congratulate you on going to receive a decoration from the Queen tomorrow at this investiture."

He said, "I am not going to be there, and I have already told them so. I am going back to Sharon, Connecticut, tonight. I have my railroad tickets, and Mrs. Hart and I are leaving here at 10:00 o'clock."

I said, "The Dutch are counting on your being there, and it would be highly embarrassing, I am sure, if one of the proposed recipients didn't show up."

I saw that I was getting nowhere at all with him, and I just finally said, "Now, Admiral, I will go one step further. My boss, the President, told me that if I couldn't persuade you to recant what you had told the Dutch ambassador and that you would show up tomorrow to receive this decoration that I should say to you that he, the President, would regard it as a personal favor if you would do this."

Well, it was quiet on the telephone, and I didn't know exactly what was happening, but all of a sudden there was this yell over the telephone that said, "Goddamn it, I'll be there."

And he slammed up the receiver and that was it. I called up Alex Loudon and said, "Don't worry, Admiral Hart will be there."

Well, every time I saw Hart after that, he would always say that I had saved him from making a terrible mistake, and each time I would deny that I had anything to do with it. I said, "I was just giving you a message from the President that he wanted you to do this." But right down to the last time I saw him he was telling me how grateful he was for saving him.*

I said, "Admiral, you saved yourself. I hadn't anything to do with it. I was just carrying a message. So there is the story. It isn't much, but it just shows you a little bit about Hart, and a little bit about the President.

I'll carry on now a little bit further. Loudon stayed on, of course. And after the President died, and I was back in Washington, and when they dedicated Hyde Park as a national memorial, Admiral Nimitz sent me up there. He told me to tell Mrs. Roosevelt he was very sorry that he couldn't get up there, which I did, ultimately.** On the way back, on this special train, I sat with Loudon, and he started in telling me what a wonderful association it had been for him to be the ambassador when President Roosevelt was in the White House. He said, "You know, we are a small nation, but he made us feel big and important. We are still a small nation, but the present President insists on making us realize that we are small."

Q: Was that Truman by that point?

---

*On 7 August 1942, in Washington, Queen Wilhelmina of the Netherlands presented Admiral Hart with the Grand Cross of the Order of Orange-Nassau.
**Fleet Admiral Chester W. Nimitz, USN, Chief of Naval Operations from 1945 to 1947. During part of that period, Vice Admiral McCrea was Deputy Chief of Naval Operations for Administration.

Admiral McCrea: It was Truman. Nothing you can say to that; there wasn't anything I could say. It was unfortunate, that is all, but that was the impression that he got. He was right about that.

I was secretary of the Pacific War Council, and the Pacific War Council met every Tuesday morning at 9:30. All the ambassadors. The Chinese were represented by T. V. Soong; then there were the Australians and the New Zealanders and the Canadians.* And when Quezon got to this country, he promptly sat in, and it was most interesting.** The President always presided.

When Mr. Churchill was here in mid-summer, he attended one of the meetings, and the President asked him to say something to the ambassadors. And I will never forget Mr. Churchill sitting across the table. He had his eyes fixed on the table and he had a pencil in his hand, and he kept tapping the table with this pencil. He never looked up, but literature just rolled off his tongue, telling what he thought about Germans--Hitler in particular--and all that sort of thing. I'll never forget his remark. He said, "We must destroy the economy of the country which permits them to do what they are now doing--these acts of wickedness against the British." That's the story, but I'll never forget Mr. Churchill sitting there tapping away, and this

---
*T. V. Soong was a representative of the Chinese leader Chiang Kai-shek and did a great deal to gain financial support for his nation's war effort.
**Manuel L. Quezon was President of the Philippines.

literature just rolling off his tongue.

Q: How much contact did you have with Admiral King?

Admiral McCrea: Well, that goes back a long ways too. I told you yesterday, I guess, that King did not like Rodman, because he said Rodman was superficial. And every time that he popped up with something like that, I, having served with Rodman, just took it on myself to stick up for Rodman. I said, "He had many traits of a military character. You might not like him personally, but he had many traits of a military character which I felt were excellent."

At any rate, I fell in with King--I go back to the Trever days now. One day, I got an order from my division commander to report. I and the commanding officer of the Wasmuth were to report to Captain King in the Lexington at such and such a time.* We got in our boats, and away we went. Captain King told us that he was going to have this night flying, and it was a difficult operation. They were experimenting with night flying, and he said, "I have to be searching for the wind all the while. I can't do it by signal to you people. One of you is to be astern, and the other is to be out ahead. The principal job of the fellow ahead is trying to keep track of me and what I am doing.

―――――――――
*Captain Ernest J. King, USN, commanded the aircraft carrier Lexington (CV-2) from 1930 to 1932.

Have your yardarm lights on so that these aviators have a point of reference to work from. That's going to be a difficult assignment."

Finally, my friend from the <u>Wasmuth</u> looked over at me--he was two classes senior to me--and he said, "John, how about you taking that assignment up ahead, and I'll take the one astern."

King stopped, and he looked up, and he said, "Which of you is senior?" Well, he knew damn well who was senior. And then he said, "As a general principle, the senior assumes the more arduous task if there is any choice in the matter."

Thereupon, the skipper of the <u>Wasmuth</u> (who now since has been gathered to his fathers) blushingly said, "Well, I'll take that assignment, and you can take the assignment astern."

Very well. The exercises started, and all of a sudden a plane hit the water about 500 yards away from us, and we swung over and we got ahold of this aviator, who by that time was in the water, and he got on board. And the exec took him down and got some warm clothes on him, and he came up to the bridge, and he said to me, "What will they do to me?"

I said, "What do you mean?"

"Well," he said, "I didn't pull the flotation gear on

the plane, and the plane sank."

I said, "You should worry about not pulling the flotation gear. You are alive, and that's it."

Meanwhile, King had sent me a dispatch. I had reported that we had recovered this aviator. It said, "Rejoin the Lexington at maximum speed."

Well, what the hell else did he think I was going to do? Of course I was going to. We were going at maximum speed, and all of a sudden a two-seater plane crashed on our starboard bow. I got over there, and we picked those two aviators off, and we got a line to the plane and snubbed the plane up as best we could under the bow of the destroyer, and I proceeded at dead slow at about four to five knots over toward the Lexington. When I got over toward the Lexington, I had to go along the starboard side so that I was between the airplane and the side of the Lexington. We got the line to the plane up to the Lexington, and then I backed clear and got off. They hoisted the plane aboard, and I gave them the three aviators that I had, and that was it. King sent a dispatch that said, "Operations for the evening concluded. Return to base." Ordinarily, one would think that somebody would say "Thank you for your services." But there wasn't any such word, so we turned and went to base.

The next afternoon I was ashore, in the bank at Coronado, and here was Captain Ernest J. King. He said,

"Good afternoon, John."

I said, "Good afternoon, Captain." And we each went our way; nothing was said about the night before. I thought to myself right quickly, "If he wants to mention the night before, it's up to him; I'm not going to mention it." And we went our respective ways. He called me John then, and from then on he called me John. That's all I can tell you about Ernest King. Oh well, there are a lot of things I can tell you about Ernest King.

Q: Please do.

Admiral McCrea: Well, I'm fearful that you will think I am trying to make too much of a hero of myself about these things, but one morning I got in early for Mr. Knox's conference. I was sitting in the back of the room, as became my low rank of captain, and I was thumbing the morning dispatches. Admiral King, who talked with a very soft voice, was sitting up right in front of the Secretary's desk. All of a sudden, there was a roar from Mr. Knox, "Admiral King, we won't discuss this matter any further. The decision has been made, and I expect you to carry it out."

Well, there was just the three of us in the room. I didn't know what the hell had gone on, and to this day I haven't any idea what the rumpus was. The next morning, after our Secretary's briefing, as I was going out the door, Admiral King said, "Come to my office, please."

"Aye, aye, sir." I fell in on his port hand, and we went up to his office. He got behind his desk, standing up, and I stood out in front of his desk.

He said, "You were in the Secretary's conference yesterday morning?"

"Yes, sir."

"You heard what the Secretary said to me?"

I said, "Yes, sir."

"I expect to make an issue of it, and I just wanted to check it out with you that you heard what the Secretary said to me. I have never been so spoken to in the Navy, and to have the Secretary say that to me yesterday, I resent it deeply."

I stood there for just a second, and then I said, "Admiral King, of course I had no idea what you asked me up here for, but now that I know, I must say that if I were in your position, I would forget it. If you make an issue of this thing, it is bound to go to the White House. And on behalf of the President, for whom I am working, I would hope that this would never get to the White House."

King whirled around, and he looked out on Constitution Avenue, out his window, and I am sure the thing that brought to his attention that I was still there was that he heard my knees knocking--that I had spoken to my commander in chief the way I had. After--I haven't any idea how many seconds it was of silence--he turned and looked at me and yelled at me, "Good day."

    I turned on my heel and beat it. Nothing ever got to the White House. I think that I gave him some good advice then, and I still think, after all these years, that it was damn good advice.

Q: It is the usual impression that King told Knox what was going on, because Knox didn't know that much about the Navy?

Admiral McCrea: That's right. I haven't any idea what the thing was about.

Q: That must be pretty unusual for something like that to happen.

Admiral McCrea: Well, Knox just let a roar out of him. As I say, I thought after I had gotten out of there that I had given him some damn good advice, and I still think so.

    Who would have been the loser? King. Who would have been the fellow to suffer the most? The chap for whom I was working, the President, would have had to be juggling the pros and cons in a row between the commander in chief and the Secretary of the Navy.

Q: How frequently did President Roosevelt go directly to Admiral King rather than through the Secretary of the Navy?

Admiral McCrea: King never came to the White House unless he was asked over there. The only time that I can really recall King asking to go over there--and I told it to you yesterday, I guess--was when we were setting up this bombing of Tokyo.

Q: Didn't you have some contact with Admiral King on the trip over to the Teheran Conference?*

Admiral McCrea: When they went to Iran, I saw a lot of King, because he was a passenger in the Iowa, and he was on the bridge most of the time, sitting around. He didn't have any place to go. We had so many people on the ship that were senior to him--Roosevelt and then Hopkins too. Then we had Leahy and Marshall and Arnold all around there, but King was senior to Arnold. They had a lot to do and a lot to think about.

I think I should go back a little bit further. When Iowa went into commission and I was given command of her, we shook down in the Chesapeake Bay. We could only have on

---

*The conference at Teheran, Iran, from 28 November to 1 December 1943, was the first meeting of the big three--Churchill, Stalin, and Roosevelt.

J. L. McCrea #3 - 219

board about one-quarter of our oil capacity, because we were virtually scrubbing the bottom all the while in the Chesapeake Bay. It was a very unsatisfactory cruising thing. I was sent up to Casco Bay, and I went in there a couple of times.

And after, we came out of Chesapeake Bay once, and I was sent up to Casco Bay. On the way in I made an error in judgment in that I delayed putting the rudder over maybe a matter of five or ten seconds--maybe 30 seconds at the most--and going into the Casco Bay, to the anchorage there, we clipped a rock that was in the entrance to the channel. Well, there was water enough there for <u>Iowa</u> to have gotten in, but it was an error in judgment on my part; I did not put the rudder over as soon as I should, and we took a cut down our port side.

The only dry dock that we could get into was down in South Boston; there was a very big dock down there. Of course, I made a report right away to the Navy Department about the misfortune that happened to us, and I felt badly. I thought I was a good ship handler, because I had been able to get the feel of every ship that I had been in, in handling it, whether it was a minesweeper or a destroyer or a battleship or whatever. But I made, and I repeat again, an error in judgment. I should have put the rudder over seconds before I did.

Of course, I knew that would be distressing to the

President, and I also knew it would be distressing to King. A court of inquiry was held right away, and the admiral, who had been aide to the Secretary of the Navy at one time, and he was the district commandant, was the senior member of the board of investigation. And when it opened up, I started right in telling them--it was about 9:00 o'clock in the morning that we assembled. About 9:30 he looked up and said, "You know, about this time of the morning I like to have my morning coffee, so I'll just declare a recess for a few moments." He looked over at the table and said, "John, won't you join me?"

I said, "Certainly," and I got up and went in.

We got inside his outer office and he said, "Do you realize what you are doing? They can use every word that you have said about this incident against you in trying you by court-martial or whatever punishment that they want to give to you."

I said, "Listen, Admiral, of course I know what I am doing. I have been in the JAG office; I know what goes on there. The ship belongs to the Navy. It is temporarily in my custody, and the Navy has every right to know exactly what went on, and I am going to give them that story--no matter what happens to me."

Well, I did, and in the end I got a letter of reprimand, which is in some one of my boxes now. I have never read it completely. I glanced at it once, I remember, and it went into one of my boxes, and I haven't seen it since. But I know I've got it someplace. They didn't need to reprimand me; I had reprimanded myself so many times since the thing happened, and I've had to live with it all these years. I knew, from what I knew about King, that he would be disappointed in me, but there was nothing I could do about it at all. I wrote a note to Admiral King, and I said, "By now, you know of the misfortune that has overtaken *Iowa* and me. Of course I regret it greatly, but I am hopeful that I won't be taken out of my ship." And I signed my name to it, and that was all.

King never responded to my note. The years passed, and finally I nailed him one day when he was retired and he was working on his book. I was in his office and I asked him about the President, what his reaction to my trouble was. He said, "We never discussed it."

I said, "You didn't speak to him about it?"

He said, "No, why should I? I knew that Brown [Wilson Brown who was the President's aide] would tell the President, and I thought if the President wanted to talk to me about it, he would bring up the subject, and he never did.* The closest that he came to it was this: when we were looking for a ship to take him to Oran [when he was going to the Cairo and the Teheran Conference], I suggested

---
*Vice Admiral Wilson Brown, USN, naval aide to President Roosevelt.

to him that I had the New Jersey here on the coast and we could use her."

And the President, according to Admiral King, said to him, "Ernie, when John left the White House, I told him I hoped that some day that I could join him in the Iowa. Is the Iowa available? Could she do this?"

And Admiral King said, "Yes," but I was up in Argentia, Newfoundland. So that was what happened. I was on my way out of Argentia this fine morning--this was after our repairs had been completed at the Boston Navy Ship Yard, and we had gone up there--and as we went out the channel from Argentia, they handed me a dispatch, and it said, "Proceed to Hampton Roads, Virginia."

The exec was there, so I said, "Just have this word passed over the loudspeaker, 'Iowa is on her way to Hampton Roads, Virginia.'" It was on the loudspeaker. It was quiet; then all of a sudden I heard this whoop throughout the ship. They realized that we were going down to Hampton Roads.

I arrived in Hampton Roads early on Sunday morning, maybe about 10:00 or 11:00 o'clock, and I went over right away to see Admiral Ingersoll.* And he said, "You know why you are here?"

"No, I haven't any idea why I am here."

---

*Admiral Royal E. Ingersoll, USN, Commander in Chief Atlantic Fleet.

He said, "The President and the Joint Chiefs of Staff are going to go to the Mediterranean for a meeting at Cairo and Teheran, and you are going to take them. Admiral King wants to see you in his office tomorrow morning. Go on up tonight on the night boat."

I said, "Admiral, I have already had orders to go alongside the dock at 5:00 o'clock tomorrow morning, because the tide will serve then. I would like to put the ship alongside and go up later."

He said, "The only way you can go up is by my plane, and I have to have my plane by 11:00 o'clock."

I said, "Very well, sir. I will assure that your plane will be back here."

So right after we got the ship under way and got her alongside the dock, I left the ship and went on board his plane and flew up to Washington.

As I went through Admiral Edwards's office, he said, "Do you know what you are going to do?"*

I said, "I was told by Admiral Ingersoll that I was going to take the President and Joint Chiefs to the Mediterranean; that's all I know."

And Edwards said, "When you get them over there and drop them where they are going, you are to return to the United States."

I went in to see Admiral King, and he told me what the

---
*Vice Admiral Richard S. Edwards, USN, chief of staff to Commander in Chief U.S. Fleet (CominCh).

President was going to do, and the Joint Chiefs, and then he said, "Now about your employment while the conference is going on."

I said, "Admiral Edwards told me that I was going to come back to the United States."

"Well," he said, "I try to keep Edwards knowing what I have in mind, but in this case I guess I missed it. You are not going to come back to the United States. The only thing we would have to bring him back in would be a cruiser, and I am not going to subject the President of the United States to a westward passage of the Atlantic in December in a cruiser."

Well, that was enough for me, and he told me what was doing. The President was going to make a talk at the Arlington Cemetery on Armistice Day and that he would, that afternoon, go by special train down to Newport News. And Iowa would be there in Hampton Roads, and he would embark, and we would start off for the Mediterranean. Then he said, "The President wants to see you."

So I got on my horse and went over to see the President. We talked about it, and he was looking forward to going. That afternoon I was busy around the Navy Department about some items that I had to look out for about Iowa, and I caught the night boat going back to Norfolk.

After dinner that night I was standing out there on deck, and I thought, "Everybody--Admiral Ingersoll, Admiral King, the President--everybody that I have talked to has said that this is a very secret mission. But if the President catches a special train and goes to Newport News, everybody in tidewater Virginia is going to know what's going on." Then I went back to the time that I had my shakedown in the Chesapeake Bay. Of course, I knew I would have to have a complete cargo of oil to start out with.

So I just stood there thinking, and then all of a sudden it occurred to me, "Why can't I come up here and meet him at the mouth of the Potomac, get him on board ship and all the rest of these people? We can come down here and fill up with oil. We can get down by 6:00 o'clock that night, fill up with oil. The tide serves about 11:00 o'clock, and it will be high water and I can go on to sea." Well, the more I thought about it, the more I felt like Jack Horner--sticking my thumb in and coming out with a plum.

As quick as I got back to the ship in the morning, I sent for the navigator and the executive, and we broke out the charts, and I was sure that we could do all this. I piled into my boat and went over and saw Admiral Ingersoll. And I told him about my conference with King and seeing the President and all that, so I said, "Here is what I propose to do. If you don't agree, I'll just forget it and go ahead and do what you told me to do."

And I told him what I suggested--that we pump out all of our oil--leave about 25% in the ship. We could get up to the mouth of the Potomac, pick up the President. The President could come down to the mouth of the Potomac on his yacht, the *Potomac*, and that would be the end of it. The only people who would know that he was leaving Washington at all would be the people there at the naval base and also the people at the Navy yard. The *Potomac* would just be missing, and she would just stay down the bay.

Admiral Ingersoll looked at me, and he said, "I approve. Take my plane and go back to Washington right now."

I got on the plane and away I went. And he sent a dispatch that I was on my way back to Washington. I went in and saw Admiral King as to my suggestion of what I proposed to do. He said, "I approve. Go to the White House and see the President."

I did, and the President said, "I approve." And that was it.

Now the only bad thing about that at all was that I wasn't quick enough on the trigger the day before when they told me about these things, but I had a lot of things on my mind. I wanted to think this thing over. And when I thought it over--I was somewhat flattered, as you can imagine, that these fellows agreed to what I suggested. Well, away we went.

We left the Navy yard and pulled out in the stream. A barge came alongside, and it was loaded with all the special equipment that FDR needed--ladders, also they brought a bathtub and all that sort of thing. And they took out my shower and installed his bathtub in there.

Q: This was in the captain's cabin?

Admiral McCrea: Yes, it still is there, too, as a matter of fact. And that is exactly what happened.

Q: Who installed the bathtub?

Admiral McCrea: The workmen from the Navy yard. They came on board, and as soon as they got on board, I heaved up, and away we went up in the Chesapeake Bay area. There we were, and we stayed there. We were quarantined, as far as I was concerned, from the shore in every direction, excepting these people who were doing all this installation. The President, after he finished his speech, came down that night, and he had a leisurely trip down the Potomac. And he came on board the *Iowa* the next morning about 8:00 or 8:30.

Meanwhile, King had gotten there the day before, along

with Marshall and Arnold and one thing and another, and King wanted to know what provisions I had made to receive the President and everything to do with it. So I showed him what we had done, and he approved completely. I said, "Admiral King, I am giving you a room right across from a bath; I haven't any room for you anyplace else. The one room we have with a bath in it I have assigned to Harry Hopkins.

He said, "That's correct." And that was the way we went.

As soon as the President got on board, we heaved up, and away we went for Hampton Roads, where I had already made provision for two tankers to come alongside to fill us up with oil. That night we anchored at around 5:30 or such a matter, and these tankers came alongside. That night the President invited me to come and have dinner in the cabin, down there in my own cabin. There was the President, Leahy, Marshall, and King, and Arnold and God knows who else. Then the President said to me, "Now what are your plans for tonight?"

"Well," I said, "Mr. President, we have high water slack at 11:00 o'clock tonight and I would like to get under way at 11:00 o'clock and go down to buoy 2CB and go on to sea."

He said, "John, this is a very important mission that we are starting on."

And I said, "Yes, it is, Mr. President."

He said, "You know that this is the Friday."

And I said, "I know that."

He said, "I'm just sailor enough to not to want to start anything important like this trip that we are going on, on a Friday. Now could you manage to get under way on a Saturday morning rather than Friday night?"

I said, "Yes, Mr. President, we still will have enough water to handle ourselves getting out of here."

That was exactly what we did. We hove short at about a quarter of midnight, and at eight bells we broke ground, and away we went.*

Time went on; years went on. Leahy wrote a book entitled I Was There, and in that book, if you have a copy of it, you will find in there how the President left Washington after his talk over there and got on the special train and went down to Newport News where he joined the Iowa and all that sort of thing.** Well, I was back in Washington, of course, and Leahy sent a copy of this book to me, autographed.

---

*"Heave short" means to heave around on the anchor chain until the anchor is at short stay, just prior to breaking ground. Eight bells were struck every four hours--in this case, midnight.
**Fleet Admiral William D. Leahy, USN, I Was There: The Personal Story of The Chief of Staff to Presidents Roosevelt and Truman: Based on His Notes and Diaries Made at the Time (New York, Whittlesey House, McGraw-Hill Book Company, Inc., 1950). On page 194, Admiral Leahy indicated that Roosevelt and his military staff boarded at Hampton Roads on Friday, 12 November, but there was no mention of a special train to the Norfolk area.

I was old enough and my hair was grey enough that I was invited by the superintendent to come and sit on the platform at graduation at the Naval Academy. I went down there and sat there, and Marshall made a very fine talk and he referred to the _Iowa_, how he had been in the _Iowa_ on a couple of trips, and he said, "As an old artilleryman, I must say that you Navy fellows have the most accurate gunfire that I can imagine, and I was in _Iowa_ when she was bombarding out in Korea."*

Well, Leahy was on the platform. After the ceremonies we had lunch at the superintendent's quarters, and I said, "Admiral, of course I wrote you a note and thanked you very much for that book _I Was There_, and I appreciate your thoughtfulness in sending it to me. But I have a growl to make about it."

And he said, "You can growl about any of my conclusions that you want to, but factually it is correct, because I used my notebook."

"Well," I said, "that's just what I am talking about. Don't you recall that you left the White House on the night of the 11th of November and that you went down to Quantico and got on the _Potomac_ and came down the river and joined the _Iowa_ at the mouth of the Potomac River?"

He said, "Yes, we did, didn't we?"

---

*George C. Marshall, the Secretary of Defense, spoke at the Naval Academy graduation exercises on 1 June 1951.

I said, "Your book says that you went to Newport News."

He said, "Goddamn it, why didn't Denfeld catch that?"*

I said, "Because the operation was so damn secret that Denfeld never knew anything about it. That's all there was to it, and this is actually what happened."

So there it is. Now Leahy's book, in which he said "I was there," has still got that in there, but it is completely wrong. So that's the growl that I had with Admiral Leahy. But all this while I saw a lot of King from time to time. And after I left the White House, and when I came back to Washington--he was still operating on all cylinders, and he hadn't had any of his troubles--I saw a lot of him.** I was very fond of him. He was a tough baby to shave; there is no question about it.

I'll get back to Iowa a moment. As I told you, I thought I had the feel of every ship that I sailed in, and I did. I thought I was a good ship handler, and I still think that I was pretty good as a ship handler. And lots of people never, no matter how much they try, ever get to be good shiphandlers, and I think I was pretty good. But I've forgotten who it was that said "Pride goeth before a fall," and it went with me. I have lived all these years

---
*Admiral Louis E. Denfeld, USN, Chief of Naval Operations from 1947 to 1949, was a protege of Admiral Leahy.
**In 1947, Admiral King suffered a stroke which impaired his ability to speak and write.

since then with the fact that my lapse in some way or other of 5, 10, 20 seconds or such a matter made a complete change of life for me. Because I have lived with that tear that we put in the Iowa's side all these years. There is not a thing I can do about it now, but think about it and regret it.

Q: You had another exciting incident during that trip when there was a torpedo fired at the ship.

Admiral McCrea: Yes, that happened too, and I can tell you about that.

When I reported to Admiral Ingersoll, he said, "I am going to send a squadron of destroyers to look out for you. Three will go as far as Bermuda or thereabouts, and then you will be picked up by another three, and then off the Azores you will be picked up by another three." So away I went. What happened--and I didn't find this out until a year or so later--the commanding officers of these destroyers were told to prepare for distant service and the chap on this destroyer--his gunnery officer told his torpedo officer to prepare for distant service, and his torpedo officer told the chief torpedoman to prepare for distant service.*

And the torpedoman, I suppose, figuratively scratched his head and took his primer and started fitting them in the locks to see whether they would fit or not. Well now, of course, when you get right down to it, that's rather a silly thing to do because--I don't know whether you have a shotgun or not, but you can always count on your shotgun shells fitting in the gun--this is about these primers fitting in the firing locks. Unfortunately, one firing primer was left in the lock, and on this Sunday afternoon we were having a little exercise on board Iowa about shooting at some weather balloons that were sent up as targets. And right in the midst of this operation there came over the loudspeaker--"Torpedo headed your way." Of course, it came from the ship that was the lead ship. The thought that flashed across my mind at the moment was that we had been ambushed, and I had been fearful about that. And I will get into that a little later.

We went to general quarters, and the boatswain's mate--right at the end of the thing when they sounded general quarters--said, "This is no drill." And it wasn't. It was no drill, all right.

---

*The destroyer was the USS William D. Porter (DD-579), commanded by Lieutenant Commander Wilfred A. Walter, USN. For another account of this incident, written by an officer who was on board the Iowa, see Commander Charles F. Peck, Jr., USNR (Ret.), "Torpedo on the Starboard Beam," U.S. Naval Institute Proceedings, August 1970, pages 90-93.

The first thing I knew, someone hissed in my ear, "Captain, what is the interlude?"

I recognized the voice as that of Ernest J. King, and I said, "Admiral King, I am just trying to find out what's going on."

And at that moment the destroyer that had made the announcement said, "I think the torpedo is mine."

Meanwhile, I had rung up full speed. We were making 25 knots, and I rang up full speed and started to swing away to run away from the torpedo, because the torpedo would be making about 45 knots or thereabouts, and I figured that--I didn't know where it was coming from, and I thought I could run away from it. Then when he said, "I think it was mine," that made it a completely different picture, and I turned and put the rudder back over and headed for that destroyer. And we were just nicely in the middle of this turn, when there was this big explosion and the whole _Iowa_ went like this. And I said to Tom Casey, my executive, "Tom, do you suppose we've been hit?"*

And he said, "No, I don't think so, Captain. If we had been hit, I think the reaction would have been much heavier than what we experienced."

This torpedo exploded in the turbulence of our wake, that's what kicked the torpedo off.

I didn't know all this until I was out in the middle

---
*Commander Thomas J. Casey, USN.

of the Pacific, and this very destroyer pulled up alongside of me, and the division commander was in that ship. He pulled in at daylight one morning to get oil, and we talked over the telephones, back and forth, and he told me the whole story about this damn thing.

Many things have been written about it; most of the things by people who do not know what they are writing about. They have something, and they embellish it in one way or another. But Leahy did say, in his book, that he thought the ship was well-handled, and that's one thing. I thanked him for that too.

Q: What was the President's reaction?

Admiral McCrea: He was up there watching the shoot, and his valet was rushing him back and forth across the bridge. As I say, he lived in my cabin, and he was out on that platform there. It was just a joke, as far as he was concerned. It wasn't a joke as far as I was concerned at all, but that's the way it worked out.

Q: How did you wind up spending the time while he was at the conferences?

Admiral McCrea: That's another story. On our way across, as I told you, Admiral King spent most of his time on the bridge of the Iowa with me. I had my little emergency cabin about half as big as this room, and I had a little kneehole desk there and a chair and my bed, and that was my equipment. I used to sit on the side of the bed, and King would sit in the chair. We talked about all sorts of things.

One time we were sitting there talking (and this is a personal item), and we got around to talking about Mahan, and I remarked to him that I had read almost everything that I could get my clutches on that Mahan had written, especially the book about types of naval officers.* And King said to me, and this is a story that I repeat with somewhat reluctance, but I've lived long enough now so that it can't follow me too much. King and I were talking about types of naval officers, and he turned on me and he said, "Now, John, you are a good naval officer, but you have an outstanding weakness."

"Oh," I said, "Admiral King, I have inventoried myself many times, and I can come up with more than one weakness. But I would certainly be interested in knowing what you think my outstanding weakness is."

---

*Captain Alfred Thayer Mahan, USN (Ret.), Types of Naval Officers: Drawn from the History of the British Navy (Boston: Little, Brown and Company, 1901). A very similar version is contained in Thomas B. Buell, Master of Sea Power: A Biography of Fleet Admiral Ernest J. King (Boston: Little, Brown and Company, 1980), pages 420-421. Buell drew upon unpublished reminiscences which Admiral McCrea had provided to the Franklin D. Roosevelt Library at Hyde Park, New York.

"Well," he said, "that's easy and I'll say it in a few words. You aren't a son of a bitch."

"Well," I said, "Admiral King, you are a good naval officer, and I have never heard anybody refer to you in such terms." He glared at me, and he jumped out of that chair, and he stomped out of the cabin, because he knew I was lying like hell. But before he got out, I said, "Admiral, I think I know when to be a son of a bitch, and I would rather have it that way." I could make up my mind when I needed to be a son of a bitch and not be the kind of subject that, every time I went out on deck, someone would say under his breath, "There's the son of a bitch." Well, that is one of my laughs about King.

So, on the way across, he never said "boo" about what the ship was going to do while they were at the conference. But I knew enough that I wasn't going to bring up the subject, because King wanted to do things his way, and I knew damn well he would not leave that ship without telling me what he wanted to do. And Admiral Cooke, whom I knew well, came to me one day--the day before we got in--before we went through the straits, and he said, "John, what are you going to do while we are at the conference?"*

I said, "I don't know."

"Wouldn't you like to know?"

"Why, of course I'd like to know."

---

*Rear Admiral Charles M. Cooke, Jr., USN, the chief plans officer on Admiral King's CominCh staff.

"Well, why don't you ask Admiral King?"

I said, "I will not ask Admiral King what I'm to do while you are at the conference. He will tell me when he wants to let me know." So that's the way it went.

I had made up my mind that if King stepped over the gangway, stepped on the upper platform to leave the ship, and had not told me what to do, I was going to ask him what he wanted me to do. Well, we went out that morning, and the early fellows like Cooke and a few others had gotten in the boat and started ashore--in Oran--to catch the plane to take them to Cairo. King was standing there, waiting for the President to come down. He reached in his pocket and pulled out a piece of paper, and he handed it to me. In his own handwriting (it is someplace in my files) it said, "At 1800 hours [so-and-so, which was the following day], depart Oran and proceed to Bahia, Brazil."

I took a look at it, folded it up, and put it back in my pocket. Those were my orders, written in his hand, and I never asked him what the hell.

All right. I got rid of all those fellows. A tanker came alongside of us and started giving us oil. So I went over to call on Admiral Cunningham (not Andrew Cunningham, but John, the vice admiral), and he was in the Sheffield. He said to me, "Captain, what are your orders?"

And I reached in my pocket, and I read this thing to

him. He said, "I am changing those orders."

"Yes, sir."

He said, "You came through the straits last night. The Spaniards, those alleged neutrals, know that a big unit went through the straits last night with all your escorts. [And I might add here that we were joined by six destroyers of the Royal Navy, so we had an escort of nine destroyers to carry us through the straits]. Unquestionably, the information that a big unit went through last night is now in Berlin. I want you out of here by 1800 hours today."

I said, "Admiral, you will have to give me another tanker then at any rate. And I don't know if we can get enough to get to Bahia, but as far as getting out, I've just got to get it [oil] out there."

He sent for his chief of staff, and by the time I got back to my ship, the Iowa, there was another tanker alongside of us throwing oil in us. And at 1800 hours that night we cast off our lines, and away we went. And Cunningham said, "I am flying this afternoon to Gibraltar, and the Sheffield is going to go with you and be senior officer for the destroyers. And will you turn our Royal Navy destroyers loose as soon as you get out of range of air attack?"

I assured him I would, and that's what I did.

Q: Was it his concern that if you stayed there you would

get an air attack?

Admiral McCrea: That apparently was his concern, but he changed my orders and flew to Gibraltar and turned over his flagship, along with the six Royal Navy destroyers that went with us, so that was the way that happened.

Q: And then you proceeded to Brazil?

Admiral McCrea: I proceeded to Bahia, Brazil. And I went ashore and called on Jonas Ingram, whom I knew well.*

Q: Where did you know him from?

Admiral McCrea: He was on Admiral Rodman's staff. I knew him well. When I arrived in Bahia, Brazil, he was there. He sent me a dispatch--I had sent this dispatch that I needed so much fuel, and he said, "I shall meet you in Bahia." Well, who was I to say he shouldn't meet me in Bahia?

When I got there, to Bahia, he was bitterly disappointed that the President was not on board. He said, "Why didn't you tell me the President was not on board?"

I said, "Admiral Ingram, you asked me a question, and I am going to ask you one. Why didn't you ask me whether

---
*Vice Admiral Jonas H. Ingram, USN, Commander South Atlantic Force.

the President was on board or not? When you sent me the dispatch and said that you would meet me in Bahia, who am I, the captain of a capital ship, to tell a three-star admiral where he can go on his station or even question what he is doing on his station?"

Well, he gave me a box of cigars, and that was it. That's the way that interview ended, and he went away disgruntled the next day.

When I got back to the ship from calling on Ingram, I got back, I guess, about 2:00 o'clock in the afternoon--we had gotten in just about noon--and when I got back, there were orders for me to proceed to Freetown, arriving by such-and-such a date, and to await orders there. The navigator had broken out the charts, and he said, "Captain, I figure we've got to leave by about 6:00 o'clock tonight to get to Freetown so that the tide will serve us and we can get anchored in Freetown by this date." And that's what we did. So I went across the Atlantic four times in a month. Going over and then back this way, across the equator, and then back to Freetown. I got to Freetown and stayed there three or four days, and I got a dispatch "Proceed to Dakar and there await orders." Which I did. And that's where I picked them up and brought them home. That was an incident, because King didn't come back with us; he went on someplace else. I have forgotten just where. Neither did Marshall.

Wilson Brown came to see me after we got under way that night. The President came on board as a passenger in a French destroyer, and it was impossible for him to have gotten up on the bridge and come across, so we brought him aboard in the boatswain's chair. That boatswain's chair, the last I heard of it, was at Hyde Park.* Hopkins and Watson came aboard from the bridge of this French destroyer to our quarterdeck, on their hands and knees across the gangway.** The President was in an uproar about them, just laughing at everything about them. They wouldn't touch the steadying lines or anything to get over there; they went on their hands and knees.

He made a talk, of course, when he left the Iowa at the mouth of the Potomac. We took him right back to where we picked him up, and the Potomac came alongside and took him back to Washington. He made a talk, and in this talk he remarked about those landlubbers Hopkins and Watson crawling on board the ship.

Q: What was the purpose in sending you to Brazil? Was that just to get you out of harm's way?

Admiral McCrea: No. Well, that may have been partially in
___
*Hyde Park, which was Roosevelt's home in New York, is now a presidential library and museum.
**Major General Edward M. Watson, AUS, Roosevelt's military aide.

his mind, but he said that I was to utilize my time making passage to Brazil to get the deep water cruising in, which I was unable to do in the Potomac and in the Chesapeake Bay area. He said, "This ship needs to be in deep water." And, of course, we were in deep water all the way going to Oran, but it was something for us to do, and it was interesting for the crew, too.

Q: What advantage did that serve the ship?

Admiral McCrea: We had all sorts of gunnery drills going on, day and night, around there and doing all sorts of things. When we got back to Freetown, the British boarding officer came off to see us, and he said he had a message from his admiral. He said, "There are some Italian ships that came in here and surrendered [men-of-war], and my admiral hopes that you will not exchange courtesies between the ships, despite the fact that they have surrendered."

I said, "Your admiral can rest assured that I shan't do that."

That night the admiral gave a dinner for us, and said that one of the first things the Italians wanted to know was what the source of women around Freetown was. And he said he was looking out for his sailors. The admiral said, "I told him that our sailors went around the bush on their own, and that's the way his people could go."

Q: What happened then after you returned to the United States and let the President off?

Admiral McCrea: We went to sea, directly to the Pacific. We left Norfolk on the second day of January 1944, and we went directly to the Canal Zone, and through to the Pacific.

That was interesting. Of course, the Iowa's beam was 108 feet, 3 inches, and the Panama Canal locks are 110 feet, which was 21 inches to split. Of course, these expert Canal Zone pilots, with all their equipment, get you through safely, even with just 21 inches. Twenty-one inches is just about like this, and you split it.

Q: Didn't you pick up Admiral Hustvedt in the meantime?

Admiral McCrea: Yes, we picked up Hustvedt and his staff.* They had stayed back in Norfolk.

Q: What kind of an officer was he to serve with?

Admiral McCrea: Pretty good. Pretty good. I had known

---

*Rear Admiral Olaf M. Hustvedt, USN, Commander Battleship Division Seven. Hustvedt's Naval Institute oral history describes his time in the Iowa.

him since he was a junior lieutenant. He had been in the <u>New York</u> on Admiral Fechteler's staff.* Fechteler, the father of William Fechteler, who was the Chief of Naval Operations.** He was known throughout the fleet as "Dutch Gus." He was born in Germany, but I was very fond of him. He had a very attractive wife and they had, I think, three daughters and two sons. One of the sons was killed--Frank was killed--and the daughters married.***

Q: You told me yesterday you had a little discussion with Admiral Hustvedt about your chief master at arms. Will you cover that, please?

Admiral McCrea: Well, he didn't like my chief police petty officer--for what reason I never could get from him, but he wanted me to get rid of him. And I told him, "He is one of the best enlisted men that I have ever known, and I know enough about the Navy to know that it is a very difficult job to be the chief police petty officer in any ship. Because he is a bluejacket who is charged with a great deal

---

*Rear Admiral Augustus F. Fechteler, USN, Commander Battleship Division Six, Atlantic Fleet, during World War I.
**Admiral William M. Fechteler, USN, Chief of Naval Operations, 1951 to 1953.
***Lieutenant Frank C. Fechteler, USN, a pilot, was killed in an airplane crash in 1922.

of authority that he must exercise over his fellow bluejackets, and this man Duncan is an exceptional man. I must say, Admiral, if you insist that I get rid of him, I shall do it, but I feel I must have the order to do so in writing."

That ended it; it was never brought up again.

Q: His name was Prince Duncan?

Admiral McCrea: Yes.

Q: How did he come to the Iowa?

Admiral McCrea: I had fallen in with him in the Pennsylvania. He was the number two in the police petty officer force in the Pennsylvania, and I thought they had a very fine ship's police force in the Pennsylvania. His boss, Prendergast, had been made an officer. As you go along in the service, you run into various officers and various enlisted men, and you sort of tag them mentally. You say to yourself, "If I ever have need for a fellow like this, that's the guy I'd like to get hold of." And that's the way I felt about Duncan. So I ran him down and got him in the Iowa, and he was tops. He just died here the other day; it broke me up about that.

J. L. McCrea #3 - 247

Q: The <u>New Jersey</u> went along with you, didn't it, during that voyage?

Admiral McCrea: Yes.

Q: What do you remember about her during that period?

Admiral McCrea: Nothing particular. She was just another ship. I was busy looking out for my own. I knew the skipper of the ship well, and that was it.

Q: This was Captain Holden?

Admiral McCrea: Holden, yes.* He later died of cancer. We had been good friends.

Q: Where did you know him from?

Admiral McCrea: Naval Academy. He was two classes behind me at the Naval Academy. He was a good officer, a topflight communicator. He knew all about something that I didn't know a damn thing about.

Q: Did you have much discussion with him during or just before this voyage?

---

*Captain Carl F. Holden, USN, who died in 1953.

Admiral McCrea: No.

Q: Did the two ships exercise at tactical maneuvers on the way out?

Admiral McCrea: Oh, yes, sure. On the way out. I don't remember where we anchored down there.

Here is another thing. I told you about this Jap cruiser we sank. They left Truk, a number of ships, and we were broken off from Spruance and the New Jersey, and the Jap ships tried to escape to the Pacific.* We caught up with them that afternoon. (One of my close friends, this fellow Hoke Smith that I told you about yesterday, was in the South Dakota, and when we left them he sent me this dispatch--"Lucky Dog.")** We had the speed, you see, that Spruance wanted. I was standing up there on the bridge, and here was this Jap cruiser off about 16,000-20,000 yards away. And all of a sudden, the wake of a torpedo passed under our stern, I guess about 1,000 yards. About the same time, looking out ahead, here was a torpedo wake that crossed our bow about 600, 700, or 800 yards ahead of us.

I just instinctively said to the gunnery officer, "Open fire on that cruiser." Just like that, you see. It

---

*Vice Admiral Raymond A. Spruance, USN, Commander Central Pacific Force.
**Captain Allan E. Smith, USN, commanding officer of the South Dakota.

disturbed Hustvedt because we let go, and the cruiser rolled over and sank. We put four salvos into her, but we didn't need to, because we hit with the first salvo. You could see these white uniforms of these people going up the side of the ship as she was sinking.

Admiral Hustvedt came up, and he said he didn't know that he could approve of what I had done.

I said, "What, Admiral? What's the trouble?"

And he said, "You opened fire on an enemy ship, without orders to do so, in the presence of an admiral and your division commander."

I said, "Admiral Hustvedt, I am sorry if you disapprove." I didn't have the courage to tell him that I once read the life of Nelson, in which he had remarked that no captain could be condemned, or should be reprimanded, for opening fire on the enemy, no matter what the circumstances were.* I have forgotten the exact wording. I didn't have the courage to remind him of that.

Other than that, we got along very well. The next time I saw Spruance's chief of staff ashore, which was just a few days later, I spoke to him about this thing, and I said, "What was the admiral's reaction?"

He said, "Not at all; he didn't pay attention to it." Well, the ship rolled over and sank and couldn't fire any

---

*Admiral Horatio Nelson, a British officer who achieved much success in the late 18th century and early 19th century with his aggressive tactics.

more.

Q: Do you think Hustvedt was overly cautious?

Admiral McCrea: Well, I think he was right to this extent--that I had ignored him and ignored Admiral Spruance. But here was this thing out there shooting torpedoes at us, and they didn't shoot any more after we put that salvo in her.

Q: A number of officers who have commanded ships of the Iowa class said that that was the high point of their naval career, because there was great satisfaction in controlling something that big and powerful.

Admiral McCrea: That's right, and you could almost spin them on a dime at times. I remember I took the Pennsylvania alongside the tender in San Pedro. I was exec, and the captain of the tender was over there, and when we were coming alongside he said, "John, I've seen them come and go all the while, and this is the best landing that's been made alongside this tender in I don't know when."

I said, "George, you had better say that out loud. I would like my captain to hear that."

My captain didn't want to have anything to do with it much. In ship handling you've got to be thinking out ahead to beat hell.

Q: Especially because a ship that big has so much momentum.

Admiral McCrea: Yes, momentum. And another thing, it doesn't have a brake under your foot that you can step on and stop it.

Q: How was the Iowa when you operated it in carrier task groups?

Admiral McCrea: They were glad to see us. I remember Sherman, Ted Sherman. He was out there and he said, "I always feel better with you fellows alongside."* Because we could make virtually the same speed that the carriers could make. And he said, "When you have launching into low winds and things like that, you've got to run up the speed. And it is always comforting to know that you've got a good battery of 5-inch over there along with us."

Q: Did you have a good crop of OODs to stand the

---

*Rear Admiral Frederick C. Sherman, USN, Commander Task Group 58.3.

watches?*

Admiral McCrea: Well, there is another thing. Yes, for the most part. We had someplace around 150 officers in the Iowa, and only 15 or 16 of them were Naval Academy graduates. I remember I had a young fellow, about your size, who came out of Ohio State University or someplace out there. (His name has just left me for the moment.) I thought that this fellow had as much promise as any of them, and I fooled around with him and got him on watch. And finally he got to the point where he was standing senior watch. I was very firm about what I wanted these guys to do. I slept on a cot right on the bridge, and I never left the bridge from when we got under way until we got back in port. When we tied up someplace, I'd go down in the cabin. I was available always up there on that bridge to be called. I had, among other things--here are my standing orders:

"Be alert and keep watch. You are in charge of the ship. Unremitting vigilance is necessary to prevent surprise encounters and to insure the safety of the ship from navigational dangers.

"Call me immediately upon sighting, visual or radar, a strange object. Identity and range can come later.

"Call me at the first shadow of doubt.

---

*OODs--officers of the deck.

"Test telephone communications every 15 minutes.

"Know the recognition signals, and be prepared for the time of changing.

"When flag is not on board, answer a direct challenge immediately. When flag is on board, neither initiate nor answer a challenge, this being a matter over which the flag has jurisdiction.

"Do not assume the light you see is the one expected. Verify its characteristics. Have a list of lights expected on hand with their characteristics.

"Allow no lights to be shown on the topside. Do not answer or make signals at night without my permission.

"Report to me any unusual schedule or any unusual movements of ships in order.

"Report to me at the completion of each course and speed change.

"Orders for the night: Keep the bridge and conning tower quiet at all times."

Well, here is my standing night order, and I would write up the various things that we expected.

This is my second volume of them--make sure what you see and all that sort of thing.

Right outside the conning tower door was where I slept on the cot, to be easily available. It just so happened that I was asleep this particular night, and this young junior lieutenant, in whom I had confidence enough so that

I had given him a watch, in some tangled-up way he got pretty close to one of the carriers. He hadn't any business being there, and if he had been alert he would have avoided the situation, which was not good. I was there; all he had to do was to touch me on the shoulder, and I would have been on my feet. He didn't do it.

The next morning, about 8:00 o'clock, I was contacted by the executive officer, and he told me what had happened in the night. Right away, I went down to see Hustvedt and tell him what had happened. Hustvedt looked at me, and he said, "I was just wondering when you were going to come and tell me about this."

"Well," I said, "Admiral, I am just as sorry as I can be, but there isn't anything I can do about it. I took every precaution that I could possibly think of to see that this ship was safely handled. It would have been safely handled if I had been called."

But at any rate, I fired this officer. Threw him off the watch list completely.

He said, "I knew you were there, Captain, but I just didn't want to disturb you."

I said, "You didn't want to carry out the night orders that I had given you, to call me at any sign of any change. Hustvedt didn't like it, I didn't like it. But the fact that Hustvedt knew about it disturbs me, and he knew about it before I did."

But he didn't say a word to me on that. Of course, I wish he had. He was waiting to see when I would come.

Q: You told me before the tape started that there was an occasion when you missed out having Admiral Spruance embarked in your ship.

Admiral McCrea: Well, I told you that maybe Spruance was just halfhearted about coming on board <u>Iowa</u>. I don't know if he was or wasn't, but if he had come and hoisted his flag in <u>Iowa</u>, he would have had to displace Hustvedt, and maybe he didn't want to do that. At any rate, I was annoyed that my executive would let me sleep through. He didn't call me, and he rather prided himself on the fact that he had scared them away.* Poor guy. He was a darn good officer that fellow, but he had high blood pressure. His father was a doctor up here in Lowell, and he had a brother who was a doctor. His mother died when we were out in the Pacific. The dispatch came to the ship, and I had orders down there in the radio place that if anything like that came through, any death notices or anything about family affairs, to route it via me so I could get ahold of the officer concerned. I sent for George and told him,

---

*Some of Spruance's staff officers had come to the <u>Iowa</u> to see about her suitability as Spruance's flagship. Captain McCrea was asleep at the time of their visit, so they wound up speaking with the executive officer, who discouraged the idea.

gave him this dispatch that his mother had passed on. He got back for it.

I ultimately got back to Washington later, and when he succeeded Tom Casey as exec, I knew that he had high blood pressure. The doctors would have sent him ashore if I had said so, but he begged to stay. And he said, "I know I have high blood pressure, but it has not interfered with my duties so far. If it does interfere, I'll be the first to check it out." Well, he finally got back here and he went to the naval hospital and he died out there in Bethesda. I went out to see him a couple of times. He was a hell of a good officer.

Q: What was his last name?

Admiral McCrea: George Leahy, of the class of '25.*

Q: Wasn't the situation that you had told him you were going to take a rest because you had been . . .

Admiral McCrea: Well, hell, I had been on the bridge for nearly three weeks, and so I just turned in when I got the ship tied up and all that sort of thing. I told him I was going to take a nap, and I said, "Just look out for things. I would like to get some uninterrupted sleep." Then with

---
*Commander George A. Leahy, Jr., USN.

almost a cheer, he told me how to take it. Spruance's boys had come over there looking with the idea of hoisting Spruance's flag in the Iowa.

Q: So he wound up in the New Jersey instead?

Admiral McCrea: He wound up in the New Jersey instead. It doesn't make any difference. I don't think he probably would have come to Iowa; he might not have, at any rate. But I didn't get the chance. I think I could have sold him something about the ship, because it was built for a fleet flag.

Q: What was the exec's reason in telling Spruance's people that he didn't want Spruance's staff on board?

Admiral McCrea: Well, I don't know how he talked them out of it, if he did. Of course, it's always a nuisance to have a flag around and all that sort of thing. I suppose that's what he said, but he had Hustvedt, so he knew that.

Q: You did have one flag officer on there later as a passenger. This was Admiral Lee, who came on board to observe the bombardment of Mili Atoll.* What do you recall about that experience?

─────────
*Rear Admiral Willis A. Lee, Jr., USN, Commander Battleships Pacific Fleet.

J. L. McCrea #3 - 258

Admiral McCrea: Well, I'm trying to line up my thoughts in a chronological way. Mili Atoll was some distance from Majuro--not too far, 70 or 80 miles or something like that. And it was occupied by the Japanese. So my admiral, Admiral Hustvedt, and Admiral Lee thought that it would be a fine target for Iowa to go down and bombard. So away we went. The intelligence reports said that Mili had 4.7-inch guns on board, and that was all they had, and a very small battery of them at that. So I figured out that we could get within about 17,000 yards, or maybe a little farther inside than that, and out of gun range from these guns, and give the island a going-over.

All right, we got out there, and almost in no time, as soon as we opened fire, fire was returned. And the first thing I knew, Iowa got hit twice, and I was trying to get out of there. Meanwhile, as soon as I saw the fire, I had the word passed that all exposed gun positions take cover, and that included the 20-millimeter and the 40-millimeter guns. So that was that.

Well, we pulled out of gun range, and we started to see what the hell happened. And we had a hole blown in the side of the ship, almost as big as that side of the house. Also, one shell hit the face of a number two turret and disintegrated. And a couple of men inside that turret in gun pointer positions got fragments of shell in their cheeks.

Well, I never did know what the hell had happened about this thing. Evidently, there was something bigger there than the intelligence people said. Some of the crew picked up a chunk of the deck of *Iowa* and made for me in the machine shop a paperweight. I've got that damn thing around there someplace. On this piece of teak they fastened this fragment of the Jap shell that hit us, and they wrote across this thing about the bombardment of Mili and the date, and so forth. It has green baize cloth underneath, and I use it.

One day when I was in the Navy Department, after the war, a young chap was standing at my desk, and he looked at this paperweight. And he saw this about bombardment of Mili and he said, "You know, I took the surrender of Mili."

And I said, "My God, you are the fellow I'm looking for. We got hit from Mili, and we were well outside of the range of the guns which the intelligence report said were on Mili."

He said, "I can tell you what you got hit with. When Singapore fell, the Japs got a number of 7-inch guns, and they brought two and put them on Mili, and you got hit with 7-inch shells."

So there it is.

Q: They brought the guns and shells from Singapore to Mili?

Admiral McCrea: To Mili, and there it was. That's how we were wounded, and if I hadn't cleared that deck, we would have lost a whole gun's crew down there, because the one that hit the face of the turret--great chunks went through this gun tub. We were lucky, lucky as hell.

Q: In general, how much shore bombardment did the Iowa do when you had command?

Admiral McCrea: Not too much. Oh, we did quite a bit. We bombarded northern Tinian and southern Saipan and all that sort of thing. Ponape. Dropped a shell or two on Kwajalein, nothing in particular. We didn't encounter any opposition excepting on Mili.

Q: These bombardments were done in company with other fast battleships, weren't they?

Admiral McCrea: Oh, yes. I suppose other vessels were with us too.

Q: But really, you didn't get much practice then, because you had to spend so much time with the carriers?

Admiral McCrea: Oh yes, we were with the carriers. I was with the carriers a great deal, a great deal. As a matter of fact, as I told you, I enjoyed that. You never knew what the speed demands were going to be. Old Fred Sherman, I knew him well. He came from Port Huron, Michigan, which is just 40 miles down the track from Marlette, where I came from. He was a good officer. I had never heard of him to speak of until the war came along. He was an aviator, and, of course, those fellows promptly sprang into life when aviation started living up to its prognosis.

That's a pretty red tree out there, isn't it?

Q: Fall is more advanced up here than it is down in Annapolis. It is still essentially green down there.

Let me just take a break, Admiral, and change the tape here, please.

Admiral, what do you recall about Harry Hopkins?

Admiral McCrea: All I knew about him was what I read in the newspapers and one thing and another. After a while, I was over there at the White House, and I got to be greatly fond of him, because there wasn't anybody around that place that worked harder for the President than Hopkins did. He worked like hell for him, and he abused himself physically in that he worked beyond his capacity to work. He really punished himself. He would work like hell and stand it as long as he could, and then he would get on an old slouch hat and a coat and go out to some bar in Washington and get stinko. I won't say stinko, but it was close to it.

Q: What made you think you wouldn't like him initially?

Admiral McCrea: Just what I had read about him in the papers. Everybody was tearing him down; all the newspapers were tearing him down, that's all there is to it. When I would say something to him--something I had read in the paper directed derogatorily at him--old Harry would just shrug his shoulders and say, "They don't really think that about me. They are just taking clouts at me to get at the President. They want to harass him all the while, and they don't dare come out and say that's what their purpose is, so I am a whipping boy for him."

He just would shrug it off.

Q: Did you ever have to take any heat on the President's behalf yourself?

Admiral McCrea: No, because if anybody started it about him, some of my friends, I would rise up and disagree with them flatly--for the most part.

Q: So you lost some of your basic Republican heritage.

Admiral McCrea: That's right. My mother was quite opinionated. They lived their politics up there in Michigan, but she finally got around to the fact--I told her about President Roosevelt and Mrs. Roosevelt and the things that they had done for me and my family and all that sort of thing. When I left the White House, Mrs. Roosevelt said something to Estelle, "What does your husband need?"

And Estelle said, "The other day I was packing his bags to go to sea, and I came across an afghan that was pretty well chewed up, to the point that I discarded it. I didn't want him to take that to sea with him."

After I had been away from the White House about six months, one day a box came to the Iowa by the mail, and it had a White House sign on the outside of this box. I opened it up, and here was a great big, beautiful, hand-knitted afghan for my bed with a note on the top: "The President and I trust that this will keep you warm in your new ship."

Now they needn't have done things like that. Neither one of them need have done things like that, but they did. And how can anyone think ill of people who are kind when they don't have to be, when they are polite and courteous to you.

The railroad association had built this big, bomb-proof sleeping car--palace car, really--for the President, and they donated it to the government. It had four bedrooms in the thing and a dining alcove and a kitchen and all that sort of thing. And when that car was put in service, the President and Mrs. Roosevelt went on the thing. Ross McIntire was on it in one of the bedrooms, and McCrea and his wife were in another one, invited to go with them to Hyde Park. Of course, it was quite an occasion in this very new, beautiful car, and the B&O people always furnished the dining service stewards and one thing and another--at least for the most part. Dan Moorman, who was the B&O passenger agent, came on board with a case of champagne.* It was an interesting experience to go there and be with these people. My wife went shopping with Mrs. Roosevelt up in Poughkeepsie, and she came back and she told me, "I don't know how that woman stands it. Every old crone in this part of New York State seemed to be in that store this morning, coming up to shake Mrs. Roosevelt's hand, and she was always polite to all of them. She must have been bored to tears about it, but there she was, being kind to people."

Q: It sounds as if President Roosevelt had a great deal of affection for you. Did this bond develop as you worked together?

---
*Daniel L. Moorman, a special operating representative of the Baltimore & Ohio Railroad.

Admiral McCrea: Oh, sure. He didn't know me. Steve Early said that he liked me, because he gave me the God-damndest things to do. That was how Steve knew that I was getting on all right with him. Whenever he said he wanted so-and-so done, I didn't ask him how or why or anything else. I'd just say aye-aye and that's it, and go my way and get it done.

Q: What are examples of some of these things that he did give you to do?

Admiral McCrea: I can't begin to tell you--all sorts of little odds and ends. I remember something he wanted me to run down about a character that he had known in the Navy--I'm not going to mention his name, and I did it for him, found out about this fellow. He was always interested in the Navy. All of the people that he knew as a young Assistant Secretary of the Navy--and mind you, he was made Assistant Secretary of the Navy at the ripe age of 31. Do you know of any 31 year old right now of your acquaintance that you would give a job to as a number two cabinet officer? Of course you don't, but President Wilson gave it to FDR, and he was just 31 years old.

When he came to the graduation exercises at the Naval

Academy in 1913, he had only been in office a very few weeks then. I remember him coming down to make the talk, and he was accompanied by Boies Penrose.* Penrose had a paunch out here like this; he had what I think is known in the medical trade as a pendulous abdomen, and he was swinging his way down. Then the fellow from South Carolina who was Chairman of the House Naval Affairs Committee in the House (Penrose was chairman of the same committee in the Senate). The fellow from South Carolina was not much behind Penrose as far as figure went, but here was this young, Greek god with his head high in the air--he always carried his head high in the air--strolling down there and bowing.

Q: That was Roosevelt?

Admiral McCrea: Yes. Here I was, a midshipman in the ranks there, and I just saw him then. I was amazed; I was about 22, I guess, and here he was 31. He was popular for the most part with the younger naval officers, and the people he knew had reached flag rank by the time he got to be President. And he would call one fellow after another: "What's ever happened to this one?" And all that sort of thing.

I told you what he told me about wanting to go in the

---

*Senator Boies Penrose (Republican--Pennsylvania).

Navy, didn't I?

Q: I don't think so.

Admiral McCrea: Well, he said that once he expressed to his mother--when he was about 12 or 13 years old--he said that he wanted to go to the Naval Academy. And he wagged his head and said, "John, she took me into the little room off the reception hall, and she gave me a talking-to, and I have never forgotten it. She didn't say too much against the Navy, but she said that she was sure there were more important things in life in store for me rather than just being a naval officer. I have never forgotten the way she went after me."

Q: Did he ever ask your advice on what officers might go into what billets?

Admiral McCrea: No, he didn't. He knew people. He had great confidence in King and many of the people. He had great confidence in Stark, and I think Stark did a good job for him. He used to send for Stark and Marshall all the while, and they would go over there and talk. Marshall always carried a chap with him; Stark never did. Stark would come back and tell me what FDR was up to, and so there you are.

One of Stark's grandchildren developed polio, and, of course, FDR knew all about polio.

Q: Did you discuss it with the President when it came time for Admiral Stark to leave as CNO and Admiral King to take over?

Admiral McCrea: No, he never said a word about it. By that time, I was in the White House.

Q: Wasn't one of the roles of the President's naval aide at that time to serve as a naval adviser? What sorts of advice did he call on you for?

Admiral McCrea: Now listen. You made a flat statement there, and I am not sure that I agree with you completely, what you say was the job of the naval aide.

Q: One of the roles of the naval aide.

Admiral McCrea: You said that he would call on me for advice. He never called on me for any advice that I know of. He didn't say, "I want your advice on so-and-so," but he might talk casually about things going on. And when I told you yesterday that when Grace Tully came in and wanted to know if he would come over and pour cocktails, and you remember I couldn't name the first fellow--I have thought of it since, and his name was Dean Landis, and he was the dean of the Harvard Law School.* He, I am told, got into trouble with the bottle later and had quite a time over at Harvard. The number two guy then was Alexander Woollcott.** I used to religiously listen to Alex Woollcott on Sunday afternoons when he would broadcast. He was most interesting to listen to. I remember one time we were, I was down in the map room, and the telephone rang. And here was the chief usher. And he said, "Captain, I think you should come up here [on the main floor of the White House]. Mr. Alexander Woollcott was here to see Mrs. Roosevelt, and he has come down from up there, and he is roaming around here. I think somebody ought to be looking out for somebody as prominent as he."

I said, "Very well, I'll be right up there." So I went up and introduced myself to Woollcott, and he told me that he had ordered a cab, and I said, "Can't we send you someplace?"

"Oh, no." He had ordered this cab, and he was going to wait for it. Then he started walking and talking and one thing and another, and he went out on the front steps in front of the White House. And, to my astonishment, Alexander Woollcott sat down on the front steps in front of

---
*James McCauley Landis, dean of Harvard Law School, 1937-46.
**Alexander Woollcott was a radio broadcaster, journalist, drama critic, and author of a number of books.

the White House. And I thought, "I've got to be courteous to this fellow, so I'll sit down too." I made a remark, and it still holds, that I envy anybody who can sit down and take the English language and do what a good writer can do with it.

And he remarked, right off of hand. "Oh," he said, "there's nothing that beats the English language." And he went on to talk about things, and he said, "I notice that you have been using a word that I regard as the weakest word in the English language."

I said, "Really, Mr. Woollcott?"

He said, "You use often the word 'very.' It's the weakest word in the English language by a long shot. And to show you how unnecessary it is, how useless the word is--if you substitute for the word 'very' and use for it 'damn,' it will come out more often right than not."

I have never forgotten that, and I avoid the use of the word "very" as much as possible, especially in writing anything. Another thing that he didn't like: "I strongly recommend." [Use] "I recommend or I don't recommend." There is a lot of merit in what the guy said. You are a writer; you must know. I don't know whether you agree or not, but that's all right. I'm just telling you what another famous writer said.

J. L. McCrea #3 - 271

Q: Where did you live at the time when you were serving the President?

Admiral McCrea: I had my own home in Washington. I bought a home there in 1929. There is an odd story about that too.

I was on the West Coast with Admiral Rodman. One of his classmates who had resigned early from the Navy and had gone into the banking business and lived in Los Angeles was a fellow by the name of James Drake.* And Admiral Rodman would refer to "Old James this and Old James that." And he had had a stroke and wasn't in too good health, but he loved to come down to the flagship and sit around and talk with Admiral Rodman. Well, it was a lot of fun to listen to these two fellows talk about the Naval Academy. And Jim Drake would come down and get a chair and sit on the quarterdeck of the New Mexico and just take that southern California sun. One day he said, "You know, I am a banker."

And I said, "Yes."

And he said, "I want to know; have you saved any money in the Navy?"

"Oh, not very much, Mr. Drake."

And he said, "Well, tell me; have you saved any?"

---

*James C. Drake and Hugh Rodman were in the Naval Academy's class of 1880. Drake resigned as an ensign and subsequently died in Los Angeles in March 1921.

And I said, "Yes, I've got a few Liberty Bonds. I think, all told, I have $1,800 worth in Liberty Bonds."

He said, "Do you want to make some money?"

"Well," I said, "of course I'd like to make some money, but I don't know how."

"Now," he said, "I'll tell you what. You sell your Liberty Bonds and buy into a company that's forming here in Los Angeles by the name of Pacific Finance Corporation. The Pacific Finance Corporation finances the purchase of automobiles. The banks in California have done this for some time, and the legislature has now fixed it up so that the banks have got to get rid of this operation. Two or three finance companies have been organized, and the one that I am thinking about is the Pacific Finance, and it's headed up by John B. Miller who is the president of the Southern California Edison Company. I have ridden along with John B. Miller in a number of things that he has promoted, and everyone has been successful. It may be odd for a banker to tell you to sell Liberty Bonds and buy that, but that is what I am suggesting you do."

Well, that was enough for me, so I sold my Liberty Bonds. In due course, my Pacific Finance went moving up and up and up, and I had gone to the China Station. And I had gotten married, and I came back. When I went to the China Station, I left my little nest egg with the Union Trust Company in Washington. One of the vice presidents,

George Fleming, was a close friend of mine, and I like him very much indeed. And he said he would keep his eye on my few shares of AT&T and Pacific Finance and a few odds and ends that I had while I was on the China Station. So when I finally got back in 1926, I still had the Pacific Finance. Then, in due course, Foxhall Village--do you know Foxhall Village in Washington?

Q: Vaguely. I'm not specifically familiar.

Admiral McCrea: Well, one Sunday morning my bride and I were living down there in Burleith, and we went out for a walk. It was pretty cool, the day was something like this, and there was this sign on there. It said, "Model house, come in." So we went in and took a look, and it was very attractive. The house was heated, and the fellow who was sitting the house and acting as salesman said, "What is your name?" And I told him. "Got a telephone?"

"Yes, I do."

Well, that afternoon, Mr. Boss of Boss and Phelps, Sunday afternoon, came to my house. Before the afternoon was all over, I had committed myself to a down payment, and I sold Pacific Finance and got considerable money out of it--nothing spectacular, about $6,500 or $7,000 or something like that. But it was more than enough for a down payment on one of those houses, and that's the way I got into owning a house. I kept it from 1928 until 1956 or 1957, and I've always been sorry that I sold the damn thing, because it tripled in value down there.

And the next thing was the reason I sold it was that Estelle--that's my wife who died--was convinced that that's where the blacks would move in. In our time, around Washington, whenever the blacks penetrated any neighborhood, no matter what, the price of the real estate went down like that. She thought that as long as I was going to stay up here, that I should get rid of it, which I did. I got into the thing, as I say, through the Pacific Finance, because James Drake suggested that I sell my poor little Liberty Bonds and get into it.

Q: You probably didn't get to spend much time there when you were naval aide to the President, did you?

Admiral McCrea: I lived in it.

Q: But you probably had to spend the bulk of your time at the White House.

Admiral McCrea: Oh, yes. Hell, I left the house every morning about 7:00 o'clock. I had a bluejacket with a little Pontiac I had, and he would be at the door at 7:00 o'clock every morning for me. That was Saturdays and

Sundays too. It was a seven-day-a-week job being naval aide to the President, especially on Sundays. I would be doing all sorts of things for him. Everybody would just scatter like that on weekends, which is understandable. I can understand it, but here was this fellow who was committed to his bed. His valet would come in and dress him, and he would get in his wheelchair if he wanted to go someplace. But he was pinned down in that room or his adjoining circular study upstairs. He liked people. He liked to talk about things that were on his mind. He would start off, "Well, I've been thinking about so-and-so," and he would talk. Talk and talk.

Q: Could you give me some examples?

Admiral McCrea: He was always asking questions, "What do you think about this? What do you think about that?" Whether it was a naval officer or a civilian or somebody, or some event, "What do you think about it?"

So very often I would say, "Mr President, I am a naval officer. I don't think . . ."

"But you are a citizen. You must have an idea." For instance, he might ask, "Could Al Smith have been elected in 1932?"*

---

*Alfred E. Smith of New York, running on the Democratic ticket in 1928, was defeated in the presidential election by Herbert Hoover. Roosevelt himself defeated Hoover in the 1932 election.

"Oh," I said, "Mr. President, I'm a naval officer . . ."

"Come on now, John, you must have an idea. Could Al have been elected in 1932?"

I said, "Well, right off the top of my head, I suppose there would have been enough bias, in the Sun Belt at any rate, to keep a Catholic from being elected President of the United States in 1932." With that, I stopped.

He didn't say "I agree with you," or "I disagree." All he said was, "Al thinks he could have made it, and that was the start of all the differences that arose between Al and me." Then he would move off to something else.

I think I was right. I think probably that he couldn't have been elected in 1932. I just feel that way. Maybe I was right, and maybe I was wrong; I haven't any idea. It was certainly a little startling to be quizzed about things that you had very little knowledge about. But he was right. I was a citizen, and I ought to have had some sort of an idea what I was talking about. That, of course, is one of the weaknesses of our system of government--brains don't always prevail at all. Which one of the Greeks was it, Demosthenes or Aristotle, who said that "Democracy carries within itself its own seeds of destruction." I don't know which one it was.

Q: I forget which one it was.

Admiral McCrea: Some famous Greek, way, way back, thought that, and every once in a while I am wondering if the guy wasn't about right.

Q: President Roosevelt--one of his great strengths was finding out the public opinion and then reacting accordingly.

Admiral McCrea: That's right, but I'm not so sure that public opinion is certain enough of itself or is the correct view. Of course, I think that the newspapers and the TV--I'll tell you, I have many misgivings about the newspapers. I'll tell you what he said about that. He said, "When I was in the Navy" [he always talked about when he was in the Navy]. He said, "I got the idea that you naval officers lived a cloistered career. I've held two press conferences a week [that, of course, in great contrast to what goes on now], and at those two press conferences every week, they come in, and they ask me questions. For the most part I encourage them to give questions to Steve, and Steve can look up answers and things like that. I want you to attend my press conferences, so you will have an idea what the rest of the country is thinking about."*

It turned out that I was one of six people who had chairs to sit in, and I sat right beside Earl Godwin who was the fellow who says, "Thank you, Mr. President" at the end of the conference.** I sat beside Earl Godwin, and there it was. I thought that FDR handled the press beautifully. May Craig would come in--they didn't have any chairs to sit in; they stood up with their notebooks, and they did this and that. He would look at May Craig and say, "Well, May, where in the world did you get that lovely hat?" and a few things like that, and people laughed and away it went.***

Vermont Royster--you know him--he writes.**** Every so often he would write something that went back in the White House, and he was around there at that time. Roscoe Drummond of The Christian Science Monitor was one of the fellows. And a Chinaman, whose name I have forgotten, but I met him on my trip to the Orient. He was in the airplane with me flying back. He came to the United States for the China News, and he was in this Pan American airplane when we were coming back to the United States. He was there, and every so often he would call me up and invite my wife

---
*Presidential press secretary Steve Early.
**Earl Godwin, a broadcaster for the NBC radio network, was president of the White House correspondents' association.
***Mrs. Elizabeth May Craig, Washington correspondent for a number of newspapers, was famous for talking back to President Roosevelt during press conferences.
****Vermont C. Royster, long-time reporter and editor for The Wall Street Journal.

and me to have dinner with him someplace. I got to know quite a few of these fellows. This Roscoe Drummond I have a high regard for.

When anybody would come up with a question that he didn't have an answer for right away, he would say, "Now just a minute, I can't answer that. Steve, see about getting me an answer for this question." And the President would turn to the questioner and say, "You can get in touch with Steve," or "We'll have an answer by the next meeting that we have." And he would move onto something else.

He had the press conference on Tuesday afternoon, I think it was, at 3:30, and the second press conference of the week was at 9:00 o'clock on Friday morning. Tuesday afternoon was for the benefit of the morning papers, and the one Friday morning at 9:00 o'clock was for the benefit of the afternoon papers. He did that every week that he was in town. If he was out of town, of course, he couldn't have it, but nevertheless, that's what he did. It was a very well-thought-out way of running things. Nowadays, these lads with their pads, they don't stand up and ask questions. They sit in comfort in the plush seats and think up insulting questions to ask the President and a few things like that, and that rather annoys me.

Now, Steve Early once, sitting on the train when we

were going out West--Steve was sitting there one night talking to me--and he said, "John, this is a great guy we are working for back here; do you know that?"

"Of course I know it. You know him so much better than I do, but I've gotten to admire him greatly."

Steve said, "We've had a little trouble. One day he called me in, and he said, 'Steven, look, I want you to pick up Drew Pearson's press pass.'"*

And Steve said, "Well, boss [Steve always called him "boss"], why should I pick it up?"

The President said, "He is a son of a bitch, and I would just like to have his press pass picked up."

Steve said, "My answer was, 'Mr. President, out of a 180 million people, there must be a lot of sons of bitches in the United States, and aren't they worthy of being represented at your press conferences?'"

Steve said, "I thought I was clever as hell, but he didn't laugh."

"And the next day, he rang me up and wanted to see me, and I went in, and he said, 'Steven, have you picked up Drew Pearson's press card?'

"'No, Boss, I haven't.'"

"'Well, I want you to do it.'"

And Steve said, "I'll go do it, and I'll bring it

---

*Andrew R. Pearson, author of the syndicated newspaper column "Daily Washington Merry-Go-Round." Pearson was a muckraker and predecessor of Jack Anderson.

right in to you, and when I bring it in to you, I'm going to bring my letter of resignation as your press secretary."

And he said, "The President said, 'Now wait a minute, Steve. Both of us may be a little hasty. I think you are hasty, and I may have been a little hasty, but we'll talk about it some other time.'"

Steve said, "That was months ago, and he's never raised the subject since."

Then the next thing that happened--when he was running in 1940 and they went to New York on campaign business, and here was the train down in Pennsylvania Station there getting ready to go back to Washington, and the President had gotten on the train. And the train was supposed to pull out at 4:30 or 5:00 o'clock or whatever it was, and Steve was with some people who were in the gallery, up in the waiting room there. He turned around and made a dash to catch the train; it was going in a couple of minutes. He got up there to the gate, and the gate was just being shut by this black. And Steve said, "I'm going down there to get on the train."

And he said, "Oh, no you're not."

And Steve said, "I just kneed this black and swung the gate, and away I went, right on down. The next morning in the papers--I had kneed this black, and he was just back on duty for the last ten days after just having had a hernia operation, and the newspaper played it up to beat hell.

I've been around this business long enough, I didn't say a word to the President. I just let it sit. I felt like a skunk, but I didn't say a word. And the President didn't say a word. I knew damn well that he must have seen it in the paper, but he never said a word, and he's never said a word yet about it. Now for those two instances I'm citing, I say we are working for a great fellow back here."

I have often thought of what Steve said--what a great fellow he was.

I told you about meeting Roy Howard out in the middle of the Pacific on Guam; we kept in touch with each other and wrote back and forth. And when I was appointed to the White House, I got a wonderful note from Roy Howard in which he congratulated me in being sent to the White House and he hoped that I would enjoy it. He said, "The President, I am sure, doesn't like me, and I don't think I like him too much. But, in all truth, when the history of this century is written, I am convinced that he is going to go down as one of our great Presidents." This was signed by Roy Howard, and it was written to me. He was on his yacht down in the Chesapeake recuperating from a heart attack or some other damn thing.

I told Steve Early about getting this letter from Roy Howard. He said, "Could I see it?"

"Of course you can see it."

And Steve said, "I feel very kindly toward Roy Howard,

because he gave me one of my first jobs in this business. I know he is in bad favor here, but I would just like to have that letter."

So he took my letter, and he showed it to the President. Well, the President remarked about it a few days later, and he said Steve had shown him this letter. And he wanted to know my connection with Howard, and I told him about meeting him on the Island of Guam when he was engine-bound there and about seeing a good deal of him both in my house and over at Government House and one thing and another. I said that I had kept in touch with him throughout the years.

He said, "You know, I suppose I should feel more kindly toward Howard, but when I was first elected here, I wanted Howard [who was head of the UP, which was strong all through South America]. I wrote and asked him if he would be good enough to make a trip on behalf of the United States down through these countries in which the UP was strong to improve the position of the United States down through South America. You know what this fellow Howard wrote to me? He wrote me a letter, and he said that he couldn't afford to take time off to go and do such a jaunt. The idea that he could put that up as a good reason not to go do something for his country. And the country had been awfully good to Roy Howard, so I just rather gently removed

Roy Howard from my circle of acquaintances."*

Now there is another side of the story. It was interesting to run onto this sort of thing. Every time I saw Roy Howard when I was at the White House, and I saw him a number of times--then when I was with John Hancock, I saw him a good deal, because the John Hancock people negotiated a loan for the Scripps-Howard, and I went down to New York when the signing took place, and Roy and I went off and had lunch. He said, "Let all those money-grubbers sit out and have lunch by themselves. I want to have lunch with you, and we'll sit and talk about Guam and the Western Pacific."

And that's the way it worked out. He was quite a guy, that fellow.

Q: As evidence of what a good guy Roosevelt was, he took care of getting you a good assignment when you left the White House. How did that come about?

Admiral McCrea: Well, I'll tell you. Wait a minute, there's something that just flashed across my mind. One day Howard remarked to me, "You know, I wish I was as tall as you are."

I said, "My God, I'm not very tall, I'm just . . ."

---

*UP--United Press, then one of the major wire services for providing news to newspapers and radio stations. UP has since merged with International News Service to become United Press International.

He said, "I'd give anything to be your height." Do you remember him? He was short, very short.

Q: I've seen pictures of him.

Admiral McCrea: "But," he said, "I get along pretty well at my size. You know, often, when the press is crowding around, with my size, I could just stoop down and go right in here like this and pop up in front of all these tall guys that are standing around there getting the interview. So, with my size, I have overcome that a bit."

Now, you spoke about going to Iowa. One day the President sent for me, and he said, "John, I've seen any number of ships christened, and so has my Mrs. But her secretary, Malvina Thompson, has never seen a ship of any size launched. She has expressed a wish to see the Iowa launched." (The invitations had come into the White House that the Iowa was going to be launched on such-and-such a day at such-and-such a time. They had to be at high water, you see, at 10:22 or something like that in the morning.) And he said, "Do you suppose you could arrange it to escort the Mrs. and Malvina Thompson to the Navy Yard in New York and see the ship launched?"

I said, "Why, of course I can. I think so, Mr. President."

And he said, "Now there is one other thing about this.

Joe Grew has just been released by the Japanese, and he has arrived in this country, and I want to talk to him. And I am going to give a little dinner party for him, and it's going to be the night before the launching of the Iowa.* I want you to be at Joe Grew's dinner, if possible."

I said, "I think I can arrange that, Mr. President. I can get passage on the midnight train from Washington to New York, and I can go join Mrs. Roosevelt and Miss Thompson there."

Well, right away I got a note from Mrs. Roosevelt saying that she would be pleased, if I could find it convenient, if I could have breakfast on the morning of so-and-so with her and Miss Thompson in her apartment in New York. Well, of course, that was easy to work out--I had already made arrangements with the commandant, and they were going to supply me a car and send a car and a driver to take us all to the Navy yard to be there at the time the ship was to be launched.

Mrs. Wallace, the wife of the Vice President, christened the Iowa, because he was from Iowa.** As I stood there and saw this ship going down the ways, the thought flashed across my mind: "Gee, that would be a

---
*Joseph C. Grew, a career Foreign Service officer, became U.S. ambassador to Japan in 1932 and remained in that post until the outbreak of war in 1941. He was returned to the United States in 1942 when American diplomats were exchanged for Japanese Embassy personnel interned in this country. The Iowa was launched 27 August 1942.
**Mrs. Ilo Browne Wallace, wife of Vice President Henry A. Wallace.

wonderful command for somebody, but it's not for me, because I would be too junior." So I just let it go.

It so happened that Randall Jacobs, who was the Chief of the Bureau of Personnel, had an office in the Navy Department directly across the corridor from my office as naval aide to the President that I had in the Navy Department. I had an office in the White House, of course, but I had this one in the Navy Department on the front corridor. And it was directly across from Randall Jacobs. One day he was in my office, and I was talking with him, and I said, "You know, when I was sent to the White House, I got gypped out of going to this cruiser as commander, and I am hoping that I can get a battleship. Do you suppose that you will have battleships available by the time that I leave the White House, which will be about seven or eight months from now?"

He said, "Hell, yes, we'll have battleships available and probably going past your bracket for command."

I said, "I just saw that Iowa being launched the other day, and it was a very wonderful sight." And with that I let it go. Came that fall in mid-September--and I have already told you, I suppose, that the President said he would release me after a decent interval, and we decided that a decent interval was a year or thereabouts, unless he had fired me first. So we were on the West Coast, down in

San Diego, and the Western Union fellow came and hunted me up, and here was a telegram addressed to me. It said, "Iowa goes in commission 15 January 1943. Are you interested?" It was signed by Bill Fechteler.* Well, I wrote an answer right away and gave it to the boy. Bill Fechteler was the captain detail officer, and what I said to him was, "Of course I am interested, but I cannot commit myself here. Wait until I get back to Washington in the next ten days, and I will see you and talk it out with you."

So that was it. I got ahold of the President and said, "I would have been here just a little over a year then, and I am just wondering if you will let me go the 15th of January to commission the Iowa?"

He said, "I think we can work that out."

And I said, "Okay, thank you." And I told Bill Fechteler that.

Meanwhile, Eisenhower made the landings in North Africa in the first week in November, as I recall. Right after election, they landed. The President knew they were going to land about that time. He never said one word. Not one word. Our war prospects at that time weren't too good, the way things had been going. He never said one word until after the elections were over and the Democrats

---

*Captain William M. Fechteler, USN, Director, Officer Personnel Division, Bureau of Naval Personnel. Fechteler was later Chief of Naval Operations from 1951 to 1953.

had lost some seats. And he said, "If Eisenhower had landed a week earlier rather than a week later, I don't think we would have lost those seats." That's the only time I ever heard him mention political things--about votes or anything like that. I think his observation was probably correct.

We move on now, and all of a sudden one day, I think it was the first week of December, about the second or third, the President called me in, and he said, "I am going to try out something on you. You know I've been in correspondence with Winston."

And I said, "Yes, I did, Mr. President."

And he said, "I want to sit down and talk face to face with Winston, and I think that we should go to North Africa. What do you think about my going to North Africa?"

And I think that's the only time he ever asked me anything about what did I think about something that had to do with taking action on his part.

"Well," I said, "Mr. President, popping this on me, I just can't give you an answer right now. Let me think it over tonight, and I'll tell you in the morning, if I may, just exactly what I think."

He said, "That's good, do it."

I thought about it that night, and the next morning I, of course, saw him with the dispatches, and he brought it up again. He said, "What conclusion did you reach?"

I said, "I think, Mr. President, that you shouldn't do it."

"Why not?"

"I'll bet you that North Africa is full of all sorts of people who would take you on for $10.00. I just don't think you should take that chance."

He said, "I want to see the GIs in a combat zone. They are taking chances; why shouldn't I take a chance?"

Two weeks later, if you will recall, Admiral Darlan was assassinated Christmas Eve in North Africa.* He knew Darlan, and Darlan's son was a polio fellow, and he had been in Warm Springs. President Roosevelt never once mentioned Darlan's assassination, and I wanted so much to say, "You see what I told you." But I didn't; I had sense enough not to. And we went right ahead with our plans to go to North Africa.

Then he said, "I must be here for the opening of the Congress. We will leave town right after that and go to North Africa, and you are going with me."

I said, "The *Iowa* is due to go into commission on the 15th of January.

---

*Admiral Jean Francois Darlan had been Commander in Chief of the French Navy, then accepted the position of Minister of Marine in the Vichy regime. He later became vice premier, but he gave up that post to become head of all French forces. He had links with both Allies and Germans, so neither side knew whether he could be trusted. General Dwight D. Eisenhower designated him as political head of French North Africa, following the Allied invasion. Darlan was killed by a French fanatic on 24 December 1942.

J. L. McCrea #3 - 291

And he said, "You won't be back for it."

"Well," I said, "Mr. President, I would hate to lose the ship."

And he said, "John, under the circumstances, I don't think they'd take the ship away from you."

Now that is exactly what happened, and we went. And when we got back, we got back on Sunday night the second or third of February. I was detached the very next day, and away I went to join the *Iowa*, and then the *Iowa* was not commissioned until the 22nd of February. But I was detached and I went right straight up to New York when they were assembling the crew and doing all that sort of thing.

Now where did I skip around here?

Q: I don't think you skipped anything. Could you move forward from that point? What activities did you get involved in as soon as you reported to the ship?

Admiral McCrea: Well, getting the ship in commission. That was the big thing, getting the thing in commission. We invited Mrs. Henry Wallace. The commandant, of course, invited Mrs. Wallace, and Mrs. Wallace's answer came through her secretary that Mrs. Wallace wanted to know if her expenses would be paid to make this trip to New York for the commissioning.* And the answer was no, because the commissioning of the ship was entirely different from the launching of the ship. And the commissioning of the ship was the commandant's and the captain's party, and that was all there was to it. Mrs. Wallace never did show, but nevertheless, that was the way it was.

Q: Was the ship essentially finished as far as building when you got there?

Admiral McCrea: Oh, yes, pretty much. But there is so much to do about cleaning up around the ship and getting it in shape. We moved on board two or three days before the ship was actually commissioned. My mother was up in Michigan, of course, and I wanted her to come down. And she wrote and said that she couldn't come down to New York. I got my brother on the telephone then and told him this was a very important thing in my life and was there anything wrong with our mother and why did she turn me down? Whereas, any time I suggested that she go to California or Panama Canal or anyplace else, she was all for going and did. He said, "No, she's all right; she can go."

I said, "All right. You make her go." So I met her

―――――――――
*The commandant referred to here is Vice Admiral Adolphus Andrews, USN, Commandant Third Naval District and Commander Eastern Sea Frontier.

at the train and took her over and set her up in a hotel. That night before the ship was going in commission, I gave this dinner party aboard ship, and I went over to the hotel to pick up my wife and my two daughters and my mother, and we came back to the ship. And here was this Marine prancing up and down in front of the brow leading up to the ship. I came over there, and he came up and said no one was permitted on board the ship.

I said, "Well, I'm the prospective captain. I'm going to be the captain of this ship tomorrow."

And he said, "My orders are that no one is to be permitted aboard this gangway."

I said, "I won't interfere with your orders. This is my mother, this is my wife and my two daughters. Would you get your corporal of the guard?" The corporal of the guard came down, and my wife and my mother stood there and laughed at my perturbation about not being able to get aboard the ship that I was going to be the captain of. They thought that was a good joke. It was, in a way, but nevertheless, we got on board. Mr. Knox was there the next day, and he met my mother, and my mother got rid of something that was on her mind. She said that she thought that ship was too big for a little fellow like me--that I was so young--and I was 51 or 52 or something like that. Nevertheless, that was it.

So it was all in good spirit, but she told Mr. Knox.

And Mr. Knox and I saw a good deal of each other when I was with Stark and also when I was at the White House, so he put in a good word for me. That was the way that worked out.

Q: Did you find out the reason for her reluctance about coming?

Admiral McCrea: She just thought she was getting a little too old to travel, she said. That was all. But she was glad she went. As a matter of fact, in that picture right up there, my mother is sitting in the front row there. She had my two daughters with her and my wife sitting alongside of them, but she was sitting in the front row there.

Q: What do you recall about the commissioning ceremony itself?

Admiral McCrea: There was one distinguished visitor there. His name was John Pierpont Morgan, and he came, by gracious, in morning coat and tophat and everything; he did it up right.* Ten days later, he died, and the obituary notice said that he contracted a cold attending the

---
*Morgan was the son of the noted financier of the same name. He had succeeded his father as head of J. P. Morgan & Company and had acted as an agent of Allied governments in floating large loans in the United States during World War I.

ceremonies of the commissioning of the USS Iowa.* He developed pneumonia and died, but that's one of the things I remember particularly well. He had been at the launching of the ship, too, in morning coat, tophat, everything. That's the way he went.

Q: Was the affair subdued in any fashion because the war was in progress?

Admiral McCrea: Not to my knowledge. There was a British ship tied up at the dock right nearby--the Ajax--and she was one of the cruisers that had taken on the Graf Spee. Those little cruisers had taken on the Graf Spee, the pocket battleship, and she had gotten into port, but she was defeated. The captain, you know, committed suicide.** Nevertheless, the Ajax was up there in the New York Navy Yard. Having served in the North Sea with the British, I wanted to make connections with the skipper of the Ajax, and I did. I went over there and called on him and told him how I had been in the North Sea with the British in the

---
*Morgan died 13 March 1943 at his winter home in Florida. Published reports attributed his death to a heart attack followed by a stroke.
**The Graf Spee entered the port of Montevideo, Uruguay, to repair battle damage. Because of international law, the amount of time she could stay in a neutral port was limited. Rather than go out to face the British ships once again, Captain Hans Langsdorff, the commanding officer, had his crew blow up and scuttle the Graf Spee. He then killed himself the night of 19-20 December 1939, while interned in Uruguay.

First World War and how I enjoyed it.

I got him to tell me about taking on the Graf Spee. He told me that it was quite a job for them to take on that pocket battleship. They were underarmed really--these light cruisers--and they dashed in like a bunch of hornets coming at you from all directions, and they knocked the thing off and did a lot of damage to the ship. And there is one thing that stuck in my mind about what this fellow said. He said, "Had it not been for the steadiness of the petty officers in this ship in remote parts of the ship, away from control of their officers, we might well have lost the ship." I have never forgotten what that fellow told me, and I cranked that thought into my talk when we commissioned the Iowa. It was very interesting to have that talk and, of course, I had him to lunch. And he had me at lunch and one thing and another. It was exceedingly interesting to be in the Navy at that time.

Q: Was there any press coverage of the commissioning?

Admiral McCrea: Now that's another thing. It had been sent out from the Navy Department that there would be no announcements in the press about the commissioning or decommissioning of ships and all that sort of thing. Boy, when the papers came out on Tuesday morning or whatever, here was a flood of things about the commissioning of the

Iowa--this brand-new, 45,000-ton battleship. The first thing that I got ahold of was this letter from this chap who was the Vice Chief of Naval Operations in which I was chided for the press coverage about the commissioning of this ship.*

I was annoyed enough about it so that I climbed on the train and I went down to Washington, and I said nothing was put out about in the way of press coverage about this ship. There were press people on board, of course, but they were told there was not to be any press coverage and they knew it; all these people knew it. And I went further than that--the commandant told me, too, that he had done everything he could to suppress it. But it turned out that Mr. Knox, newspaperman that he was, as soon as he got back in Washington from the commissioning of Iowa, he let fly in all directions.**

So I said to the Vice Chief of Naval Operations, "I think this letter should really be withdrawn, but I am not going to ask you to do it, because how can I tell the Secretary of the Navy that he can't release to the press something about the commissioning of a ship? That's the spot I'm in, and here I am being chided in this letter about the press coverage that was given, and the Secretary of the Navy was the guy who did it all himself."

---
*Vice Admiral Frederick J. Horne, USN, was Vice Chief of Naval Operations.
**Secretary of the Navy Knox was also publisher of the Chicago Daily News.

Well, we just laughed about that and let it go, and I got on the train and went back to New York.

Q: Did Knox have a part in the commissioning ceremony?

Admiral McCrea: Oh, yes, he talked. Yes, of course he did. I wish I had a copy of what I said at the commissioning, but I haven't got one handy.

Q: Did you have a hand in picking the crew at all?

Admiral McCrea: I wanted to pick the heads of departments. I was told I couldn't do it. I said, "Now look, there is one fellow I want as gunnery officer of Iowa. And you people pick out people and send them where you think they can best serve. But I've got to live with this fellow that I want, and I want you to give him to me."

"Well, we'll give you a chance to decline acceptance of some people."

The executive officer of the ship I had never seen until he reported on board. I went along with him; his name was Tom Casey, and he came from Boston. I went along with his selection, because Turner Joy told me that he had served with Tom Casey, and Turner tried to get him to come as his exec of a cruiser that he, Joy, was going to get command of, and the Navy Department said he wasn't available.* I knew Turner Joy to be a good naval officer, and I didn't think he would put his stamp of approval on anybody who wasn't passable. So I took Casey without ever having laid eyes on him. And all the rest of them I had never laid eyes on. George Leahy I had laid hands on, because he had been the captain of the Potomac, the President's yacht, when I was first at the White House. But when the Secret Service refused to let the President use the Potomac, we took out the officers we had there, and the men, and we sent them elsewhere.

Q: Did you get the gunnery officer that you wanted?

Admiral McCrea: Yes, Quiggle. I told you about Quiggle; a fine officer that fellow, one of the best.**

Q: Did you have radar right from the start in the Iowa?

Admiral McCrea: Yes.

Q: How well did that work?

---

*Captain C. Turner Joy, USN, commanded the heavy cruiser Louisville (CA-28) from September 1942 to June 1943. Joy later went on to a distinguished career as a flag officer, including service as Commander U.S. Naval Forces Far East during the Korean War.
**Commander Lynne C. Quiggle, USN.

Admiral McCrea: Pretty well. Of course, it was by the experimental stages then. Somewhat by it, but it was good. As a matter of fact, I knew Blandy well, who was the head of the Bureau of Ordnance.* One day playing golf with him (I used to play golf with him a lot), I kept after him about the uses of radar. Finally, I got after him about this thing, and he said, "Listen, please stop, John, please stop talking about it. We've made the breakthrough." Then he came to me a few weeks later and said, "If the President is interested, we would be glad to take some films about what we have done with radar over to the White House."

I told the President, and he said, "Certainly, I would be glad to see them." And they came over and put on a good show in the cabinet room as to what they had accomplished. It was well worth seeing, because we knew what was going off.

Q: What was your estimation of Blandy as a naval officer?

Admiral McCrea: Tops. He made one mistake in his life that I know of. He was a five-striper at the Naval Academy, which was in command of the naval brigade, and he stood number one in his class of 1913. In the fall of 1912 we went to Philadelphia, and we got out of the trains up

---

*Rear Admiral William H. P. Blandy, USN, Chief of the Bureau of Ordnance. Blandy later became a four-star admiral and served as Commander in Chief Atlantic Fleet.

there--we were supposed to stay in the vicinity of the Franklin Field--and we had to march on at such and such a time.* Well, Blandy was in love, and his gal had come to Philadelphia, and he went to see the gal. He didn't get back to the formation to march them on, and he was busted. He went from a five-striper to a clean-sleever at the Naval Academy in his first-class year. I don't guess he ever lived that completely down. He was the Navy's selection to be the Chief of Naval Operations. He was Nimitz's number one guy, but Denfeld got it because of Admiral Leahy's association with President Truman. Of course, Denfeld left an aborted cruise as Chief of Naval Operations.

Q: He was fired by Louis Johnson.**

Admiral McCrea: Yes. But Blandy was tops, completely so.

Q: Do you know why Leahy preferred Denfeld?

Admiral McCrea: Well, when Leahy was in the office of Chief of Naval Operations, Denfeld was around there and Freezman and somebody else (who was the next guy, I have

---

*Franklin Field was the site of the 1912 Army-Navy football game, which the Naval Academy won, 6-0. The 1913 <u>Lucky Bag</u>, the Naval Academy yearbook, congratulated Blandy for the good grace with which he took his demotion as a result of the incident.
**Louis A. Johnson was Secretary of Defense in 1949-50.

J. L. McCrea #3 - 302

forgotten). But at any rate, I must say that I didn't think too much of Leahy's choice of people. He passed up a lot of good guys, and Denfeld got the job because of Admiral Leahy's close association with the President.

Q: Leahy knew Blandy well enough, too, because when Leahy commanded the New Mexico, Blandy was his gunnery officer.

Admiral McCrea: Well, I know what I am talking about about this, because I was there with Nimitz when the selection was being made; I was one of Nimitz's deputies. He had five deputies when he was Chief of Naval Operations, and I was the deputy for administration. We had the biggest office in the office of the Chief of Naval Operations. I had relieved Conolly; Conolly had gone to London.*

Q: How long after the commissioning did the Iowa remain at the Navy Yard there in New York?

Admiral McCrea: I can't tell you exactly--about six weeks, five weeks. I know that everybody in the Iowa delegation in the Congress came to the commissioning excepting one lone congressman. The governor came on too, Governor

---

*Vice Admiral Richard L. Conolly, USN, became Deputy Chief of Naval Operations (Administration) in January 1946. In September of that year, he received his fourth star when he became Commander U.S. Naval Forces Europe.

J. L. McCrea #3 - 303

Hickenlooper.* He told me that they had all the silver that came from the old _Iowa_ out in the state museum out there, and he wanted that silver to go back in _Iowa_. So he wrote down to the Navy Department, and I was told by the Navy Department to go out to Des Moines and accept this silver, to put it on board _Iowa_, but that I should accept it and then ask the state of Iowa if they would still continue to hold it there until after hostilities, when it could be put on the ship. That's what I did. I went out there, and they had a joint session of the state legislature, and the governor made the presentation, and I accepted it and all that sort of thing. He had a reception for me afterward, and I can assure you that I thought at the time--and I still think about it every once in a while--I looked into more honest faces that afternoon than I had seen in a long while, because these people radiated character.

Q: I am amused by that observation.

Admiral McCrea: I hope that you don't think that it is too lighthearted.

Q: Not at all.

---
*Governor Bourke B. Hickenlooper, Republican.

Admiral McCrea: One of the things about going as skipper of the Iowa, which was a little bit of a tragedy as far as I was concerned--one of my close friends at the Naval Academy was a fellow by the name of Homer William Graf, and he came from Des Moines. And he was on duty at the Naval Academy, and I was on duty in Washington, of course. He and his wife came up and came to our house one night for dinner.* Homer and I had gone to the store for something that Estelle wanted, and we walked. And on the way back he said, "I suppose you will be going to sea soon."

And I said, "Well, I hope to."

And he said, "You know, I want to go to sea, and I've got my heart set on one thing."

I said, "Good, what is it, Homer?"

He said, "I want to have command of USS Iowa."

I said, "Homer, listen, I hadn't intended to tell you this, but my orders to command USS Iowa on its commissioning arrived in my office this afternoon. You must know that I hate to cross you up in anything that you had your heart set on, but there it is; that's all I can tell you."

He walked along for about a block, and he didn't say a damn word. I felt so damn badly about it, and I still do. He passed on four or five years ago.**

---
*Captain Homer W. Graf, USN.
**While McCrea was commanding the Iowa, Graf served as chief of staff to Commander Seventh Fleet. Graf retired in the rank of commodore; he died 12 March 1970.

Q: Where did you go on your shakedown? Was that the Chesapeake Bay thing you were telling me about?

Admiral McCrea: Yes, that was the shakedown thing--to get out of the Navy Yard and just put the hook down someplace and just keep people aboard the ship and work like hell to get the ship cleaned up and get all the Navy Yard trash away.

Q: How did you spend the time between that period in the Chesapeake and then when you took the President over to Oran?

Admiral McCrea: I told you that after we bumped the rock we went to the Boston Navy Yard in South Boston, and we had the repairs completed. Then, directly that was over, we were sent up to Argentia, because the Tirpitz had moved out into the Norwegian Coast, and they sent us up there for the Tirpitz watch.* It was very bad sailing up there, because the weather was bad. The holding grounds were very, very bad. There was no holding ground at all, and we were tied up at an anchoring ring that had three cement

---

*The Tirpitz was a German battleship. As long as she was in Norway, she posed a potential threat to the Atlantic shipping lanes. Her sister Bismarck had gone out into the Atlantic as a surface raider in 1941.

blocks tied up to this upriser that went through a buoy. We were up there, and we had to keep steam at the throttle most of the time, because when the wind would hit the ship, the ship would tend to drag, and it would make these three great cement blocks pull together. And what little holding capacity they had really didn't amount to so much. It didn't amount to anything. So we had one hell of a time keeping that thing. I was delighted to get away from that thing. The bottom up at Argentia was solid rock; there wasn't any soil; there wasn't anything for anchors to bite into at all.

Q: Did your crew get any liberty at all during that period?

Admiral McCrea: No. Well, we let them go ashore right at the bowling alleys right at Argentia's naval base there and things like that. There are no gals around there, if that's what you are driving at. There is nothing around there. We were just down there; that's all there was to it.

Q: We have covered the succeeding period. Then moving ahead about a year, you were involved in the Battle of the Philippine Sea in 1944.

J. L. McCrea #3 - 307

Admiral McCrea: Yes, that was in '44.

Q: What do you remember about that operation?

Admiral McCrea: Well, it was just an interesting operation; that's all there is to it. We were going out to the westward, and the airplanes, our planes, had pursued these Japs out there, right to the limit of their fuel. I was on the bridge, and this kid came running up from the signal bridge, and he said that he had heard a whistle. He was sure that he had heard a whistle from a downed plane. It wasn't evident to us on the bridge at all, and right away we sent a destroyer and told him we had every reason to believe that a plane was down astern of Iowa and to go look for it. They went out there, and they found this doggone plane and got this aviator out of the thing. Well, the very next day, the destroyer that picked this fellow up came alongside to get fuel from us. We were always pumping fuel to the destroyers. And this destroyer came along, so I said, "Where is that aviator that you picked up last night?"

They grabbed ahold of him, and I said, "You stand right there now." And I called down to the signal bridge and said, "Come on up here [and I recognized the guy]. I want you to introduce yourself to that young lieutenant over there." And to the lieutenant I said, "This is the fellow that heard you whistle on your police whistle. None of us heard it in the bridge, so you ought to be friends for some time."

That's one little vignette.

Q: You had command of that ship longer than most COs having battleships in that period did.* You were fortunate in that regard.

Admiral McCrea: Yes, it was a new ship. I remember that Quiggle was an outstanding man; no question about that. We did a lot. We gave the Missouri a copy of every single thing that we did, including the organization of the ship and the organization of the turrets. And, so far as I am aware, we have yet to receive a note from Missouri to thank us for it. I know that worried Quiggle. And one of my good, good friends was in command of the Missouri, but I never brought the thing up.

Q: Was that Admiral Callaghan?**

Admiral McCrea: Yes. I don't suppose that he knows. I'm sure he doesn't know it.

---

*COs--commanding officers.
**Captain William M. Callaghan, USN, first commanding officer of the USS Missouri, which was also built by the New York Navy Yard. The Missouri went into commission 11 June 1944.

J. L. McCrea #3 - 309

When you told me this thing about--talking about _Iowa_--and when I told you that I was afraid that we had been ambushed, here is something that happened.

When FDR decided he was going to go to the Casablanca Conference, of course, it was all so damn secret; that's all there was to it. One day this fellow called me up and wanted to know if he could come over and see me. And I said sure, so he came over. He said that he had just received a call from a taxi driver out in town, and he wanted to know if he could come and see Starling.* Starling was really the advance man; whenever the President went out in the country, Starling went ahead to see that everything was set up. He was really too handsome for the job, because any time that anybody saw this guy Starling come in an area, right away they would say, "God, the President must be coming this way."

So Starling wanted to know if he could come over to see me, and then he said, "Is there anything going on about the President that I ought to know about?"

And I looked him dead in the eye, and I said, "No, Colonel, there isn't anything going on about the President that you need to know." And I bore down on that, that he "needed to know about."

"Well," he said, "I'll tell you what's on my mind. A

---

*Edmund W. Starling, supervising agent of the White House detail, Secret Service Division, Department of the Treasury.

taxi driver out in town called me up an hour or so ago and wanted to know if he could come by and see me at the White House. He said that he understood that I was the security man at the White House. This chap came in, and he said he had answered a call to the British Embassy, and he had picked up two women at the British Embassy, and they drove to Woodward & Lothrop, which was downtown in Washington, and that one woman said to the other (and the taxi driver overheard) 'Have you heard that the President of the United States is going to North Africa to meet with the Prime Minister?'"*

I said, "Colonel Starling, do you believe any such preposterous thing as that?"

He said, "It was a little bit hard for me to believe it, but, you know, all sorts of things can happen."

I said, "Colonel, whatever the President has in mind you need not know about at this time, so you can deny it-- whatever you have heard."

So when we got this dispatch that a torpedo was coming our way, immediately it flashed across my mind, "Have we been ambushed?" You can't tell what light talk will do. But for this taxi driver who had known something about Starling's responsibility there at the White House calling him up and coming over, and here Starling comes to me-- that's about three weeks before we are to shove off to go

---
*Woodward & Lothrop is a chain of department stores in the Washington area.

over there.

Q: Why couldn't you tell him that the President was planning to go?

Admiral McCrea: The President told me no one is to know anything about this unless they need to know, and I emphasized that point to him that there was nothing that the President had in mind that he needed to know.

Q: Did Starling come back at you later?

Admiral McCrea: He knew about it. I went over there and talked to him about it.

Q: As soon as the President authorized you to do so?

Admiral McCrea: Sure. The airplane people--I got those fellows all straightened out. The idea of a couple of women talking.

Now before I was going to Casablanca, I was at a cocktail party with a friend of mine. On the way home my wife said to me, "John, I know you are going someplace, and I don't want to know where you are going, but I was asked by this good friend of ours and told that you were going on a very interesting trip with the President. I don't want to know anything about it."

I give her credit for that. But why this flag officer in the Navy would talk to my wife about something that I was going to do for the President--it was just somewhat of a shock to me that people would do that sort of thing. I have always had my reservations on that guy ever since. He didn't need to--loose talk.

All my wife knew was that I took white uniforms with me and blue uniforms. And she knew that I was going to be in the tropics, because I was taking white uniforms, and that's all. But she didn't know a damn thing about where I was going or anything else till I got back. She knew where I had been then.

Q: Did you frequently make travel arrangements for the President?

Admiral McCrea: No, not at all. Dewey Long did all that. He was an expert at that. But what the President was referring to in those fitness reports, and those remarks he made . . . We went by train to Miami from Washington, and the President stayed in town. He went right after he opened the Congress, and we went by train to Miami, and then we got on board this Pan Am chartered plane. And this fellow said to me, "Is that the President of the United

States?"

And I said, "Yes, it is."

He said, "I was told that we were going to take some VIPs and go to Africa with them. I never want to have my passengers impress me too much."

I said, "Now listen, don't get too impressed with the President. You just remember to fly the plane as best you can; that's all we want out of you." And so we went from Miami to Trinidad, spent the night there, then flew on down to Brazil. The place we stopped there for the night was at the mouth of the Amazon. And then the next morning we got up and flew from there to the west coast of Africa, and there the Army took us over. We then flew up to Casablanca; we passed over Dakar on the way up. We spent the day there, and the fellow who was representing the Army on board the ship was C. R. Smith, who was president of American Airlines.* He was a brigadier and he represented the Army. I got ahold of all of these fellows. It all worked out.

Q: Jumping ahead again, when did you find out that you had been selected for rear admiral?

Admiral McCrea: I took the selection board over to the President to be approved, and he was getting his sinuses

---
*Cyrus R. Smith.

packed. He turned to Ross McIntire and said, "Ross, John has been selected for skull and bones. What do you think about that?" He was referring in a light way to the Yale fraternity Skull and Bones. He signed it, but King didn't let anybody go to flag rank until they had had their ship command, so I didn't actually get tied up until I was detached from <u>Iowa</u> and went to the Aleutians up there. I got a dispatch from the Navy Department that I was to assume the rank of rear admiral, which I did.

Q: This was in about August 1944.

Admiral McCrea: It was in the latter part of August.

Q: And you were relieved by Captain McCann?

Admiral McCrea: Yes, I was relieved by Al McCann.* He was a good officer, that fellow.

Q: He was best known as a submariner.

Admiral McCrea: That's right, and I was glad to get him. Those submariners are, for the most part, damn good officers.

---
*Captain Allan R. McCann, USN.

J. L. McCrea #3 - 315

Q: Where did the change in command take place?

Admiral McCrea: In Eniwetok.

Q: A much less ceremonial occasion than when you took command.

Admiral McCrea: Oh, sure. And right alongside of me was this supply ship. We were clear up at the other end of Eniwetok lagoon, and right alongside of me was this supply ship, and it was leaving the moment that our command ceremonies had taken place. It was leaving to go to Pearl Harbor, and so I just moved my stuff on over there at about 11:00 o'clock in the morning and took my little sleeping pill and got in my bunk, and there I stayed for the rest of the day. I went sound asleep--shuffled off all my problems while I slept, of course.

Q: Did you get your rear admiral uniform then when you got to Hawaii?

Admiral McCrea: The ship took me to Hawaii. I had my trunk of odds and ends, and I gave it to--I've forgotten the name of that fellow, too. His son was graduated from the Naval Academy, and he was with the British during the war and was decorated with all sorts of things. He was with a bomb disposal outfit.

Q: Draper Kauffman?

Admiral McCrea: Yes, Draper Kauffman's father. He looked out for all my luggage and had it sent to the Aleutians for me.* I had a uniform altered, and that was all there was to it.

Q: Your flagship up there was the . . .

Admiral McCrea: <u>Richmond</u>.

Q: What a contrast from the <u>Iowa</u>.

Admiral McCrea: Yes it was, quite a contrast.

Q: What did your duties entail up there in the Aleutian waters?

Admiral McCrea: We went out to the Japanese-held Kuriles. I went out there once a month, went out in the dark of the moon, shot up some particular target we had in mind, and then came back. We had quite a problem up there looking

---

*Rear Admiral James L. Kauffman, USN, Commander Destroyers and Cruisers Pacific Fleet. His son was Lieutenant Commander Draper L. Kauffman, USN, whose oral history is in the Naval Institute collection.

out for the men. No shoreside stuff excepting at Adak and also Dutch Harbor, where the bowling alleys and the gyms and odds and ends like that were connected--movies ashore. We had, of course, all the movies we needed aboard ship, but it was different for them to get ashore and get a can of beer and all that.

Q: How many ships did you have under your command?

Admiral McCrea: Well, I had the three cruisers and nine of the big destroyers, and we used to go on out there and shoot them up and try to arrive on the target area just about dark and give them 20 to 30 minutes of bombardment and then pull out and go back.

Q: What was the intended purpose of these bombardments?

Admiral McCrea: We went against military targets out there. They had the targets well spotted. We couldn't get any air cover out that far because the air cover could not get from Attu out there. So, they always dropped us about the day before. The last day was always a critical day. When daylight came, you would run in and try to get in just a little bit before dark. They never sighted us coming in at any time; at least, we never were aware that they were. They chased us every damn time. When we shoved off, they came out and went after us.

Q: Did you use the cruiser floatplanes for spotting?

Admiral McCrea: No. Oh, no. We didn't do any spotting at all; we just shot up the Jap installations. We knew where they were. I said many times that it didn't make a damn bit of difference. If you tipped all the Kuriles on their side, it wouldn't have stopped the war one minute sooner. And in a way, I thought that sending ships out that far was putting them in more jeopardy than the situation warranted. But Frank Jack Fletcher, for whom I worked, was in command of the North Pacific, and he said, "You run your own show.* Just keep me informed, and if I don't like what you have in mind or what you propose to do, I'll tell you so."

I don't know whether I could have, if I had been in his spot, trusted somebody that I didn't know at all to that extent, but that's what he did. He never stopped me or anything.

Q: Did you personally feel kind of a letdown in that this wasn't nearly as active as the Iowa's service had been?

---
*Vice Admiral Frank Jack Fletcher, USN, Commander North Pacific Force and Ocean Area. He had previously been a carrier task force commander in the Battles of Coral Sea, Midway, and Guadalcanal.

Admiral McCrea: No. I'll tell you. It was more strenuous than the _Iowa_ in a way, because going out there to the Kuriles--there was always considerable hazard with it. I always felt that when you had air cover, you are all right. But we couldn't get air cover for the last day out there, ever. The Air Force would come out as far as they could, and they would have to go back--that's all there was to it.

Q: Plus your antiaircraft capability in the ships wasn't as good either, was it?

Admiral McCrea: Oh, no. And the weather was atrocious at times.

Q: Did you lose any people over the side?

Admiral McCrea: No, not to my knowledge. I took these people ashore. I prepared for all these runs out there. We knew where the target was going to be, and we set everything up on the game boards over there, and I would go over it with them and explain what we hoped to accomplish. I always laid stress on that--what we hoped to accomplish. And if anything interrupts what we are about to do, we will have to make changes of plans right on the spot, and let it go at that. And that's the way it was. As a matter of fact, I had just come off the game board up there at Attu, and I was back in. Just as I came through the door in the <u>Richmond</u>, it was 12:00 o'clock noon up there and it was 6:00 o'clock in Los Angeles, and the first thing I heard--this was the 12th day of April--Mrs. Roosevelt had sent a dispatch to all of her sons who were in the armed services, and I knew right away that probably he had died. I listened that night, it was coming from Los Angeles at 6:00 o'clock, but we were getting it at noon up there, and that's the way it worked out. Then, within 12 days, I was ordered back to Washington right away.

King was going to send me back to the White House to be with Truman, according to Sam Rosenman. King never told me that, and I never asked him. I never asked King anything--at least, I can't remember asking him anything. And I think that was the way to get along with King too. He'd tell you if he wanted you to know. I never quizzed him about anything.

Q: What kind of boss was Frank Jack Fletcher to work for?

Admiral McCrea: I just got through saying that I don't think I would have trusted a subordinate to the extent that he trusted me. He said, "You are to go out and shoot up the Kuriles. Make your own plans. Just keep me informed as to what you propose to do, and if I don't like what you are doing, I'll tell you so."

And that's the way I went. I went over and had dinner with him a couple of times a week when we were out there at Adak, and that sort of thing. We were close friends. I had never served with him before. He came back, you know, and he went down below Washington, down there at Indian Head in Maryland; he had a house down there. A tragedy happened there once. He had this colored family there, and I think they had six or seven kids, and the house caught fire and all of them were killed or something like that. It was one night when their parents were away. I have forgotten what it was all about. Anyway, it was quite a tragedy.

Q: He sort of got shunted aside after having been in the South Pacific.

Admiral McCrea: Well, he didn't get on too well down through there with Nimitz, for some reason or other.* I don't know what happened. Maybe it was Spruance that he didn't get on with, I don't know. But Fletcher was a good officer. His uncle was Frank Friday Fletcher, and he was Commander in Chief of the Atlantic Fleet. Frank Jack

---

*Admiral Chester W. Nimitz, USN, was Commander in Chief Pacific Fleet. Historians generally conclude that Fletcher, a non-aviator, was relieved as a carrier task force commander because of his lack of aggressiveness in using the carriers tactically.

J. L. McCrea #3 - 322

Fletcher came from someplace in Iowa out there.

Q: Then you came back to Washington. What did your duties involve there?

Admiral McCrea: My duties--it just so happened that I arrived there a day or two after a fellow who was in the Central Division had had a heart attack, and they dumped me in that job. It continued right on through, and I stayed there with the war winding down. When Nimitz came back and brought the staff in there, I don't know how many people I had in that Central Division. I had more damn things going on than you could shake a stick at. We had intelligence; and we had this, that, and the other thing. And they finally took intelligence away from me and gave it to the War Plans. That was all right; they needed to do that sort of thing. But we had all sorts of personnel problems to look out for. Then, when Nimitz showed up--my office was right across the corridor and up a door from his, and I used to be in and out of there all the while--he would give me jobs to do.

Q: What were some of the assignments he gave you?

Admiral McCrea: It seemed to me that he gave me odd jobs. I had down here yesterday, and I was going to keep it and let you see it, I think I told you yesterday about the dealings of naval officers with contractors and all that sort of thing. You had to be like Caesar's wife, beyond reproach. I took a letter for Nimitz--wrote this letter-- and it was sent out to the fleet. When Forrest Sherman came along as Chief of Naval Operations, he reissued the letter, just as I had written it for Nimitz years before; he didn't change a word.* There was a good officer, Forrest Sherman. I thought he was excellent.

Q: Did you ever serve with him?

Admiral McCrea: Never had served with him before. He was Admiral Bloch's aviation officer when Admiral Bloch was in command of the fleet.** I saw a lot of Forrest out there. Forrest was an excellent officer, intently ambitious. Well, that's all right, as far as I am concerned. He stood two or three in his class academically, and he had his eyes set on being the Chief of Naval Operations one day. I am sure of that. I couldn't have done that, I don't think. I am sure I couldn't, but he did and he got there.

He lived just a few doors from me in Washington, and we were close friends, as close as anybody ever got to Sherman. And when he left, by that time I was in the

---
*Admiral Forest P. Sherman, USN, Chief of Naval Operations from 1949 to 1951.
**Admiral Claude C. Bloch, USN, Commander in Chief U.S. Fleet (CinCUS) from 1938 to 1940.

Department of Defense over there. And one day he dropped by my office and said that he was going to Europe. He said, "I have something in mind for you when I come back. I'll get ahold of you, and we'll talk it out. It's a good job; you'll keep your third star."

I thanked him. I didn't ask him what it was or anything in mind. I hadn't the remotest idea what he had in mind. He came back all right, but he came back in his casket, and I was over at the airport to meet the body when it came in.* I haven't the remotest idea what he had in mind, because he didn't say. And in accordance with my not asking questions, I have often been curious about what he had in mind.

Q: Do you think he pushed himself too hard?

Admiral McCrea: Well, I'll tell you he probably did, because that was his way of doing business. He was quite intense; he had a fine mind, no question about that. He pushed himself a lot.

Q: In the Central Division, at the beginning of the war, I think Roscoe Schuirmann had had that job.**

---
*Admiral Sherman died at the age of 54 on 22 July 1951 after suffering two heart attacks. He died at Naples, Italy, following visits to Madrid, Paris, and London--an exhausting trip.
**Captain Roscoe T. Schuirmann, USN, Director, Central Division, OpNav.

Admiral McCrea: Roscoe Schuirmann, yes.

Q: And this involved liaison with the State Department also.

Admiral McCrea: That's right, and I inherited all that stuff with the State Department. I used to go over there a lot. When the war was really winding down, Mr. Grew was over there, and I used to go see him. We would come up with dispatches--they would refer to various attitudes on the part of the Japanese--and he could always identify these people in the dispatches. He would say, "Well, I'm not surprised at this fellow thinking this way or that."

He was a very able person, that fellow Grew--at least I thought he was.

Q: Who were some of your other contacts in the State Department?

Admiral McCrea: What was the name of the purple tie guy? He was the Groton fellow. He and Cordell Hull never got on very well--the Under Secretary of State.*

---

*Sumner Welles was Under Secretary of State from 1933 to 1943. Cordell Hull was Secretary of State from 1933 to 1944.

Q: Stettinius?

Admiral McCrea: No, a tall fellow.

Q: Sumner Welles?

Admiral McCrea: That's the guy--the purple tie guy, as I said. You know his problem; I'm sure you do. He was a Groton chap, and FDR was Groton. It was interesting to do business with Welles, because whenever I went over there, I never went in his office that he didn't stand up, right behind his desk. He always stood very erect behind his desk, and we conducted all of our business standing, and that was it. Then I got the hell out of there and came back.

Q: What kinds of business would you have between the Central Division and the State Department?

Admiral McCrea: All sorts of things. For instance, Summerlin was another fellow that I did a great deal of business with over there.* He was the Chief of Protocol. The President looked out for all these fellows when they came--he would have them for lunch--like the Prime Minister

---
*George T. Summerlin, Chief of Protocol, Department of State.

from Poland and this and that. Then the Duke of Windsor, and all these fellows he would have for lunch. I remember once the President handed me a list and said, "Here is the luncheon list." The Prime Minister of Poland was there, and it was in his honor.

I quickly ran down the list and I said, "Mr. President, you've got my name down here, but I think you had better strike me off, because on this list you have given me are 13 people. I haven't any objection to being 13, but a lot of people would have. If I strike myself off, there will be 12."

"Not a bit of it," he said. "Tell Sumner Welles to come over here for lunch."

So I said, "Very well," and I started over to Welles's office. And, of course, he stood behind his desk and I told him the President would like very much for him to come for lunch that day if he could find it convenient to do so. And he was greatly honored to be invited to the White House and everything.

And I got back and told the President that Mr. Welles would be here. He said, "What did he say?"

"Well, he said he felt he would be greatly honored to be invited to luncheon at the White House."

"I hope you didn't tell him that we were only asking him because there were 13 at the table."

I said, "No, Mr. President, I didn't do that at all."

Q: This was about the time that the United Nations was being set up. Did you get involved in that at all?

Admiral McCrea: To this extent--President Roosevelt, I will say now emphatically, had great, great hopes for the United Nations. He felt that we just had to come to that sort of thing, and I got together a paper--I have them around here someplace--and I talked many times. I talked over at Harvard and talked to the meeting at the business school about FDR's hope for the United Nations. Of course, it hasn't exactly turned out that way, and I don't know what the answer is. I haven't the remotest answer. He would hope to beat everything--that everybody would rally around and try to have peace. Of course, they have done that more or less, only the various individuals want peace their way. I guess everybody wants it something different. I am sure that this thing that has gone on for the past couple of years around here would depress him no end. I am just sure of that.

Q: Alger Hiss was in the State Department then. Did you deal with him?

Admiral McCrea: Never saw him in my life. What's the name

of the chap who is up at Smith College? I think his name is Weinstein.* He wrote a book called <u>Witness</u> or something like that, and he started out to write a book that defended Hiss in every direction, and he wound up saying that he was everything that they said he was. I got the book. I read it; it's around here someplace. And Bill Buckley turned loose on him too.**

Of course, one of the great troubles with the world, I suppose, is rapid communication. (I'm taking the thread right out of the air.) We haven't at all learned how to live with rapid communication. That's all there is to it. When Napoleon was whipped at the Battle of Waterloo, it was three or four days before the news got out on the streets of London. Now, by gracious, you know what's going on instantly, every place in the world. People don't seem to be able to keep up with it. I don't know what the answer is; no one knows. We've just got to hope that people would like to have peace, and do it in a reasonable way.

I don't see that book, but Weinstein, this professor up at Smith, wrote the thing, and he felt that Hiss was

---

*Allen Weinstein, <u>Perjury: The Hiss-Chambers Case</u> (New York:Knopf, 1978). Whitaker Chambers, an admitted Communist, charged that Hiss had passed government secrets to him. Hiss denied the deed under oath and was subsequently convicted of perjury, although the statute of limitations had run out for the offense itself. Since Hiss's trial, there have been a number of attempts to exonerate him.
**William F. Buckley, Jr., trenchant conservative editor-in-chief of <u>National Review</u> magazine, syndicated columnist, author, and television personality.

getting a dirty deal. But when he got through with his book, he decided that Hiss was everything that everybody thought he was, particularly Whitaker Chambers. Bill Buckley was inclined to agree with him too.

Q: While you were there in the Navy Department, the title was changed from Central Division to Deputy Chief of Naval Operations for Administration. Why did that come about?

Admiral McCrea: When Conolly came in with Nimitz, he was in charge of administration. The way Nimitz set the thing up, he had Aviation and Personnel and Administration and War Plans and Material. Stark had to be relieved, and Nimitz wanted Conolly to do it. Conolly was an outstanding officer. Conolly once told me, "If it had not been for the war, I would never have got to flag rank."

And I said, "Why? What makes you say that?"

He said, "I don't have any personality, and I have noted right along in the Navy that people who get to the top have distinctive personalities, and I just didn't have it."

Of course, he did a splendid job out there in amphibious warfare. I saw a lot of Conolly, and I was very fond of him, and he was my boss. When they wanted to send Conolly to London, he came in to see me one day. I didn't know this was even in the cards, nor did he. But Nimitz decided they wanted to send him to London. He came in and he said, "John, I'm going to go to London."

And I said, "That's good."

"And I'm to relieve Admiral Stark, and you are going to relieve me."

I said, "Oh, no, I couldn't relieve you. Admiral Nimitz has brought all these people in here, and I've never served with him, so he doesn't know anything about me."

He said, "I've told him. My nomination to relieve me is you."

And Nimitz said, "I'll give it a thought."

Well, in about ten minutes Nimitz sent for me, and he said Conolly was going to London. I acted surprised and said, "I'm sure it would be a good job for Conolly and also for the Navy." And that was it.

And he said, "Will you join my mess tomorrow?"

And I said, "Yes, thank you, sir." And away I went.

I did a lot of things for Nimitz—all sorts of odd jobs for him. He had both Fechteler and Radford.* Both wrote with very sharp pens, and if there was one thing that Nimitz was, he was a gentleman at all times. No matter how provoked he might be, he was a gentleman about it all. And so often he would send for me, and he would hand me a letter written by one of these two guys, and he would say,

---

*Vice Admiral William M. Fechteler, USN, Deputy Chief of Naval Operations (Personnel). Admiral Arthur W. Radford, USN, Vice Chief of Naval Operations.

"Prepare it so I will sign it. The ideas are there, but I can't be so insulting to this fellow."

So I was always doing odd jobs for him. I enjoyed him a lot. When he retired and went to the West Coast, he stayed out there, you know. And I was with John Hancock and I went all over this country, and every time I went to San Francisco I would always see Nimitz.

The city of San Francisco gave this party for Nimitz's 75th birthday, and I was invited to go out there. Archbishop Spellman was brought in from New York to be the speaker, and I was sitting with Nimitz at his table.* He leaned over to me and he said, "When my 80th comes up, there is going to be nothing like this."

Well, it was San Francisco, Oakland--all those bay cities gathered around, and they had this dinner at the Palace Hotel. Nimitz was a very retiring sort of fellow. I enjoyed him a lot.

Q: Did you have a good staff when you were in that job?

Admiral McCrea: People I inherited from Conolly, and we went along; we did all right.

One of the things that was most interesting was that my office was right across the corridor from John Nicholas Brown, assistant secretary for air, and he used to come

---
*Cardinal Francis J. Spellman, USN, Archbishop of New York. Fleet Admiral Nimitz's 75th birthday was in 1960.

over there. And he would bring over these papers and he would say, "You know, I don't know anything about naval aviation. [He was assistant secretary for naval aviation.] Take a look at these papers and tell me what your recommendation is about signing them."

I said, "Well, Mr. Secretary, I'm not an aviator; I don't know."

He said, "There are such conflicting ideas here. Won't you look at them for me?"

Of course I looked at them for him, but he was a delightful fellow to be with, and he had money pouring out of all of his ears. He did an awful lot for the United States Navy. He came in and he said, "I am in a quandary. I don't know what to do. The Naval Athletic Association put a box at my disposal at the Army-Navy game. It seats six, and Mrs. Brown and I asked four guests to come with us. And the Secretary of the Navy just sent for me, and he said that I am the junior one of the secretaries in the office, and I am going to have the duty on the day of the Army-Navy game, and I can't go to the game. What will I do?"

I said, "Oh, Mr. Secretary, that's beyond me. I think you ought to go down and tell Mr. Forrestal that this is what you are up against.* And he might adapt things so

---
*James V. Forrestal, Under Secretary of the Navy (1940-1944); Secretary of the Navy (1944-1947); Secretary of Defense (1947-1949).

you could work it out." He was quite a guy.

Q: Did you have much contact with Mr. Forrestal directly?

Admiral McCrea: Yes, some very pleasant and some not so pleasant. When Forrestal came down there, he was one of the first of the under secretaries. You know, they had the idea that they would have these under secretaries and that they would be career people and, along with the way the British worked, their number two people. And they would stay on forever around there, and they were the contacts. Forrestal came down there full of beans and butter, and he wanted to run the Navy. Well, he didn't do too well with Mr. Knox.

Here is one instance. President Roosevelt told me, when I reported to him, "You are to be my eyes and ears in that Navy Department. I know a lot about the Navy, but I want you to keep me informed about what goes on in the Navy. I don't want to be informed about useless things or things that don't amount to too much. I will leave it to your judgment to select the things that I should see."

I told all those bureaus down there that the President was greatly interested in the Navy and that when they sent things to me, I would ultimately get them to the President if, in my judgment, they were the sort of things that he would want to see.

One day a letter came through that Forrestal had signed; it said: "From this date on, all the shipbuilding contracts will no longer be handled in the office of the Judge Advocate General. They will be handled in the office of the Under Secretary."

I just picked this thing up, along with all the rest of the things, and took them to the White House. President Roosevelt was sitting there getting his sinuses packed, and he came to this and he said, "Well now, just what does this mean?"

"Well, all I know, Mr. President, is just what it says here."

Then he said, "How long has the Judge Advocate General been doing this thing--looking after the contracts for the Navy?"

I said, "Ever since the office has been established--since 1885."

He said, "Doesn't this put the office out of business?"

I said, "It does as far as shipbuilding contracts go, apparently."

The President folded it up and put it in his side pocket, and the next thing I knew, three or four days later, I was sent for by Mr. Forrestal, and he said, "Did you take this to the White House?"

I said, "Yes, Mr. Secretary, I took it to the White House."

"Why did you do it?"

I said, "Mr. Secretary, when I came to this job, the President said I was to be his eyes and ears over here and to bring him anything that I thought would interest him. His interest in the Navy is profound, because he was around here for eight years as Assistant Secretary. That's why I did it."

Then he said, "I know who told you to take this to the White House."

"No, Mr. Secretary, you don't know how it got there. I am just telling you. It was put on my desk, and I took it over there. Nobody asked me to take this to the President."

He said, "I am being humiliated."

I said, "I am sorry about that, Mr. Secretary."

"Yes," he said, "the President has directed that I cancel this letter."

"Well," I said, "Mr. Secretary, I am not surprised at all, because you ran up against the fact that the Judge Advocate General's Office has been looking out for this since 1885, and there was no reason stuck in this letter as to why contracts were now going to be reviewed in the office of the Under Secretary."

We got along all right, though, and one day he sent for me, right at the end of the war. His aide Smedberg came down to see me and said that Mr. Forrestal wanted me to come and have dinner with him a couple of nights hence at 7:30 or 8:00 o'clock.*

So I said, "That's fine. I'll be glad to do it."

The day of the dinner he was on board the yacht--I have forgotten the name of the yacht--and the telephone rang. "Mr. Forrestal wants to know if you can come tonight on board the yacht at 6:00 o'clock rather than 7:30. He wants to talk to you."

I said, "Certainly, I'll be glad to."

I got down there--the thing was at the Navy yard in Washington. Right away he said, "I want to talk to you about your dealings with FDR."

I said, "Very well, Mr. Secretary."

He said, "I'd like to know your opinion of how the President worked it out with Stalin." [The President was dead by that time.] "Do you think that Stalin hoodwinked the President, or that he came under the influence of Stalin?"

I said, "Of course not, Mr. Secretary, of course not."

"Well, what makes you think not? Why did they do so much for the Russians?"

---

*Captain William R. Smedberg III, USN, whose Naval Institute oral history discusses his service with Secretary Forrestal.

J. L. McCrea #3 - 338

I said, "Well, Mr. Secretary, it is very easy. If I have heard him say once, I've heard him say dozens and dozens of times--both when I was with him and when we were at the conferences abroad--that the Russians were in contact with the enemy, and they needed help. And we were manufacturing all these goods; that is why so much went to the Russians. He said time and time again in the Pacific War Council that every one of the Germans that are knocked off leaves one less shooting at our people when we hit on the continent."

I made a point with him.

Forrestal's son had just come back; he was an ensign or something, and he had been in Moscow. Another thing, too--the reason he got me there for the dinner early that night, the other dinner guest was Wellington Koo, the Chinese ambassador, and so we talked about it.*

I got to know Forrestal exceedingly well, and then when I went to the Pacific out there as second in command in Pearl--I came back in March--I left a note with his gal that if he wanted, I'd like to see him. He sent for me. God, I must have been in his office close to two hours, and I concluded that he was losing his grip. He talked about everything in the world, and, of course, Drew Pearson was after him every damn minute--every damn time the paper came out.

----
*Dr. V. K. Wellington Koo.

As Bill Fechteler said, Forrestal would send for him and tell him to release the people, no matter whether the ships got tied up or not.* He couldn't understand why, as soon as a ship came back, it couldn't be turned loose-- tied up in the Navy yard and no laying up or anything else, and Drew Pearson was giving him hell. Pearson even wrote something in one of his columns once where he challenged Forrestal's personal courage when some holdup man snatched Mrs. Forrestal's bag or some other damn thing. I don't know what it was all about.

As I say, I got to know Forrestal well, and one day he said, "When I came down here to Washington, I didn't like, and I viewed with suspicion, every one of you flag officers."

I said, "Mr. Secretary, I'm sorry about that, but how come?"

He said, "I figured that anybody that worked for the peanuts that you flag officers do in the Navy, that you didn't amount to anything."

Now that, of course, is a funny attitude in a way. I wasn't in the Navy for the money of it, and none of my friends that I know of were in the Navy for the money that was in it, because if they were, they were greatly disappointed. But that was his thought. After he was

---

*As DCNO (Personnel), Vice Admiral Fechteler had a considerable role in overseeing orderly demobilization of the fleet after the war ended.

around there a while, he really got to be the greatest booster in the world for naval officers. He made a talk before the Cleveland business bureau or something once out there, and I heard it on the radio. I turned to my wife and I said, "Gee whiz, Forrestal has certainly changed his tune." He thought that the naval officers, the flag officers particularly, that ran the Navy were the tops in the country. Oh, yes, Forrestal was quite a guy in a lot of respects.

Q: Did you get involved when the Navy had the big hassle with the Air Force over strategic bombing?

Admiral McCrea: No.

I'm thinking about Forrestal again. Forrestal didn't like Nimitz, not at all. Why, I don't know. He wanted Edwards to be the Chief of Naval Operations, but Edwards was a sick man; that was all there was to it. And he was a chain cigarette smoker in the first place, and he just literally folded up physically.* He couldn't have hung on as Chief of Naval Operations. He had the mind to do things, but physically I am sure that he couldn't have stuck it out.

---

*Admiral Richard S. Edwards, USN, who held a number of top posts, including Deputy CominCh-Deputy CNO and Vice Chief of Naval Operations.

Q: You say that Forrestal was not a supporter of Nimitz. Do you think that's the reason he didn't take Nimitz's recommendation of Blandy to succeed him?

Admiral McCrea: No, not particularly. I would think Forrestal was smart enough to know what Blandy was, but they couldn't push down Admiral Leahy. He was at the White House, and he was at Truman's elbow, and that was that.

Q: Then you moved on from there to the Pacific Fleet. What were your duties there?

Admiral McCrea: I was number two.

Q: You were working for Duke Ramsey?*

Admiral McCrea: Ramsey, yes.

Q: What things did he have you handle?

Admiral McCrea: That's hard to say. It seemed to me I was handling almost everything. He was away a great deal; he went to the South Pacific. He had never been down through that area, and he wanted to see it all. We got a heavy cruiser there, and he went. And then he was back in

---
*Admiral DeWitt C. Ramsey, USN, Commander in Chief Pacific Fleet, 1948-1949.

J. L. McCrea #3 - 342

Washington a lot. When he first went out there, he saw MacArthur. And he wouldn't go back out there again, so I told you. He said MacArthur pushed him around, and those are the exact words he used.

One day--he had been in Washington and he came back--he called up from the West Coast on the telephone. He was sobbing on the telephone, and I said, "Goodness, Admiral, what's the trouble?"

He said, "I am just calling to tell you that I am retiring from the Navy, and in so doing, I am doing you a dirty trick."

I said, "Oh, I don't believe that, Admiral. What is it?"

He said, "I asked you to go out there for two years, and here I am running out on you."

I said, "Just forget it."

He said, "I want you to tell my wife that I am retiring from the Navy. I am telling you, but it's not for the information of my wife. The Aviation Association has made me such an offer that I cannot refuse it. They are going to pay me $40,000 a year to be the head of it, and that's just that."

He came back a couple of days later, and he was getting all squared away. But I was awfully fond of Duke Ramsey. He was softhearted as hell, just as softhearted as could be. He had more troubles than you could shake a stick at at home.

Q: Did you say he picked you for that job when he found he was going to be commander in chief?

Admiral McCrea: He invited me, asked me to come over and talk to him, and he told me what he had in mind, and would I like to go with him? He said, "I've got to take a straight line officer with me, and I know you. Would you like to go?"

I said, "Sure," and I did.

Q: Where did you know him from?

Admiral McCrea: He was Vice Chief for Nimitz, and his office was a couple of doors down the corridor from me--I was the only one of the deputies whose office was on the front corridor. Ramsey would be away a great deal; he went here and there and all over. And whenever he went any place, he always called me in, and I sat in his office and handled things on the way to Nimitz, because it was so close to my own office that I didn't have any trouble.

Q: When you were out in Hawaii, did you handle a lot of the day-to-day business for him?

Admiral McCrea: I wouldn't say that, because the day-to-day business wouldn't be much. We had the closest sort of relationship. Whenever he would pick up and go anyplace, of course, I stayed in my own office. But I always signed everything that had to do with the fleet. We got along fine. I was awfully fond of that guy.

When he collapsed, he really collapsed, and I don't know what sort of physical trouble he had. When I was with John Hancock, I would go to Washington, and I used to go around there, and I saw him once. When I went around again, Wright, the chief yeoman that he had taken with him out there from the Navy Department, said, "He's in the hospital, Admiral. Don't go and see him; you'll be so disappointed--he might not recognize you."

Q: Did fleet operations come under your purview in that job?

Admiral McCrea: Certainly. A lot of things came under my purview in that job that I can't associate exactly with fleet operations. The fleet was pretty well on the downside at that time because the war had just wound up. We had a number of ships out on Asiatic Station, and they worked out there along with MacArthur, and Berkey was out there.*

Q: That was the time of a big economy drive also.

Admiral McCrea: God, they had a hell of a time about personnel, funds, everything.

Q: Did your tour get cut short then because Radford wanted his own man?

Admiral McCrea: No, no. Raddy came out there, and he said, "John, you can stick along here."**

I knew Raddy well because he had lived across the corridor from me at the Naval Academy when he was a plebe and I was a youngster. So we knew each other well. He said, "You can stay here if you want to, because I am not going to replace you. You can stay here until your normal tour ends. I think that we can economize on officers. When the war stopped, it was set up that the commander in chief out there, if he was an aviator, would have a vice-- who was a straight line officer and vice-versa. Towers relieved Nimitz, and then Denfeld relieved Towers, and

---

*Vice Admiral Russell S. Berkey, USN, Commander Naval Forces Far East.
**Admiral Arthur W. Radford, USN, took over as Commander in Chief Pacific Fleet in May 1949.

Denfeld's vice was an aviator who was Sallada.* Then Wellborn, who was straight line, and I relieved him.** Wait, that doesn't make sense.

Q: Wellborn was junior to you.

Admiral McCrea: That's right. He was considerably junior to me, and I'm trying to think how it worked in. At any rate, Ramsey was an aviator, so I was straight line, and that's why he asked me to go over there.

I am trying to think what happened out there. I think Sallada relieved Wellborn. No, he didn't, because Wellborn came to Washington and he moved into my house--I rented my house to him. Well, I have forgotten how it worked out, but at any rate the idea was to balance one off against the other.

Q: So Radford said he was just going to economize at that point.

---

*Admiral John H. Towers, USN, Commander in Chief Pacific Fleet in 1946-1947. Admiral Louis E. Denfeld, Commander in Chief Pacific Fleet from February through November 1947 until relieved so he could become CNO. Vice Admiral Harold B. Sallada, Denfeld's deputy, took over as temporary commander in chief of the fleet until Admiral Ramsey arrived to assume command.
**Rear Admiral Charles Wellborn, USN, was chief of staff to CinCPacFlt from March through November of 1947, then in December 1947 relieved Admiral McCrea as Deputy CNO (Administration).

Admiral McCrea: Yes, he said that the Navy said they had to economize on flag officers and the commander in chief could handle all of this.

And I said, "Well, that's fine with me." So I just picked up and left. I told him that I didn't want to stay out there any longer.

"Well," he said, "I expect to go around and see what's going on in the Pacific. You can stay out here as long as you want to."

I only had about seven or eight months left to do, but that was all right. My family wasn't too keen, particularly about being out there. My older daughter got married out there; she married young Niles, who was Duke Ramsey's flag lieutenant, and Niles was later killed at Newport in a fire.* My daughter Meredith had four children, and the house caught on fire one night, the coldest night in the winter. He got them all out, and he went back to get the dog, and he didn't get out. That's one of those damn tragedies. She is now married to a retired colonel in the Army who was top assistant to Trudeau, who he had served with in France during the war. They have a place down here at Oyster Harbor, which is at Osterville, and they shoved off this morning for her place in Florida.

---
*Commander Richard M. Niles, USN.

Q: Then you headed back to Washington again after you left Hawaii?

Admiral McCrea: Yes.

Q: Did you have a specific request for a job at that point?

Admiral McCrea: No. Let me see how this worked out. I went out there in 1948, and I came back in '50. When I came back, I went to the Department of Defense, and I was the director of staff of the Personnel Policy Board. That was a pretty good office, a pretty good job, and I had my third star. Then the commandant, the job up here, was coming up vacant, and they sent me up here.

I didn't care particularly about coming up here, but I had met, when I was out there in Hawaii, the president of John Hancock, and he was a close friend of mine. And George Sumners was the president of American Factors, and American Factors was the correspondent for John Hancock here.* The president of American Factors had been in the class behind me at the Naval Academy, and we were close friends. Clark and his wife were out there for a month on a winter vacation. We saw a good bit of them, and on the last day of the vacation, he gave me a poke in the chest

---
*George W. Sumner, whose name was changed from the original George W. Sumners.

and said, "When you get through with this Navy of yours, you come and see me. We could use you in our outfit."*

Well, I finally came up here, just through a fortuitous circumstance, I hadn't any idea that I was ever going to come up here. I knew enough, of course, to keep my mouth shut. I didn't remind him up here of all that he said on the dock in Honolulu--I just knew enough to keep my mouth shut. One day, about four or five months before I retired, I got home one night, and my wife said to me that Mr. Clark's secretary was looking for me. So I called her up, and she said, "Mr. Clark wants to know if you can come and have luncheon with him on such-and-such a date."

And I said, "Let me take a look at my book." So I did, and I could, and away I went.

He had, in this small dining room, the president (he was the president), the executive vice president, the head of the personnel department, and the head of the public relations department. They sat down, and the first thing he said was, "You are going to retire soon."

"Yes."

"What are you going to do?"

"I don't know."

"Are you going to work?"

"Yes."

---

*Paul F. Clark was president and chairman of the board of the John Hancock Mutual Life Insurance Company.

"Who are you going to work for?"

"I haven't any idea."

"How would you like to work for Hancock?"

"I don't know whether I would or not."

He said, "Why do you say that?"

"Well," I said, "I say it for this reason. If I came to John Hancock, with my gray hair and my years and my retired naval rank, it is obvious that I couldn't come here as an office boy. There might be somebody working long and faithfully for this company who might aspire to do the job that you must have in mind for me, if you are going to ask me. If that eventuated--the Chinese have a name for that; they call it 'breaking somebody's rice bowl'--and I don't want to break anybody's rice bowl. And more than that, if I came here and accidentally, inadvertently broke a rice bowl, some friends of theirs might make it awfully tough for me. I just have to think that over carefully."

He said, "Well, I can set your mind at ease. There isn't anybody on the payroll of this company that will do the job that I want you to do."

I said, "Well, that's all right." So then we started in talking. I also told him, "I told my wife years ago that I was going to call all the shots in the Navy. When I retire, then she can say what she wants to do about where we lived and a few things like that." And I said, "I don't know whether she wants to stay up here or not, and I will have to consult with her."

Then he said, "Will she keep her mouth shut about what I have just said?"

I said, "Of course she would."

I told Estelle about it, and she said she wanted to think it over, and the next morning she said, "Very well, if you want to stay up here, I'll be glad to stay."

So Clark said, "I am going on vacation. You let me have your answer when I get back. I'll be away for a month."

A month passed and the telephone rang, and my secretary came in and said, "Mr. Clark is on the phone, and he wants to talk to you."

And he said, "You promised to let me know your decision about coming to Hancock."

I said, "I'll write it to you this afternoon, and you'll get it tomorrow morning."

He said, "What's it going to be?"

And I said, "I'll put it in the note." So I just wrote him, "Dear Paul, unless somebody offers me a better job between now and the first of July, I will be pleased to come to John Hancock."

We never talked about salary or position or anything else, and that's the way it wound up. And I stayed there 13 years, and I had to quit when I got to be 75. Meanwhile, I had gone all over this country for the John

Hancock company. I talked here and there and all over, and I enjoyed it. I ran into a lot of very fine, upstanding people in industry, and I ran into a lot of people, also, that I had to stop and wonder how the hell they got where they were. That was easy to do too.

I think the service has a lot to offer in a lot of ways, especially people who go to sea. When you go to sea, you've got to be able to make a decision and ride with it.

Q: Oh, yes.

Admiral McCrea: Well, that's the way it worked out.

Q: When you were in this job in the Defense Department in Personnel Policy, wasn't that surprising, since you had not had any BuPers duty?*

Admiral McCrea: Somewhat, but the whole business was developing the personnel. I had the Army and the Navy and the Air Force and the Marines, and we had a high-powered civilian who was the chairman of this thing. I had this fellow Tom Reed, who had been with McCormick over in Baltimore, and he was topflight. Then he went to Ford, and he was relieved by Howard, who was the president of a big coal company out in the Midwest. Then Howard was relieved

---
*BuPers--Bureau of Naval Personnel.

J. L. McCrea #3 - 353

by Tom Snyder, who had been on Pershing's staff in the First World War, and he had been in business someplace.* Those were all political appointments, and I was the chief of staff. I had to go around the country and talk up personnel.

Q: This was the time when the Korean War came in, and you had to build up strength quickly. What demands did that place on you?

Admiral McCrea: None whatsoever that I know of. As I recall, there wasn't anything. I was pretty much interested in the Navy, of course, as to what we were doing. You know that it takes a different kind of person to be in the Navy than it does to be in the Army; that's all there is to it. I am sure of that, and our enlisted personnel, I think, are pretty superior to most of the ones that you get in the Army. I really do think this.

Jimmy Hall, I remember, was down at Norfolk, and he was looking out for personnel down there, and I had to go down there and talk to him about it.**

Q: Did President Truman have any reluctance about calling up the reserves when the Korean War broke?

---
*General John J. Pershing, USA, Commander in Chief American Expeditionary Force.
**Vice Admiral John L. Hall, Jr., USN, Commandant of the Armed Force Staff College at Norfolk from 1948 to 1951.

Admiral McCrea: I haven't any idea whether he had any reluctance or not. I will assure you this, however, that the political aspects of it were given close attention. Bill Hassett, who wrote this book about working for FDR, stayed on with Truman, and he told me once, "There is no subject discussed at our 8:30 conference every morning but what the political aspects are given consideration many, many times when I don't think that any political consideration should be given to what we were discussing. You know, FDR, while he was a good politician, nevertheless, time and time again, I heard him say, 'The best politics are no politics.'" I never discussed politics with President Roosevelt except just casually, about odds and ends. But that is something that I think is interesting to recall and think about, "The best politics is no politics."

That is one of the things that has always annoyed me about Eisenhower. No one ever owed anybody any more than Eisenhower did to General Marshall, and here the President of the United States and a Republican let this fellow McCarthy just blackguard Marshall from hell to breakfast and never once raised his voice about it when he should have told that monkey to shut up.* That's all there is to it.

Q: Truman said he lost a lot of regard for Eisenhower over that, because he held Marshall in very high esteem.

Admiral McCrea: I know he did. If Truman had had anything to do about it, he would have promoted Marshall to a saint.

I'll tell you one thing, and this is what Stark told me. One day he came back, and as I told you earlier this morning, that Stark and Marshall used to go to the White House all the time. And Stark came back one day--this was in the summer of '41--and he said, "George Marshall and I have been good friends for a long time, but something happened this morning. I don't know whether it will get in the way of our friendship or not, and I'll tell you what it was. The President said at this conference we were having, 'I am fearful that we are going to have war some time in the Pacific. If war should come, is there something that we could do today, which had we not done it, we would regret tomorrow that we hadn't done it if war should come?'"

Stark said, "I just piped up, and I said, 'Mr.

---

*Senator Joseph R. McCarthy (Republican-Wisconsin) attacked General of the Army George C. Marshall, USA, as part of his anti-Communist witch-hunt in the early 1950s. Dwight Eisenhower, running for President in 1952, did not rise energetically to Marshall's defense.

President, I think there is one thing that should be done. I think that the Army dependents should be gotten out of the Philippines and brought home.' President Roosevelt said, 'George, are those dependents still out there? I noticed months ago in the paper that the dependents were coming back from the Pacific.'

"And Stark said, 'Those were Navy dependents, Mr. President, and Admiral Hart ordered them out in November of 1940.'"

When I went out there in January, the first week of 1941, there were still repercussions about Stark sending these people home when the Army was sending out aviators for fighter planes and was bringing their dependents out on the next ship.

Then Stark said, "The President turned to George Marshall and said, 'George, you get those dependents home at once.'"

And so he did.

Now I go on a little further. I read the statement that General Marshall made to the committee that was investigating the war and all that sort of stuff. In this statement, he said that by August of 1941 he had concluded that the possibility of war was such that he should get the dependents home from the Philippines. He got them home, by gracious, because FDR told him to get them out of there at once.

Now this fellow Hart, I'll tell you about that guy. When he was out there, Stark wrote him a note, and he said, "I think that we ought to get these dependents home. I am perfectly willing to order them home, but if I order them home, I am fearful that more significance would be attached to the Chief of Naval Operations doing this than if you did it. But you do just as you please. If you don't wish to issue the order, I'll do it."

Hart, right away--like the guy he was--issued the order for the dependents to go home. This was in November of '40, and I got out there in the first week in January 1941 and there were more growlers sitting around there, mad as hell. Their families had been sent home, but the Army dependents were sitting around there, and it took them months to get them out of there.

Q: Could we, just to wrap it up, talk a few minutes about your time as commandant and what your principal duties were? That was your last tour.

Admiral McCrea: It was more of a public relations job than anything else that I had around there. As a matter of fact, I enjoyed it a lot. There is another thing, too; I took a great interest in the naval ROTCs that we had.*
We had five of them up there. We had one at Harvard,

---

*ROTCs--Naval Reserve Officer Training Corps units.

Tufts, Dartmouth, Brown, and Holy Cross. I was greatly interested in those things and I went out, of course, and saw them a lot. When I got up there, I touched base with almost everybody around here. And I called up and wanted to see Dr. Conant, the president of Harvard. I called up and got his secretary, and I said I would like to speak to President Conant.* She said, "May I ask what you want to speak about?"

I said, "Yes, I could . . ."

She said, "President Conant is a very busy man."

And I said, "As a matter of fact, I am myself. I would like to talk to him about naval ROTC at Harvard."

She came back, and she said that Dr. Conant would see me a couple of days hence at 4:00 o'clock in the afternoon, or whatever it was. So I went over there to see him. It was announced that I wanted to talk to him about naval ROTC at Harvard. And I said, "Yes, I do, sir. I would just like to ask you this question. Does the naval ROTC unit contribute anything to Harvard University?"

"Well," he said, "that's a most unusual question."

I said, "I don't know whether it is exactly unusual or not. I will just draw a parallel. Suppose Harvard University came down to the Naval Academy and set up an operation in the corner of the Naval Academy. I would like to know whether they were contributing in any way to the

---

*Dr. James Bryant Conant, president of Harvard University from 1933 to 1953.

Naval Academy."

"Oh," he said, and he tossed his head back. He said, "I think it does contribute."

I said, "Well, thank you very much, Dr. Conant. That's all I wanted to know." And I jumped up and went. That was the end of it. I didn't see him again until I saw him in Berlin when I was over there for a Crusade for Freedom or some other damn thing.* But he was amazed. Now the fellow who was in charge of the Army reserve unit at Harvard--he and his wife came to call on me and my wife, over at the commandant's one Sunday afternoon.

And I told him that I had been over and had seen Mr. Conant, and he said, "You have? I have been here two and a half years and have never gotten to see him yet."

This kid's father was the Chief of Staff of the Army once, but he couldn't get in to see Conant. He said, "How did you get to see him?"

I said, "I just called up and said I wanted to come over and talk to him. And I put the question to him as to whether or not he thought the naval ROTC contributed to Harvard. I got my answer, and I backed out."

Well, this kid said he had been here for two years and a half and had never been able to get in to see him. That's all right, that was his problem, it wasn't mine. I saw him and I got out of him what I wanted.

---
*Dr. Conant was U.S. high commissioner for Germany from 1953 to 1955 and U.S. ambassador to West Germany from 1955 to 1957.

Q: Did you have dealings with the Naval Reserve also?

Admiral McCrea: Yes, they had Naval Reserve classes down here at night, and at the behest of the people in charge of the naval reserve around here, I went down and talked to them. I talked to all these fellows. They had a lot of nice chaps.

Well, anything else?

Q: We're at the end of the tape and at the end of a superb naval career, so I thank you very much.

APPENDIX A

UNITED STATES SHIP NEW YORK
Battleship Division Six
U.S. Atlantic Fleet

November 21, 1918

Extract from Deck Log, U.S.S. New York

8:00 a.m. to meridian:

Steaming as before, following movements of the 5th B.S. Standard speed 12 kts., course 270. At 8:20 c.c. to 90. At 8:42 in obedience to signal from Commander-in-Chief Grant Fleet c.c. to 157 and proceeded to form Red Fleet as per operation order "ZZ." At 8:56 c.c. to 90. At 9:16 sighted H.M.S. Cardiff with kite balloon in tow two points on stbd., bow. At 9:18 went to battle stations. At 9:20 astern of H.M.S. Cardiff standing in a westerly direction were sighted 5 battle cruisers, 9 battleships, 7 cruisers, and 49 destroyers of the German High Seas Fleet, which surrendered for internment. At 9:43 in obedience to signal, squadron leaders turned through 180 degrees, steadied on a westerly course, and proceeded to conduct the surrendered enemy vessels to the Firth of Forth. At 11:20 c.c. to 245. Throughout the remainder

of watch, speeds various keeping station astern
of H.M.S. Agincourt.

                    J. L. McCrea
                    Lieutenant, U.S. Navy

APPENDIX B

SECRET

The Navy Department cleared this sometime in the mid seventies

Op-12A-7-MM

February 5, 1941

MEMORANDUM FOR ADMIRAL STARK

The highlights of my trip were:

1. Departed Washington, 13 December 1940, by plane and was grounded at Kansas City, Missouri, about 2400 the same date. Proceeded by Santa Fe Rail Road to Albuquerque, New Mexico, where at 1200, 15 December 1940, I enplaned for Los Angeles.

2. Had to charter a commercial plane and shore boat to get to PAA float at San Pedro in time to catch clipper for Pearl Harbor on 15 December 1940.

3. Arrived San Francisco about 1430, 16 December 1940, after about 22½ hours in the air. Clipper had completed about one-half the distance to Pearl Harbor before it turned back because of adverse weather. Delayed in San Francisco because of adverse weather until 20 December 1940.

4. DelDelayed in Pearl Harbor, T. H., until 1 January 1941 (six days) due to fact that no plane could get through from the coast.

5. Delayed one day in Midway due to engine trouble.

6. Arrived in Manila, 6 January 1941. Contacted Captain W. R. Purnell, USN., Chief of Staff to CinCAF, who was about to proceed on detached duty (the nature of which I shall privately inform you), and made available to that officer the papers I had in my custody.

7. Reported to CinCAF at Olongapo, P. I., on 10 January 1941, and remained with him in his flagship until my detachment on 19 January 1941.

8. Departed Manila 0300, 20 January 1941, arriving Pearl Harbor 22 January 1941.

9. Had conferences with CinCUS and prospective CinCPac and their respective and prospective Chiefs of Staff and War Plans Officers.

10. Departed Pearl Harbor, T. H., 1500, 28 January 1941, arriving San Francisco 0945, 29 January.

11. Departed San Francisco 1230, 29 January 1941. Grounded at Cheyenne Wyoming at 2230, same date.

12. Departed Cheyenne, Wyoming, at 0930, 30 January 1941 and arrived Washington at 2200, same date.

13. Reported for duty in Navy Department 31 January.

The summary of the conversations which I had with various persons follow. Where quotation marks are used I have quoted directly the person concerned.

CONVERSATIONS WITH CinCAF

CHINA
Marines

Our commitments in North China, insofar as the Marines are concerned, should be reduced. In the event of hostilities the Marines at Tientsin could not conceivably get out except under the most favorable circumstances. The Marines at Peiping, if given slight warning, could evacuate to the Western Hills. Shanghai Marines could get away and it is planned that they will strike out for the Guerrilla Country. This evacuation will offer no difficulty because the guerrillas are fighting close to Shanghai. Plans have been made for the above. In this connection those not physically fit for roughing it (older sergeants, etc.) are being slowly gotten out. Admiral Hart is retaining all Marine replacements arriving on the China Station in the Manila Bay area. The Admiral remarked that Col. Peck was doing a fine job in Shanghai.

Ships

The MINDANAO, OAHU and LUZON would be quite useful in the Philippine Islands as mine sweepers. Admiral

SECRET

Hart does not, however, expect to withdraw them for a variety of reasons, chiefly among which are:

 (1) Monsoon season is now on;
 (2) It would be "doleful" for Americans in China to be without them;
 (3) It would be a most conspicuous move to withdraw them and for that reason it would be particularly bad at this time;
 (4) The presence of these ships in China "keeps up the pressure".

  The Admiral remarked that Rear Admiral Glassford was doing an excellent job in China.

TULSA AND ASHEVILLE

  Only one of these vessels is now being kept in China at a time. This in order to reduce the numbers of men who might otherwise fall into the enemy's hands.

PERSONALITIES

High Commissioner

  Admiral Hart does not tell him everything. Cannot take him into his full confidence because he is "leaky". The Secretary of Interior has made the High Commissioner appear very badly in a number of instances. Tell Admiral Stark that Admiral Hart wants the President to know that he (Hart) thinks it was a bad mistake to put the P.I. under the Department of Interior. The High Commissioner does not fit socially in the job. Very religious and very much of a pacifist. Until a couple of months ago thought U. S. participation in war in the Far East entirely out of the question. Now thinks war is possible to the extent that he is beginning to worry greatly about it. A very conscientious man but not astute. Lives in a social vacuum. Does not mix with Filipinos. He is a direct contrast to Mr. McNutt, who was a grand play-boy and who, because of his social graces and association with the Filipinos, was able to get almost anything he wanted, particularly from President Quezon. The High Commissioner has gotten "in the way" a couple of times in that he has prevented certain moneys due from the United States to be made immediately available to the Philippine government. The High Commissioner felt that if they got this money they would squander it, which they no doubt would have done. However, in so doing he incurred the wrath of both President Quezon and General MacArthur, both of whom state that their defense work has been greatly embarrassed by non-receipt of these funds.

NOTE: In accordance with your instruction I called on the High Commissioner. Admiral Hart accompanied me on the call and talked to the High Commissioner for a few moments about a matter the nature of which I will inform you privately. Admiral Hart then withdrew. I presented your respects to the High Commissioner as directed. Almost immediately he started talking about war --- wanted to know what the feeling in Washington was --- what your views in particular were, etc. I told him that, of course, all hoped to avoid war but that we must reckon with the possibility. He remarked that he had earnestly hoped that war was something the world would not again experience. He informed me that he had recently received a three page letter from the President and that he gathered therefrom that war was not far off. The High Commissioner then read a three page despatch which he had recently sent to Washington in which he invited attention to the fact that, in event of trouble in the Far East he had some 10,000 American civilians --- most of whom are in the Manila area, who should be evacuated if possible. In the despatch he invited attention to the fact that underground bomb proofs in Manila area are not practicable due to the nature of the soil and that fact that surface water is encountered at very shallow depths. The despatch further stated that most of the Americans lived and had their offices in the type of buildings which would be easy and inviting targets for bombers, etc. He made no recommendation as I recall it but merely pointed out his problem. In one item his despatch was destinctly in error. He stated that there were some 500 navy dependents still in the Manila area. I asked the date of his despatch and, upon being informed that it was drafted as of 6 January 1941, I suggested that this number might be in error. In this I was sure of my ground because in conversation with Admiral Hart I had been informed that there were remaining in the Manila area some 40 navy dependents, the greater number of whom were expectant mothers and that as soon as they had had their babies and could travel that they were being evacuated. The High Commissioner then called for Colonel Carswell, U. S. Army, his senior aide. The Colonel was directed to check the figures with the 16th Naval District and he shortly returned with information which substantiated the point I had made. I only cite this to point out that since the despatch was in considerable error in this point that it might well be in others.

The High Commissioner remarked about his difficulties with Mr. Quezon. "He's a remarkable fellow --- temperamental, flighty --- in fact most of the ear marks of a genius. Despite his outward friendship for me I can

count on periodic vitriolic tirades against me --- I suppose he does this for political purposes."

The High Commissioner stated that he felt "the distance from Washington". Stated that no one seemed really interested in the Philippines. That it was a comfort to have so solid a person as Admiral Hart close at hand. He further stated that one thing in administering his job that distressed him was that he could not frankly discuss his views regarding his many problems with Washington, because his correspondence, no matter to whom it was addressed, always leaked through to the Philippine Islands and to Mr. Quezon. And this, he said includes the letters I write to the President. "I don't think any one would deliberately let my correspondence get adrift but I must recognize that it does happen." He concluded his remarks along this line by stating that he felt there should be some one in Washington to whom he could frankly bare his heart in confidence.

NOTE: (I was somewhat bewildered by the frankness of his remarks, but I concluded that I had just happened along at a time when he felt impelled to say something to someone about his troubles).

The High Commissioner asked if I would take luncheon with Mrs. Sayre and himself. I replied that I had to call on General MacArthur at noon and that that would preclude accepting. He then remarked:

> "Oh, you can call on the General allright and get back here by one p.m., can't you? We would be glad to have you and I am sure Mrs. Sayre will be glad to see you again and have many questions to ask about Washington."

With that, I accepted.

Luncheon was a very pleasant affair. Mrs. Sayre talked of her Red Cross work and asked many questions about Washington. The High Commissioner talked at length about his recent fishing trip in the "Isabel" to the island of Palawan. Shortly after luncheon I withdrew. The High Commissioner accompanied me to the port cochere and as I bade him "good-bye" he put his hand on my shoulder and said "Tell Admiral Stark that I hope with all my heart our country can be spared the horrors of war".

My personal estimate of the High Commissioner: From what I gathered from officers and civilians in the islands and from his remarks I think he has been an optimistic pacifist until very recently --- that he is now plenty

scared and wants to help, but doesn't know what to do --
rather feels that Washington doesn't give him much thought.
His regard for Admiral Hart is most pronounced.

Commanding General, Philippine Department.

Admiral Hart feels that General Grunert is fundamentally sound. He is industrious, strong, positive, not bright, in fact a little on the stupid side. He thinks that there might be a war, differing in this respect from other Army officers in the Philippines, who seem to regard war as highly improbable. Admiral Hart takes General Grunert into his confidence much more than he does the High Commissioner.

General MacArthur

Admiral Hart states that this officer is positive in his views. Knows a lot but at the same time "knows many things that are not so". "Is leaky". Has very little regard for General Grunert and they do not get on well together. Admiral Hart stated that he had "shrewd guess" that if it weren't for the salary that General MacArthur would "duck out, because he doesn't appear to be too happy in the job".

NOTE: In accordance with your instructions I called on General MacArthur. He stated that there was "a bond" between you and him since you were 1903 at Annapolis and he was 1903 at West Point. He reviewed the war to date, with particular reference to the crumpling of the Italian resistance. At this point he introduced many stories about his experiences with Italian troops in the last war -- none to the particular credit of the Italians. He remarked that Germans had missed their chance to win the war because they apparently didn't have a Robert E. Lee nor a Phil Sheridan nor a Forrest on their general staff, because if they had had such an officer they would have overwhelmed the British at Dunkirk and followed it by an invasion of the British Isles. "No sir, he said, "the Germans just couldn't resist tasting of the lushness of Paris". A head-line in the morning paper lying on the table caught my eye and I wondered" as to "our getting into the war". His reply: "It is inevitable that we will actively participate in this war. Do you think we will build up a twenty billion dollar machine and not use it?" I turned the conversation to the Philippine Army. The best that I could get out of him was that the Army was making satisfactory progress and would be of help when needed.

- 6 -

I reported the results of my visit to Admiral Hart. He dryly remarked "General MacArthur has been generally wrong in his views thus far on the war".

U. S. ARMY

General

There are at present approximately about 4,000 American troops in the Philippine Islands. The Army contemplates no reinforcements of this number. The Army is still bringing their dependents to the P. I. Admiral Hart thinks they should not do this and that they should take out the ones that are now there.

Air Forces

Army air forces are not good. Have but 63 pursuit planes. There are about 1/3 too few pilots for planes available. Admiral Hart's idea is that the Army should maintain enough planes "on the alert" to thoroughly punish any initial day air attack that ORANGE might make to such an extent that it would never again be attempted. The Army should go "full out" on air defense in reference to fighters.

Corregidor

This is another matter. It would be a hard nut to crack. There the Army is thoroughly organized and on a wartime basis. However, the fixed and mobile A.A. defenses of the island are woefully weak (12 3" 50's only). No main battery gun is adequately protected from air attack. The underground development is extensive. There is much underground storage for reserve materials; a completely equipped 200 bed hospital, etc.

Mines

That part of the mine defenses of Manila Bay that belongs to the Army will take, according to Army officials, some 17 days to lay. Admiral Hart thinks this is excessive. He states that our part of the field is three times as large as the Army's and he feels that we could lay ours in 6 days and he regards this estimate as a most liberal one.

PHILIPPINE ARMY

This Army consists of 12 divisions on paper. Nothing larger than a battalion has ever been drilled. Not well equipped and has very little ammunition on hand. The U. S. Army has very little regard for the P. I. Army. Admiral Hart is afraid the P. I. Army is not going to move fast enough to slow up an enemy attack, which it could do, he feels, if everyone was on the alert and well trained and providing much attention was given to demolition activities.

POLITICAL SITUATION

"It can be generally said that most Filipino politicians are grafters." President Quezon seems to be the only one that can keep in order. Whenever he contacts a case of out and out grafting he deals with the grafters ruthlessly. At the present time Mr. Quezon is a very sick man. Has a recurrence of his tubercular trouble. Both the High Commissioner and Admiral Hart stated that it would be a calamity so far as our government is concerned if anything befell Mr. Quezon. The civilians whom I contacted are somewhat skeptical about our giving up the islands in 1946. I was informed that the man in the street is now beginning to wonder whether independence for the islands would be a good thing.

<u>Admiral Hart directed that I carefully bring to Admiral Stark's attention the following:</u>

"It could well happen that the Philippine Government might take the position that they do not want to be dragged into a war by us and take a position of appeasement toward ORANGE. ORANGE is vigorously cultivating the Filipinos and is making much headway". (NOTE: In this connection I was told by a civilian of long residence in the Philippine Islands and one whom I have known for some twenty years, that ORANGE is exerting its utmost efforts in courting the Filipinos, and that middle class Filipinos are now sending their children to school in Japan in numbers, where they are coddled, made much of, and treated as social equals).

FRONT DOOR

NOTE: Admiral Hart habitually refers to the "Front door" with reference to the entrance of Manila Bay. He refers to all other parts of the island of Luzon and particularly that area where land attack may be expected, as "The back door".

The old conception of our defense in this regard was the denial of Manila Bay to enemy ships. There it rested until recently. Admiral Hart feels strongly that the "Front door" should not be nailed tight, but should be kept so that we can open it for our own use as opportunity offers. In this connection, booms and nets are necessary. Some correspondence has taken place between the Navy Department and Admiral Hart in regard to this. Admiral Hart feels that the Navy Department is not fully conversant with his problem and he has requested that I ask Admiral Stark to give him "carte blanche" to go ahead and install such boom and net defenses as he, Admiral Hart, thinks necessary. He states that all but a very small part of the material necessary can be purchased locally. While I was in Manila a despatch was received from the Navy Department granting Admiral Hart an allotment of $20,000 for experimental purposes in this regard. All of the Navy's mines in connection with the defenses for Olongapo are stowed at the old Naval coaling station at Olongapo and are ready for laying. The Army has informed Admiral Hart that, on declaration of hostilities, a company of white troops will be sent to Grande Island for the protection of this mine field.

BACK DOOR

The security of the back door is very doubtful and must be regarded as a very uncertain affair. Most susceptible to espionage, sabotage and politics. Admiral Hart pointed out that worry in this regard contributed very largely to Admiral Smeallie's illness.

Admiral Hart doubts that an ORANGE landing could long be held off on any part of the coast of Luzon outside of the Manila Bay area.

DRY DOCK DEWEY

It is planned to take the dock to Mariveles Bay when and if hostilities become imminent. Moorings for this dock will not be planted. The dock has been equipped with all necessary anchors and chains and can be moved on short notice. The DEWEY is now over due for self docking. This operation takes about 6 weeks and must be accomplished during the dry season. In view of the international situation, Admiral Hart states that he will not attempt the self docking of the DEWEY this winter.

16TH NAVAL DISTRICT

One thing that contributed largely to Admiral Smeallie's illness was the anxiety about the large concentration of explosives in the casemates in Cavite. Admiral Hart stated that "probably all known safety precautions are being violated in this regard".

Generally speaking, the 16th Naval District is well organized for war. Rear Admiral Bemis stated to me that he wished that I could so inform Admiral Stark when I returned to Washington.

The best thing the 16th Naval District has is the underground development of Corregidor. The security unit from Shanghai is now established there and Admiral Hart states that the usefulness of this unit has increased threefold since removed from Shanghai. This station is all ready for use as a man radio receiving station in time of war.

Considerable underground stowage is now available at Corregidor for Navy use. The further development of this stowage is proceeding apace.

In the Manila Bay area there are a number of shops and shore plants which could be used to effect minor repairs to certain craft. The 16th N.D. is organizing these facilities for use in case of necessity.

While the War Plans of the 16th Naval District have not yet been approved, they are regarded as satisfactory and in good order. The acquisition of reinforcements from time to time of submarines and aircraft require the plans to be changed with particular reference to logistics. It should be remembered that storage space is limited and that it is now taxed to capacity.

ASIATIC FLEET

"The original conception was that the 'S' class of submarines would "Live or die close to Manila'. With the acquisition of more submarines this thought has been changed. "The punch' that this fleet has lies in its submarines and we expect to use this arm agressively. Admiral Bemis will be able to help me a lot in this regard due to his submarine experience in the World War."

The Chief of Naval Operations in a letter to Admiral Hart requested information as to whether or not additional submarine facilities were required at Cebu and Iloilo. Admiral Hart feels that extensive facilities in these areas are inadvisable since they could be easily destroyed and are outside the area intended by the War Plans to hold. He does not desire to scatter his main tending effort. On the other hand, satisfactory services afloat are vital and the outstanding need of the Asiatic Fleet is an additional submarine tender.

AIR FORCES

"The most puzzling problem I have is with the air. The air people don't understand me and I evidently don't understand them. I feel that the patrol planes can operate with less facilities than they seem to demand. I want them to content themselves to go 'full out' on information, recognizing, of course, that they should take advantage of inviting targets as they present themselves. However, as for bombing Formosa, The Pescadores, Spratley Island - No! Out here we must depend on dispersal and concealment for defense of our material on the ground. The same holds for submarines. We have investigated a number of 'rest' places for both these types and have made much progress in this regard. One of the best places I have in mind for patrol planes is the fresh water Lake of Lanao (on the Island of Mindanao 2,000 feet elevation). The strategic location of this body of water is fair. Gasoline required can be gotten in with little difficulty. We will make much use of it. A similar hideout is being developed near the mouth of the Cagayan River. Olongapo has little strategic advantage as compared with Cagayan River. I will have no more to say about the LANGLEY. I have 'shot my wad' and still feel that I am right. The Chief of Naval Operations stated in his letter of 30 December 1940, that we have no planes which the LANGLEY can tend. My aviators believe it possible that a squadron of VJ utility type could be assembled from various activities and sent to this station." It should be remembered that a great deal of the area over which our planes will fly will not require planes of long radius of action. The next plane reenforcements ought to be something the Langley can tend."

FUEL

(Note: A complete report on this subject has been made to the Navy Department since my departure from Washington.)

"The Army is much worse off than we are. They expect to rely heavily on requisitioning supplies of ordinary gas and 'pepping' it up with chemicals."

Admiral Hart is not worried in regard to fuel, diesel, and lubricating oil. He has been in conference with the Standard Oil Company representatives in the Dutch East Indies and he states that this company owns 4 tankers and charters 12. Admiral Hart states that he knows he could get as many as 3 tankers from Standard Oil any time he needs them. The Asiatic Fleet has 3 months supply of aviation gas on hand for war purposes.

RAINBOW THREE

References referred to are pages and paragraph numbers in the PLAN. All remarks are direct quotations by Admiral Hart.

Page 6

"I doubt that Washington will be able to do anything in time and that all that will be accomplished must be done locally."

1301(g)

"I accept this. I absolutely must have 4 cargo ships."

2102(a)

"I regard this as very questionable (especially subhead (1). I feel that ORANGE may possibly try the whole venture leaving us out of it. I consider it highly probable that they may feel that our fears for the Atlantic and our known apathy for things in the Far East will keep us out of hostilities in the Orient."

2103(a)(1)

"I would be perfectly satisfied if 'for supporting other offensive operations' were underlined in all copies."

2104

"Give me these and I am ready for war."

3111

"I hope the priority of tasks fits the order in which they are laid down. I suppose that they are laid down in order of importance and I approve."

3121

"I can raid them with submarines but I am not permitted by War Instructions to wage that kind of war. If I were writing this paper I would leave out '(a)' and insert (Cc)' and '(b)' in that order.

3121(c)(1)

"Are the limitations of the Malay barrier indicated by this paragraph? If these geographical locations were not given I would be much freer to act. Note: The term 'Malay barrier' does not bother me much, nor would it hamper my movements in any way, but I would like this cleared up. I suggest a definition 'Asia to Australia'."

3455

"I consider the last sentence the way this thing will be done."

GENERAL OBSERVATIONS ON RAINBOW THREE

"The Navy Department should try to get the Army to do all possible in connection with its efforts in the Philippines. The Army just doesn't think we should be fighting out here. The Army has planned to tell ORANGE that the Camp Hohn Hay and Fort McKinley are non-military zones so that women and children can be assembled with safety at those points. Ridiculous!"

"The most fortunate circumstance about our problem is that ORANGE is desperately in need of oil. The Dutch are thoroughly prepared to destroy all oil fields. ORANGE knows this and accordingly realizes that they must proceed most carefully."

"Can I expect that all merchant shipping under our flag will be given as much warning as possible regarding eventualities?" Note: I answered the above in the affirmative.

"I accept all the assumptions but it does not appear to me that they have been thought all the way through.

ORANGE can initially:

    (1) Go to Philippines.

    (2) Go down East Coast of Philippines and roll up the Netherland East Indies from East to West, staying clear of the British, or

    (3) Staying West and strike British first, including British North Borneo. I feel that we can rule out (1) because I think they will hope to the last to keep us out of it."

"I feel it altogether possible that ORANGE will use combination of (2) and (3) above."

"Can a reissue of 'Regulations governing U.S. Navy in War (1917)' be expected? I wish a definite answer as to this point."

"The ORANGE Navy and own government are very cautious. I feel that it also highly probable that they will creep cautiously to the Southward. I also feel that they won't jump us unless they feel certain that in so doing they can attain a tremendous initial advantage in doing so. I do not feel that the destruction of the entire Asiatic Fleet would be regarded by them as such an 'initial advantage'."

"I have given much thought to the Allied Command Areas. Air Marshall Brook-Popham has command of all British land and Air forces out here. These forces are defensive forces. Far and away the best set up would be unified command for the air and naval forces and the British have already set up something in the way of this as pointed out above. I feel that our war efforts in this theater would be considerably weakened if a cooperative principle is decided upon, rather than a <u>unified command</u> for air and naval forces. I wish to point out very strongly that I have no personal ambition in this regard. I view this matter with so much importance that I wish it to be pressed most strongly before the Navy Department."

"Are the territorial and naval forces going to help hold the Malay Barrier? If so, that is all right, but if they are to be utilized to defend Sydney and Auckland that is all wrong. I would like to get a definite agreement on this point. If their employment is to be restricted to a cooperative principle I would like to know it and I wish to impress that that cooperation will have to be damned whole hearted to be effective."

"I feel that I must withhold orders to my submarines to sink ORANGE merchantmen until an American ship has been so sunk. I cannot submit my submarine captains to the ignominy which would befall them if they were to sink a merchant ship 'without warning', and in consequence cause much loss of life."

"With reference to this plan I feel that with the acquisition of DesDiv 52 I am better equipped for mine-sweeping than anything else. I had hoped that these vessels would be equipped as mine layers and have anti-submarine equipment as well."

"The crying need for Singapore in aircraft is for fighters."

"Get all the information possible on Port Darwin and send it to me."

"I was informed some time ago that the ORANGE 8,500 ton cruisers had shifted their batteries from triple 6" mounts to twin 8" mounts (5 of them). Rumor now is that they have had one target practice since their alterations were completed and as a result of same two captains are being removed and one is being court-martialed for the poor performance of his ship. I am further informed that these ships suffered much structural damage during this target practice."

"Our old CA's are 'soft'. They cannot absorb punishment as could the SAN FRANCISCO class."

GENERAL REMARKS

"I consider that the Asiatic Fleet should be given priority in all things. This is the front line trench. Above all I want priority of attention from the Navy Department. I do not want to have to send follow-up despatches. It goes against my grain and principles to do so. From my position out here I feel that the Department is altogether too slow in answering my despatches. Some of my recommendations have evidently been completely ignored."

"Admiral Hart talked at length about what he termed the ponderousness" of War Plans generally. He thinks there

- 15 -

is altogether too much form for the substance involved. He feels if we were sure that we had a year of peace ahead of us it would be a good thing to scrap our planning system entirely and start anew from scratch. He states that one of the contributing matters to Admiral Smeallie's breakdown was worry about War Plans. "The whole system needs simplification. The average Naval officer sitting down to do the planning - especially the sort who are sent to the 16th Naval District - gets quickly lost in the maze of details in connection with the planning and seems quite incapable of catching up. Our system of War Plans should not be beyond the capabilities of the average officer."

MAINTENANCE

"The alteration of putting in gasoline and negative tanks in the submarines has been put by me in a deferred status."

"The matter of camouflage for our ships has given me much concern. Has Yards and Docks any suggestions as to how I can effectively camouflage the DEWEY?"

"The bottoms of combatant ships, plus the big auxiliaries, have now been painted with plastic paint."

"Everything gets one week for docking. I have moved the supervising constructor from Shangai down to Cavite. He is of much assistance to us here."

"Splinter protection has not yet been accomplished because of non-receipt of material."

"The degaussing project is going ahead most satisfactorily. The same can be said for the echo sound equipment project. The Commandant of the 16th Naval District and I have plans for requisitioning commercial stocks of anything we may need in the event of emergency.

(NOTE: A contractors representative for the echo sound equipment is now in the Philippine Islands. He states that the equipment is functioning better in the P. I. waters than it ordinarily does elsewhere.)

The following remarks were made to me by Admiral Hart and his Fleet Intelligence Officer concerning certain ORANGE Flag Officers:

Admiral K. Oikawa - Minister of Marine

"Careful. Not rapier witted. Rather slow thinker. Probably won't make many mistakes. Reputed to be wealthy. Can be counted upon to make decisions and stand by them."

<u>Admiral I. Yamamoto</u> - present Commander-in-Chief, combined fleets.

"Energetic. Highly able. Bold in contrast to most who are inclined to be cautious. Decisive. He has American viewpoint. Formerly Naval Attache in Washington. London Arms Conference delegate. Well versed in international affairs. A wounded veteran, having lost two fingers at Tsushima. Highly thought of by rank and file of ORANGE Navy. Personally <u>likes</u> Americans. Plays excellent bridge and poker. Alert in every way. Very air minded."

<u>Admiral S. Shimadu</u> - Commanding China Seas Fleet

"Unable to definitely size him up. Pretty good I think. Cagey. Always has defenses well organized. Great admirer of the Prussian system. Strict disciplinarian. Cold and calculating. One of the foremost of southern expansionists. Mean."

<u>Vice Admiral A. M. Hibino</u> - Commandant, Kure.

"Rather well disposed towards Americans. Handsome. More than average mental equipment. Understands American mentality well. Cautious thinker."

<u>Vice Admiral S. Iwamura</u> - (Formerly liaison officer at Shangai)

"Bright, able, upright and straightforward. Pro-American. Decidely anti-Axis. Has had much general staff duty. Strikes one as knowing his business."

<u>Rear Admiral T. Oka</u> - (Formerly Chief of Staff, 3rd Expeditionary Fleet). Now Chief of ONI General Staff.

"Young. Splendid mind, but not particularly forceful. Smartest of the younger Admirals. Estimate him to be about 48 years of age."

<u>General remark:</u>

"One does not have to see many ORANGE Naval Officers until one realizes that there is a wide variety of quality."

The day before I left Admiral Hart called me in and remarked he wished the following emphasized:

"The two important items of disagreement we have with the Navy Department are as follows:

(1) Nets and booms.

We know what we want and the easiest way out for the Department is to let us do it our way. My first thought was to plant piling from Sangley Point to Manila breakwater and equip same with torpedo nets. However, we must keep the entire Manila Bay available for the use of the Fleet should it be needed. The later plan of securing the "front door" by mines and booms at Corregidor is by far the best.

(2) Air Basing

We do not want extensive bases outside the defense area. They must be temporary at best. Dispersion and concealment is the answer. Why the complete air base in Manila Bay when we are leaving in 1946?

Tell Admiral Stark that I regard the following as important:

"I have a shrewd guess that General Grunert would welcome an order from the War Department to keep wives and children at home and get those now out here home."

"Something should be done with the press services about publishing ship movements. We cannot expect to conduct operations if these operations are to be broadcasted to the world."

"There are four (4) fine ships of the Maersk Line (Danish registry) out here which are now not in use. Three (3) are in Manila and one (1) is in Ceba. They are diesel engine powered, about 7,000 tons, twin screw. The Navy Department should keep this in mind and should things get to the point where we are grabbing shipping grab these. They would be most useful in time of war.

"Last words to Admiral Stark" - CinCAF

"You are defending our home fires. Don't let the home guards get too much under your feet and absorb too much of your attention." I asked Admiral Hart to enlarge on "home guards". His reply "the army and the continental Naval Districts".

CONVERSATION WITH COMMANDANT 14th NAVAL DISTRICT

"Tell Admiral Stark that he should drop everything and pay the Fleet and this district a quick visit. It would do him good and at the same time help us." Admiral Richardson told me he agreed heartily with the above.

"Tell Admiral Stark that we must have good officer personnel if this district is to accomplish anything. Our output will be no better than our personnel."

"Give my best to Admiral Stark and tell him I hope he is enjoying his job."

CONVERSATIONS WITH ADMIRAL RICHARDSON AND REAR ADMIRAL KIMMEL. - Present also Captain Smith, Captain Delany, Captain McMorris and Commander Murphy.

Admiral Richardson stated that his interpretation of paraphrased despatch before him was that it had been sent by the Chief of Naval Operations on his own responsibility in order that CinCUS and CinCAF could have plans in hand to carry out "Plan Dog" should occasion arise. This would mean more "alert" and increased measures of security and plans for action east of Longitude 160 E. Our position would, therefore be essentially a defensive one.

Admiral Richardson remarked that the anti-aircraft defenses of Pearl Harbor left much to be desired. "They are, in my judgment, wholly and completely inadequate." To this, Rear Admiral Kimmel quickly agreed. Admiral Richardson continued

"The Army must realize that the protection of this base is their paramount consideration of the Pacific. The principle thing that is needed here now is:

(1) Increased Army land plane strength.

(2) Increased a.a. guns up to 5" and 37 mm.

(3) A most liberal supply of ammunition for target practice and action."

The above defensive measures should be taken at once - the planes procured and manned, the guns installed and manned.

The attention of the Navy Department is especially invited to the fact that the Army mobile defenses of Pearl Harbor are now as follows:

(1) 9 batteries of 3" guns, 4 guns per battery

(2) 36 fighter planes, 19 of which are 6 years old. 17 of which are 4 years old.

(3) 53 bombers, 6 years old. ("Army calls them obsolete" - Admiral Richardson).

(4) 109-50 caliber machine guns.

There are not enough pilots for these planes. There is no prospect of receiving additional planes before the middle of 1941.

"There are no 37 mm guns on the island" - Rear Admiral Kimmel."

Rear Admiral Kimmel remarked that he felt consideration should be given to establishing a balloon barrage in and near Pearl Harbor ---- that one might be useful at Lualualei Ammunition Depot as there is no protection there now at all. He remarked that effort in this direction should not be diverted from getting additional planes which are badly needed. Admiral Richardson remarked that he did not think a balloon barrage would be of much assistance ---- and that it might be of much annoyance to us. Admiral Kimmel remarked that he thought the mere reported presence of a balloon barrage might act as a deterrent. Rear Admiral Kimmel suggests consideration be given to providing torpedo nets for ships in Pearl Harbor. He remarked that the technical difficulties might be "almost insurmountable."

Admiral Richardson remarked and it was agreed to by Rear Admiral Kimmel that, with reference to "Plan Dog", "CinCPac should be informed as soon as possible ---- even a tentative decision would be helpful ---- as to the numbers and types of craft which are to be withdrawn from this fleet."

"The battleships were brought around Ford Island the last time the Fleet came in. This will be done habitually in the future. This obviates the winding of the ships in the vicinity of their berths to head them to seaward."

Admiral Richardson's personal plans are as follows:

He will stay in Honolulu until about 14 February. He expects to then proceed to the coast and upon arrival will proceed to Long Beach and pack his personal effects. He expects to motor east via New Orleans. Unless hostilities eventuate he does not intend arriving in Washington prior to 15 March 1941. Probably will arrive in the Department about 11:50 on that date.

CONVERSATIONS WITH REAR ADMIRAL KIMMEL

The admiral stated:

"Head this 'Things I am thinking about'."

The following must be done by the air people (Army and Navy) in connection with the defenses of Pearl Harbor, T. H.:

    (1) Communications between the Army and Navy air fields should be instantaneous.

    (2) Provision for the standing of alert watches should be such as will not wear out personnel and material.

    (3) Provision must be made for the prompt detection of enemy air craft.

    (4) The command arrangements for the local air defenses must be worked out.

    (5) We must have satisfactory aircraft recognition signals and all personnel, ground and ship, must be so trained that they will be able to recognize our own and enemy aircraft.

    (6) The army plans should include provisions for landing on Navy Fields and practice should be had at same. The Navy shore based aircraft should practice using the Army Fields.

Tell Admiral Stark "I am either going to be good friends with the Army and get things done or I am going to have a hell of a fight with them. My preliminary conversations with General Herron and his air man indicate that we are going to be good friends but we haven't yet got down to 'cases'. I am perfectly willing to make concessions to get the answer and I'm not going to get too much obsessed with any one thing. However, the defenses against aircraft for Pearl Harbor must be improved.

"Tell Admiral Stark that I will do my utmost in this job. I will be guided in what I do by what I think is best for the country. Further I will do exactly as I think right. I shall not attempt to curry favor in any quarter. I have certain convictions about the job and I will administer it with all the vigor I can muster. I am well aware of my own short comings. I am getting about me the best staff I can pick. I further feel a deep sense of responsibility of the job that has been given me."

CONVERSATION WITH REAR ADMIRAL BEMIS

"Tell Admiral Stark and Rear Admiral Sharp that from a cursory inspection I am well pleased with the readiness of the 16th Naval District for war."

CONVERSATION WITH REAR ADMIRAL DRAEMEL - (Comments are with reference to Rainbow III)

"I do not feel it possible to maintain any show of force in the Pacific without committing ourselves beyond hope of withdrawal."

"I do not particularly like the assignment of units to task forces by the Navy Department example. The assignment of a 16 torpedo ship to a task where an 8 torpedo ship with more guns would seem to be indicated." Again, suppose the 'plug is pulled' when an assigned unit is under going overhaul."

PERSONAL OBSERVATION

Midway

The project at Midway is progressing rapidly. The contractors have about 1,000 men there. They are a rough looking lot but Lieutenant Ventres (C. E. Corps Reserve) tells me they are workers. No hard liquor is permitted but the men can get two cans of beer per day. There are cases of insubordination from time to time, but the bosses get on with the men surprisingly well. The food for them is excellent and plentiful. I was delayed there one day and I had an opportunity to inspect the project in its-entirety with the exception of the activities on Eastern Island. Ventres told me (2 January) that 141 acres of runways were cleared on that island and ready for surfacing. The whole project should be finished by 1 October, and the station will be ready for use about 1 July 1941.

The officer in charge of the Marine detachment tells me that the Army engineers left the place in an "awful mess". They just weren't good first lieutenants and the Marines have been kept fully occupied clearing up rubbish and debris in all parts of the island that was left by the Army.

Wake

The U. S. S. Burrow arrived 9 January 1941. When I passed through Wake east bound (22 January) she was moored to a buoy off the reef. From Peel Island I could see the contractors mess hall on Wake which I was told was rapidly nearing completion. The first contingent of contractors men, I was told, numbered 80 some.

Guam

The typhoon did a great deal of damage. Its results were every where evident and the island presented a rather sad appearance in contrast to my recollection of it. Governor McMillin informed me that much headway had been made in rebuilding the place. He feels that the rebuilding of the Marine activities should be held in abeyance until it is definitely determined that the present location of the barracks, etc., will not interfere with projected air fields, etc. He feels that the plateau which they presently occupy would make a splendid air field.

I visited the new reservoir and it is progressing rapidly. When completed, it will make a fine target for bombing. That is bad, but I know of no remedy. Some sort of concealment should be worked out because without an adequate water supply Guam would be almost uninhabitable for a force of any size.

J. L. McCREA

APPENDIX C

McCREA MEMOIR

I know men are not generally selected for positions of power because they inspire loyalty and affection amongst those around and beneath them. But something in my feelings for John and the remembrances of several Navy "bluejackets" who attended John's funeral made me turn to Webster's Dictionary to see if the word "admiral" was related to the word "admiration." I found among numerous other derivations of "admiral" a small notation: "influence of the Latin admirabilis, meaning admirable." The apparent insignificance of this derivation was disappointing.

For me, the word "admirable" characterizes John far better than "admiral." This was not always the case, however. When I met John some 27 years ago, he was strictly an admiral to me. My thoughts today are about John's transformation in my eyes from admiral to admirable. The subtitle of this memoir is "The Admirable Who Prevailed Through Disarmament."

I did not welcome the appearance of an admiral on our doorstep to court my mother. I had adored my father, and I was very independent. Moreover, I was a member of the flower generation. I believed in liberal ideals--in love, not war. The vision of this tall, erect figure with a shock of white hair, a booming voice, and an air of command was dismaying. Inclined to the view that this was an alien who could not possibly understand or appreciate the sensitive values of a young person like myself, I kept a cautious distance.

This was the state of affairs when I first experienced the force of John's disarmament techniques. At the time, I was into folk music, singing, and playing the guitar. One day John arrived with a present for me. I knew that I had not been particularly warm to him; I suspected that this offering was some sort of a bribe. I wondered as I opened it what sort of inappropriate thing he could have gotten to soften me up. I was amazed to find an album of folk music filled with unusual songs sung by wonderful singers--nothing ordinary or commercial. I was simultaneously thrilled and racked with guilt for my evil thoughts. To this day I do not know how he managed to pick out such a perfect present, but for the first time, I sensed that this admiral had a lot more on the ball than I had given him credit for.

As time passed, it became more and more difficult not to be disarmed by John's obvious enthusiasm for my mother. The widow Tobey, like her daughter, did not initially embrace the concept of remarriage. John, the boy two doors down the street, tackled this obstacle with what I now know to be his usual resourcefulness and determination. As might be expected, he wined and dined her and brought her flowers. He also called her regularly from wherever he might be when he was traveling on business for John Hancock Life Insurance. He brought her back little presents from his trips. And he repeatedly told her--and my brother and me--what a wonderful person she was.

The coup de grace to any lingering misgivings about the marriage came after mother finally consented to marry him. John went out and had a little metal plaque made up. It said, "On this spot she said `Yes,'" and it gave the date. He would take it out every now and then, plunk it down on the actual site--the library sofa--and tell us how lucky he was that she had agreed to marry him.

They were married when he was nearly 75. Not unmindful of the possibility that this marriage would not be a long one, John made up for lost time by celebrating anniversaries by the month rather than the year. After four years of marriage, John went into a card shop and asked the salesman if he had any cards for a 50th wedding anniversary. Seeing this elderly gentleman who looked the part of husband for a half-century, the salesman got all excited and started to carry on about how wonderful it was and how unusual to have achieved so many years of marriage. At that point John had to confess that he had been married only 50 months, not 50 years. Thereafter, the celebration of monthly anniversaries tapered off because no cards were made with such high numbers. As it turned out, in defiance of the actuarial tables, they were married for 25 years--or 300 months!

I soon discovered that one dividend of being a stepdaughter was that I received support from an unexpected quarter. Many of you may not know that John's mother had aspirations for him not as a naval officer but as a violinist. For many years he retained both a three-quarter and a full-sized violin as evidence of his early artistic endeavors. John did not share his mother's enthusiasm for the violin, however. He said that he had frequently advanced the hands on the practice room clock so that he could prove to his mother that he had practiced for the obligatory amount of time that day and then go play baseball. His career as a violinist ended abruptly when the shaved the tip off one of the fingers on his left hand in a fan. He recalled that his first thought at the time of the accident was, "Thank heavens, now I can't play the violin!"

During his early years as my stepfather, John's none too passionate love of music was subjected to the acid test. I had just started to play the cello, and whenever I was at home, I practiced long and regularly in the living room. John endured these practice sessions in silence, in part, I suspected, because his hearing was not too sharp. In a few years, however, he started to comment that I was getting pretty good on that thing and tell me about the lady cellist on the Lawrence Welk Show. Still later, he would ask, "When is our Jude going to try out for the Boston Symphony?" When I heard that, I knew how hopeless his mother's aspirations for him had been. But however misguided, I was grateful for the inquiry.

Despite a sometimes crusty exterior, I discovered that John had many charming and endearing ways that revealed unexpected facets. Of course, he was always correct in his demeanor, bearing, and dress. He opened doors and pulled out chairs for ladies. He always wore a jacket and tie, even on casual occasions, and if it was summer, he frequently wore a rosebud in his lapel. He was also incredibly punctual, monitoring departures and arrivals as if the success of the Normandy invasion depended upon it.

But he was not stiff. A good-looking woman always brought a twinkle to his eye, and he was generous with compliments. When he respected character or conduct, he was direct about expressing his feelings. With unabashed admiration, he often remarked on my brother's fine character and values and on the courage of a judge we knew who dared to sentence Mafia leader Tony "Pro" to a jail term.

He also relished a good, high-spirited conversation and struck these up without regard to the age or status of his counterpart. Once John, my mother, and I got into a cab in New York City. To make more room for the ladies, John sat in front with the driver, out of earshot behind the glass divider. We had hardly gone a block when John and the driver were engaged in animated conversation, which continued for the duration of the ride. At our destination, they exchanged very cordial good-byes, and we asked what they had been talking about. "Baseball," was the answer. The admiral from Massachusetts and the cabby from the Bronx had been talking baseball as if they had known each other for years.

Two activities which I found particularly special were his exercising and his gardening. Virtually every morning until he was 95, John would get down on the floor--"on the deck," as he called it--and do bicycle exercises with his legs in the air. The determination necessary to keep this up year after year I found truly awesome.

The gardening struck a different chord. For someone who was a career naval officer, John showed no interest in the sea. To my knowledge, he never once set foot in our Herreshoff 12-1/2 foot sailboat--too small, no doubt. Instead, he fixed his sights firmly on the garden. He was purported to have introduced the tomato to the island of Guam, although that story may be apocryphal. In Chestnut Hill he raised amaryllis and tomatoes from seed in the cellar. In the summer it was roses and dahlias. Although I never would have thought of him as the organic gardening type, he used to order shipments of ladybugs which he launched in the rose garden to attack the aphids. His efforts seemed perpetually successful, for the house was always full of flowers. And whenever I visited Marblehead in the summer, there was always a bud vase with a fresh rose on my dresser.

And then, of course, there were John's stories. He had had extraordinary experiences during his lifetime. I recall sitting with him watching TV pictures of Neil Armstrong walking on the moon and realizing that this man had been born in a house that probably did not have electricity and had witnessed the first automobile, the first radio, the invention of penicillin, the first airplane, the first TV, the first computer, the atomic bomb, and now a man on the moon. In addition, he had spent a significant amount of time at the very center of world affairs. He had known at least three presidents, worked for FDR, met Churchill and numbers of other world leaders, and had an important naval career. His phenomenal memory seemed to enable him to remember all of these experiences vividly. I came to regard him as a sort of human reference library.

John took great pleasure in relating his experiences, not as a reflection of his own achievements, but to share events and personalities that he found "exceedingly interesting." And his enthusiasm for his subjects was infectious. At first I was interested only in civilian matters: the Roosevelts and the personalities in the Roosevelt administration, the time when Wallace Simpson, later Duchess of Wales, tried to flirt with John. I loved his description of opinion day at the United States Supreme court and of Mr. Justice Brandeis, tipped backed in his chair with eyes on the ceiling, delivering the opinion of the Court in flowing prose without visible assistance of notes.

Another favorite was the tale of Winston Churchill, in a propriety-be-damned mood, accompanying FDR and John to their very early morning plane dressed in pajamas, bathrobe, and trench coat, completed with walking stick and cigar.

Later, as the names of the officers began to stick, I became more interested in his Navy stories. When the bluejackets called him on Christmas or his birthday, I wondered what John was like as a commanding officer. Were these bluejackets just a few zealous Navy loyalists, or did John inspire something special in these men? A glimpse of an answer came from John himself.

John told me once that a naval vessel was a very small community and that in war, particularly, the whole crew had to work closely together for the ship to function effectively. Rancor and bad feelings could not be allowed to fester because they could physically endanger the men and the ship. Accordingly, John said it was his practice whenever he dressed someone down to have a pleasant word with him later that day so that the sailor would not go to bed feeling angry or resentful.

This practice struck me as brilliant--pure winning through disarmament. But the practice itself revealed much about the man who used it. I suspect that the qualities that made John concerned about his men's thoughts when they went to sleep had more than a little to do with the presence of the loyal <u>Iowa</u> bluejackets at his funeral, men who had served under him for only two years some 46 years before. To my mind, it is just these qualities that made John truly an admirable.

Julia C. Tobey
31 January 1990

Index to

Reminiscences of Vice Admiral John L. McCrea

U.S. Navy (Retired)

ABDA Command
    The Dutch government in exile presented an award to Admiral Thomas C. Hart in August 1942 to take the sting out of the loss of the ABDA ships in the Pacific earlier that year, 207-210

Ajax, HMS
    British cruiser that fought the German battleship Graf Spee in 1939 and was at the New York Navy Yard at the time of the commissioning of the USS Iowa (BB-61) in February 1943, 295-296

Alcohol
    Drinking to celebrate the transfer of the battleship Idaho (BB-24) to Greece in 1914, 29; Rear Admiral William Standley sometimes ignored Prohibition in the early 1930s, 198

Altrock, Nick
    Washington Senators pitcher who coached Naval Academy midshipmen pitchers in 1915, 36-39

Anderson, Commander Walter Stratton, USN (USNA, 1903)
    Senior member of board that examined the destroyer Babbitt (DD-128) in the early 1920s asked McCrea to be his executive officer, 74-75

Asiatic Fleet, U.S.
    Operations of the minesweeper Bittern (AM-36) in the Far East in the early 1920s, 64-71, 101-105; Commander Husband Kimmel got a Far East tour of duty in the early 1920s so he would be ready for war with Japan, 83-85

Astoria, USS (CA-34)
    McCrea assigned as navigator of from 1934-36, 130-131, 133-134

Athletics
    McCrea's father deplored, 6; Midshipman Walter Seibert pitched a perfect baseball game at the Naval Academy in 1913, 9; status of at U.S. Naval Academy circa 1912, 35-39

Australian Navy
    The cruiser Canberra, sunk at Savo Island in August 1942, was honored by the subsequent naming of a U.S. heavy cruiser the USS Canberra (CA-70), 146-150

Babbitt, USS (DD-128)
    Destroyer mothballed by McCrea in San Diego in early 1922, 57-58, 72-74

Baseball

Midshipman Walter Seibert pitched a perfect game for the Naval Academy in 1913, 9; McCrea was Naval Academy team manager in 1915, 35-39

Beach, Captain Edward L., USN (USNA, 1888)
Commanding officer of the armored cruiser Memphis when she went aground in the Caribbean on 29 August 1916, 126

Beardall, Captain John R., USN (USNA, 1908)
McCrea's predecessor as President Franklin D. Roosevelt's naval aide became superintendent of the Naval Academy in early 1942, 138

Belknap, Commander Charles, Jr., USN (USNA, 1903)
Advised McCrea in 1919 to serve under Admiral Hugh Rodman, 52-53

Bidwell, Commander A. Trood, USN (USNA, 1908)
Served as executive officer on board the armored cruiser Rochester (ACR-2) in the early 1930s, 119-120; while in the Bureau of Navigation in 1940, assigned McCrea to work for Admiral Harold Stark, the CNO, 120-121

Bittern, USS (AM-36)
Minesweeper that McCrea took command of in the Asiatic Fleet in 1924, 64-65; took scientists on an expedition to the Dutch East Indies in the mid-1920s, 65-71; provided assistance for the commerical passenger ship Irene near Chefoo, China, in July 1925, 101-105

Blandy, Rear Admiral William H. P., USN (USNA, 1913)
Discussions in 1942 with McCrea about the capabilities of radar, 300; reduced in rating as a Naval Academy first-class midshipman in 1913 because he didn't get to formation on time, 300-301

Boston, Massachusetts
McCrea's first trip to during midshipman cruise in 1912, 22; tour with his wife, 23-24

Boston Navy Yard
USS Constitution's deteriorated condition in this yard in 1912, 22; manufactured battleship anchor chains in 1912, 22-23; repaired damage to the battleship Iowa (BB-61) in 1943, 219, 305

Brooke, Senator Edward
Influence on the Panama Canal Zone decision in 1977, 116

Brown, John Nicholas
Asked McCrea for advice while serving as Assistant Secretary of the Navy for Air shortly after World War II, 332-334

Casablanca Conference
    British Prime Minister Winston Churchill's participation in this January 1943 conference, 145-146; rumors circulated in Washington, D.C., in 1942 that President Franklin D. Roosevelt was planning a trip to North Africa, 309-312; Roosevelt traveled to the conference by a series of airplane hops, 312-313

Casey, Commander Thomas J., USN (USNA, 1923)
    Was executive officer of the battleship *Iowa* (BB-61) when a torpedo was inadvertently fired at the ship in late 1943, 234; highly recommended for job as XO of the *Iowa*, 298-299

Cassard, Commander William G., CHC, USN
    Chaplain who got midshipmen disciplined for misbehavior during choir practice at the Naval Academy in 1911, 201-202

Chatfield, Admiral Alfred E. M., RN (Ret.)
    Former British First Sea Lord who made speeches against Prime Minister Winston Churchill during World War II, 144

China
    The minesweeper USS *Bittern* (AM-36) provided assistance to the commercial passenger ship SS *Irene* that ran aground near Chefoo in July 1925, 101-105

Churchill, Winston
    British Prime Minister visited the United States in 1942 to confer with President Franklin D. Roosevelt, 140-144; at the Casablanca Conference in January 1943, 145-146; addressed members of the Pacific War Council at a meeting in Washington, D.C., circa 1942, 211

Coast Guard Academy, U.S.
    Senator John F. Kennedy's views, expressed in the mid-1950s, concerning admission of candidates, 78-79

Conant, Dr. James Bryant
    As president of Harvard University in the early 1950s, met with McCrea concerning the status of the university's NROTC unit, 357-359

Conolly, Vice Admiral Richard L., USN (USNA, 1914)
    Nimitz's deputy for administration in the Office of Naval Operations in mid-1940s, preceding McCrea to that post, 131, 302, 330-331

Constitution, USS
    Deteriorated condition of this aged frigate at Boston Navy Yard in 1912, 22

Cooke, Rear Admiral Charles M., USN (USNA, 1910)

Conversations with McCrea aboard the Iowa (BB-61) regarding his assignment after reaching Oran in November 1943, 237-238

Crehan, John F. (USNA, 1946)
Former aide of McCrea's on duty at White House in the early 1960s during John F. Kennedy's administration, 82-83

Cutts, Captain Elwin F., USN (USNA, 1908)
Commanding officer of the battleship Pennsylvania (BB-38) in May 1940 when orders came for the fleet to remain in Hawaiian waters, 87-89

Daniels, Josephus
As Secretary of the Navy gave orders to discharge personnel right after World War I, 54-55

DeMille, Cecil B.
Hollywood director who made the 1944 movie The Story of Dr. Wassell, based on the experiences of a Navy physician in the Dutch East Indies, 206

Denfeld, Admiral Louis E., USN (USNA, 1912)
Chosen as Chief of Naval Operations in 1947 through the influence of Fleet Admiral William D. Leahy, 301-302

Dixon, Sir Owen
McCrea's interaction with this Australian ambassador to the United States regarding renaming the Pittsburgh (CA-70) the Canberra in 1942, 147-150

Donahue, Midshipman Alfred Hyde, USN (USNA, 1913)
Introduced McCrea to choir "racket" at the Naval Academy in the summer of 1911, 199-200

Drake, James C. (USNA, 1880)
Banker who visited the USS New Mexico (BB-40) around 1920 to see Admiral Hugh Rodman, 271-272

Dutch East Indies
The minesweeper USS Bittern (AM-36) visited Sumatra and Java as part of an American scientific expedition in the mid-1920s, 65-71

Dyer, Lieutenant Commander George C., USN (USNA, 1919)
Flag secretary to Admiral J. O. Richardson who had orders in May 1940 for the fleet to remain in Hawaiian waters, 87

Early, Stephen
Press secretary who was involved in finding a retreat for President Franklin D. Roosevelt in 1942, 152-154; comments to McCrea about Roosevelt, 265; declined to pick

up press pass from columnist Drew Pearson in 1942 when asked to by Roosevelt, 279-281; unpleasant experience with black railroad porter, 281-282

Edison, Charles
As Secretary of the Navy, visited the fleet flagship Pennsylvania (BB-38) in the spring of 1940, 50-51, 76

Edison, Thomas A.
Famous inventor who toured the battleship New York (BB-34) at New York Navy Yard in the mid-1910s, 47-50

Education
McCrea attended the Robert L. Werntz preparatory school in Annapolis in 1911, 13-14; McCrea studied at the Naval War College in 1922, 61-62; McCrea's law studies at George Washington University in the late 1920s and early 1930s, 106-113

Edwards, Admiral Richard S., USN (USNA, 1907)
News related to the Atlantic crossing of the battleship Iowa (BB-61) to the Mediterranean in November 1943, 223-224; was Secretary of the Navy James Forrestal's choice to be Chief of Naval Operations after World War II but wasn't up to the job physically, 340

Eisenhower, President Dwight D. (USMA, 1915)
McCrea's reaction to Eisenhower's decision to give Panama the Canal Zone in the 1950s, 116; renaming of President Franklin D. Roosevelt's Shangri-La, Camp David, 155; landings in North Africa in November 1942, 288; McCrea lost respect for Dwight D. Eisenhower beause he tolerated attacks on General George Marshall in the early 1950s, 354-355

Ermine, Natalio
Panamanian attorney who challenged McCrea in the early 1930s about presumptions regarding the Panama Canal, 115-116

Fechteler, Rear Admiral Augustus F., USN (USNA, 1877)
As Commander Battleship Division Six in the summer of 1917 had his flag in the USS New York (BB-34), 45-46

Fechteler, Rear Admiral William M., USN (USNA, 1916)
As director, Officer Personnel Division of BuPers, assigned McCrea to command the Iowa (BB-61) in 1943, 288-289; sharp-penned writer for Chief of Naval Operations Chester Nimitz in the mid-1940s, 331-332; comments on Secretary of the Navy James Forrestal's style of issuing demobilization orders at the end of World War II, 339

First Naval District
McCrea's role as commandant in the early 1950s emphasized

public relations and work with NRTOC units, 357-360

Fletcher, Vice Admiral Frank Jack, USN (USNA, 1906)
Delegated authority and trusted subordinates while serving as Commander North Pacific Force in 1944-45, 318-322

Formosa
General Douglas MacArthur spoke in the late 1940s of the value of a U.S. base on this island, 193-194

Forrestal, James V.
Had a squabble with the Navy Judge Advocate General while serving as Under Secretary of the Navy early in World War II, 334-336; quizzed McCrea about President Franklin D. Roosevelt's World War II dealings with the Soviet Union, 337-338; gave evidence in the late 1940s of losing his grip mentally, 338-340

Ghormley, Vice Admiral Robert L., USN (USNA, 1906)
Was reassigned from London to duty as Commander South Pacific Area in 1942, 170-171

Glassford, Rear Admiral William A., Jr., USN (USNA, 1906)
Navigator when the USS *Idaho* (BB-24) was sold to Greece in the summer of 1914, 28-29; passed on the story of Dr. Corydon Wassell's medical exploits in the Dutch East Indies in 1942, later the subject of a Hollywood movie, 205

Graf, Captain Homer W., USN (USNA, 1915)
McCrea's Naval Academy classmate who in 1942 expressed the wish to command the new battleship *Iowa* (BB-61), but the job went to McCrea instead, 304

Greek Navy
Bought the USS *Idaho* (BB-24) in the summer of 1914 and renamed her *Kilkis*, 27-29

Grosvenors, Mr. and Mrs. Gilbert and Melville Bell
Stop offs on Guam in 1930s and McCrea's subsequent visits with in Washington, D.C., 181-183

Guam
McCrea sought to avoid duty in Guam in the mid-1930s because it was not considered career-enhancing, 131-132; McCrea's duties as executive officer of the naval station in the 1930s, 172-174; provision of fresh water for the island in the mid-1930s, 173-179; the Navy and Pan American Airways cooperated on the island, 179-184, 189-190

Gunnery--Naval
British and American capabilities in World War I

compared, 90-91, 96-98; shooting of the USS Iowa (BB-61) in 1944, 98-99; ships of the U.S. North Pacific Force bombarded the Japanese-held Kurile Islands in 1944-45, 317-318

Guns
   Inventor Thomas A. Edison examined the 14-inch guns of the USS New York (BB-34) in the mid-1910s, 47-48

Hallaran, Charles Francis George Thomas, RN
   Discussed British and American naval philosophies with McCrea during World War I, 91-92

Hart, Admiral Thomas C. Hart, USN (USNA, 1897)
   Commented on Admiral Harold Stark's order for McCrea to meet with Admiral Husband Kimmel in February 1941, 86; personal correspondence between Stark, Hart, and Kimmel, 95; met McCrea at Los Angeles Chamber of Commerce ball for Pacific Fleet Navy personnel in 1930s, 173; as Commander in Chief Asiatic Fleet in the early 1940s, view of General Douglas MacArthur, 193; reluctantly accepted decoration from the Dutch government in 1942, 206-210; role in sending Navy dependents home from the Philippines in 1940, 355-357

Harvard University
   As commandant of the First Naval District in the early 1950s, McCrea worked with the president of Harvard University concerning the status of the school's NROTC unit, 357-359

Hickenlooper, Bourke B.
   Iowa governor who presented state silver service to the new battleship Iowa (BB-61) in 1943, 303-304

Hoover, Charles L.
   McCrea's meeting with this consul general in Batavia (Dutch East Indies) in 1924, 67

Hopkins, Harry
   McCrea's high regard for this special assistant to President Franklin D. Roosevelt, 261-262

Howard, Roy W.
   United Press official who had a mixed relationship with President Franklin D. Roosevelt over the years, 282-284; comment about his height, 284-285

Hughes, Admiral Charles F., USN (USNA, 1888)
   One of five captains in McCrea's four years on the New York (BB-34), 1915-19, 41

Hull, Cordell
   McCrea's clever exchange with President Franklin D.

Roosevelt's Secretary of State in 1942, 140

Hustvedt, Rear Admiral Olaf M., USN (USNA, 1909)
As battleship division commander embarked in the Iowa (BB-61) in January 1944, 244-250; criticism of McCrea regarding a near collision of the Iowa with a carrier, 254-255; recommended the Iowa's bombardment of Mili Atoll in March 1944, 258-259

Idaho, USS (BB-24)
In the Mediterranean when World War I broke out in the summer of 1914 and subsequently sold to the Greeks, 26-29

Ingersoll, Admiral Royal E., USN (USNA, 1905)
Conveyed the news in the fall of 1943 that McCrea would take President Franklin D. Roosevelt and the Joint Chiefs of Staff to the Mediterranean aboard the Iowa (BB-61), 222-224, 226

Ingram, Vice Admiral Jonas H., USN (USNA, 1907)
As Commander South Atlantic Force, was disappointed about not meeting President Franklin D. Roosevelt in Bahia, Brazil, in late 1943, 240-241

Intelligence
Establishment of a map room in the White House in 1942 to display war intelligence for President Franklin D. Roosevelt, 162-163, 165-167

Iowa, USS (BB-61)
Fueled destroyers in the Pacific in 1944, 76-77; commissioned in February 1943, 93, 287-298, 302-303; Admiral Husband Kimmel aboard for visit at New York in 1943, 93-96; shooting capabilities in 1944, 98-99; Atlantic crossing to Teheran conference, November 1943, 218-219, 222-235; McCrea scraped the ship's bottom through a miscalculation in Casco Bay early in 1943, 219-222, 231-232; through Gibraltar en route to Bahia, Brazil, December 1943, 239-240; deep-water cruising experience, 242-243; through Panama Canal to Pacific, January 1944, 244; Prince Duncan as her chief police petty officer, 246; sank a Japanese cruiser off Truk in February 1944, 248-250; maneuvering capabilities demonstrated during Pacific Fleet operations in early 1944, 250-251; officers of the deck, 252-255; Admiral Raymond Spruance's staff officers turned away in 1944, 255-257; bombarded Mili Atoll in March 1944, 258-260; launched in August 1942, 285-287; radar aboard and its efficacy, 299-300; shakedown in Chesapeake Bay and repairs in Boston Navy Yard early in 1943, 305-306; Battle of Philippine Sea, June 1944, 306-308

Iowa (BB-61)-Class Battleships
Maneuvering capabilities demonstrated during Pacific

Fleet operations in early 1944, 250-251

Irene, SS
　Passenger ship that was assisted by the minesweeper USS Bittern (AM-36) after running aground near Chefoo, China, in July 1925, 101-105

Jacobs, Rear Admiral Randall, USN (USNA, 1907)
　Chief of Naval Personnel in 1942 who assigned McCrea as naval aide to President Franklin D. Roosevelt, 139; McCrea asked him in late 1942 for command of the Iowa (BB-61), 287

Japanese Navy
　Surface ships tangled with the battleships Iowa (BB-61) and New Jersey (BB-62) at Truk Atoll in February 1944, 248-250

Java
　Visited by the minesweeper USS Bittern (AM-36) in the mid-1920s, 67

John Hancock Mutual Life Insurance Company
　Boston company for which McCrea worked following his retirement from active naval service in 1953, 348-352

Joy, Captain C. Turner, USN (USNA, 1916)
　Recommended Commander Thomas Casey as executive officer for the battleship Iowa (BB-61) in 1943, 298-299

Judge Advocate General (JAG), Office of
　McCrea's work for during law school in the late 1920s and early 1930s, 106-110; Under Secretary of the Navy James Forrestal tried to take contract review authority away from JAG early in World War II, 334-336

Juliana, Princess
　Dutch princess who lived in the United States during World War II and visited Hyde Park, New York, in 1942, 71-72

Juneau, USS (CL-52)
　Cruiser that sank in November 1942 with five Sullivan brothers on board, 150-152

Kennedy, Senator Edward M.
　McCrea's presentation of a marine painting to in 1963, 81-82

Kennedy, Senator John F.
　Expressed views in the mid-1950s about admitting candidates to the service academies, 78-80; made a talk to Boston blood donors in the 1950s, 80-81

Kennedy, Joseph P., Sr.
   As U.S. Ambassador to the United Kingdom in the late 1930s, opinion of the British on the threshold of World War II, 90

Kimmel, Admiral Husband E., USN (USNA, 1904)
   Visited the British fleet in World War I to inspect gunnery, 83-84, 90, 96-97; as Asiatic Fleet destroyer division commander in the early 1920s, quite interested in readiness for war, 84-85; became Commander in Chief Pacific Fleet in February 1941, 85-86; McCrea's praise of, 86; worked ships hard near Pearl Harbor in 1941, 92-93; visited the new battleship Iowa (BB-61) at McCrea's invitation in 1943, 93-96; compared with Admiral William Standley, 197-198

Kimmel, Dorothy
   Wife of Commander Husband E. Kimmel, stayed home to take care of family while her husband went to the Far East in the early 1920s, 84-85

King, Admiral Ernest J., USN (USNA, 1901)
   Criticisms of Admiral Hugh Rodman, 59-60, 128-129, 212; role in sending McCrea to the White House as President Franklin D. Roosevelt's naval aide in 1942, 121, 138; attempt to secure post for McCrea as naval aide to President Harry Truman in 1945, 129; briefed Roosevelt on plan to bomb Tokyo in early 1942, 168-169; style of command as Commander in Chief, U.S. Fleet, 171; McCrea's dealings with while King was captain of the carrier Lexington (CV-2) in the early 1930s, 212-215; in a row with Secretary of the Navy Frank Knox in early 1940s, 215-217; passenger on board the Iowa (BB-61) en route to Teheran conference in November 1943, 218, 227-228, 234-238; expressed delayed reaction to McCrea after the grounding of the Iowa in 1943, 220-222; FDR's confidence in, 267

King Orry, HMS
   British ship that towed targets during gunnery exercises in World War I, 98

Knox, William Franklin (Frank)
   As Secretary of the Navy in early 1940s in a row with Admiral King, 215-217; as publisher of Chicago Daily News, released news in early 1943 about the commissioning of the battleship Iowa (BB-61), 297

Kurile Islands
   Ships of the U.S. North Pacific Force bombarded the Japanese-held Kuriles in 1944-45, 317-319

Law
   McCrea took the legal course at George Washington

University in the late 1920s and early 1930s while working in the Judge Advocate General's office in Washington, 106-110; McCrea passed his bar exam in the Panama Canal Zone, 110-113

Leahy, Commander George A., Jr., USN (USNA, 1925)
Suffered from high blood pressure while serving as executive officer of the battleship Iowa (BB-61) in 1944, 255-256

Leahy, Fleet Admiral William D., USN (USNA, 1897)
Question about accuracy of a portion of his book I Was There, 229-232; association with and influence on President Harry Truman in selecting Admiral Louis Denfeld as Chief of Naval Operations in 1947, 301-302

Lee, Rear Admiral Willis A., Jr., USN (USNA, 1908)
Observed the bombardment of Mili Atoll in March 1944, 257-259

Lexington, USS (CV-2)
Conduct of flight operations in the Pacific while under the command of Captain Ernest J. King in the early 1930s, 212-215

Lion, HMS
McCrea went aboard for a tour of Vice Admiral David Beatty's flagship during World War I, 97

Loudon, Dr. Alexander
As Dutch ambassador to the United States in 1942, coordinated his government's decoration of Admiral Thomas C. Hart, 207-210

MacArthur, General of the Army Douglas, USA (Ret.)
Married Jean Faircloth in New York in 1937, 185; meeting with McCrea in Japan in the late 1940s, 190-194; recalled from the Far East by President Harry Truman in 1951, 193-195; intimidated Admiral DeWitt C. Ramsey, Pacific Fleet Commander in Chief, in the late 1940s, 342

Maine, USS (BB-10)
Sent to the Mediterranean to pick up the crew of the Idaho (BB-24) in the summer of 1914, 27, 30-33

Marshall, General of the Army George C., USA
Addressed Naval Academy graduates in 1951 as Secretary of Defense, 230; criticized by Senator Joseph McCarthy in the early 1950s, 354-355; delayed bringing home U.S. Army dependents from the Philippine Islands on the eve of World War II, 355-356

Massachusetts, USS (BB-2)
Conditions on board during midshipmen's summer cruise on

the East Coast in 1912, 18-22

McAdoo, William G.
Former Secretary of the Treasury who discussed his business experiences with McCrea on Guam in the 1930s, 183, 186-88

McCandlish, Captain Benjamin V., USN (USNA, 1909)
As Governor of Guam and commandant of U.S. Naval station there, assisted McCrea in 1930s in finding sources of fresh water on Guam, 174-179

McCrea, Vice Admiral John L., USN (Ret.) (USNA, 1915)
Served from 1915 to 1919 in the New York (BB-34), 1, 38, 41-51, 90-91, 96-98; 99-100, 126-127; birth and boyhood in Marlette, Michigan, 2-8; parents of, 2-8, 12-13, 17, 27-28, 32-33; midshipman at the Naval Academy, 1911-1915, 5, 17-40; duty as naval aide to President Franklin D. Roosevelt in 1942-43, 12-13, 71-72, 137-171, 203-206, 262-291; Robert L. Werntz preparatory school in Annapolis, 13-14; acceptance to U.S. Naval Academy in 1912, 16; executive officer of the USS Pennsylvania (BB-38), the fleet flagship, in 1938-40, 50-51, 76, 87-90, 132-133; aide to Admiral Rodman, Commander in Chief of the Pacific Fleet, on board the New Mexico (BB-40), 1919-21, 51-55; mothballing of the destroyer Babbitt (DD-128) in 1922, 57-58, 74-75; shore duty in 1922 at the Naval War College, 61-63; commanded the minesweeper USS Bittern (AM-36) in the Asiatic Fleet in the mid-1920s, 64-71, 101-105; executive officer of the USS Ramapo (AO-12) in early 1920s, 74-76; commanded the new battleship Iowa in 1943-44, 76-77, 93-96, 98-99, 218-224, 227-235, 239-246, 248-251, 255-261, 263, 287-308; contact with John F. Kennedy in 1954-55, 78-82; in the late 1920s and early 1930s studied law at George Washington University and served in JAG office in Washington, 106-113; on board flagship Rochester (ACR-2) with the Special Service Squadron in Panama, 1930-31, 113-120; worked for Admiral Harold Stark, then Chief of Naval Operations, in Washington in 1940-41, 120-122; commanded the destroyer Trever (DD-339) in the early 1930s, 123-128, 196-197; command of North Pacific Task Force in 1944-45, 129, 313-322; assigned as navigator of the Astoria (CA-34), 1934-36, 130-131, 133-134; assigned as executive officer of the naval station on Guam in the mid-1930s, 131-132, 134-135, 137-138, 172-189; promotion to rear admiral in 1944, 313-316; duty in Central Division of the OpNav staff in Washington, D.C., under Fleet Admiral Chester Nimitz 1945-46, 322-341; as Deputy Commander in Chief Pacific Fleet in the late 1940s, 341-347; Department of Defense Personnel policy work, 1952-53, and retirement with John Hancock, 348-352

McIntire, Rear Admiral Ross T., MC, USN

White House physician who was involved in finding a retreat for President Franklin D. Roosevelt in 1942, 152-154

McMorran, Henry
Republican representative who sought candidates from Michigan's seventh congressional district for appointment to the Naval Academy around 1910, 10-11

Medical Problems
Crew members of the USS New York (BB-34) were felled by influenza in 1918, 43-44

Merchant Ships
Passenger ship SS Irene was assisted by the minesweeper USS Bittern (AM-36) after running aground near Chefoo, China, in July 1925, 101-105

Mili Atoll
Bombardment of by the Iowa (BB-61) and other ships in March 1944, 258-260

Military Academy, U.S.
Senator John F. Kennedy's views, expressed in the mid-1950s, concerning admission of candidates, 78-79

Missouri, USS (BB-63)
First crew did not express appreciation for the help provided by the Iowa (BB-61) in 1943 in getting the ship and turrets organized, 308

Montgomery, Lieutenant (junior grade) Robert, USNR
Movie actor who served as a Naval Reserve officer in World War II, including duty in the White House, 162-165, 167

Morison, Samuel Eliot
The genesis of his assignment as naval historian by President Franklin D. Roosevelt during World War II, 159-162

Movies
Story of Navy doctor in the Dutch East Indies in 1942 inspired a Hollywood movie, The Story of Dr. Wassell, released in 1944, 204-206

Naval Academy, U.S.
Baseball games in the early 1910s, 9, 11, 35-39; Lieutenant Commander James J. Raby was a member of the Academy's Board of Examiners in 1911, 15-16; summer training cruises, 1912-14, 18-33; hazing of midshipmen in the early 1910s, 39-40; Senator John F. Kennedy's views, expressed in the mid-1950s, concerning admission of candidates, 78-81; midshipman shenanigans in connection

with choir practice in 1911, 199-203; George C. Marshall, as Secretary of Defense, addressed graduates in 1951, 230; Assistant Secretary of the Navy Franklin D. Roosevelt impressed McCrea during a vist in 1913, 265-266

Naval Reserve Officer Training Corps (NROTC)
As commandant of the First Naval District in the early 1950s, McCrea worked with the president of Harvard University concerning the status of the NROTC unit, 357-359

Naval War College
Junior and senior classes underwent essentially the same course in the early 1920s, 61-62

Neal, Commander George Franklin, USN (USNA, 1901)
As skipper of the oiler Ramapo (AO-12) in the early 1920s, demonstrated a fine sense of humor, 76

Netherlands
The Dutch royal family lived in the United States while their country was occupied in World War II, 71-72; Queen Wilhelmina presented a decoration to Admiral Thomas C. Hart in August 1942 for his role in the Far East at the beginning of World War II, 207-208; comparison of attitudes toward the Netherlands by U.S. presidents Franklin Roosevelt and Harry Truman during the 1940s, 210-211

New Jersey, USS (BB-62)
McCrea's contact with her skipper, Captain Carl F. Holden, in 1943-44, 247-248

New Mexico, USS (BB-40)
First electric drive battleship, assigned to Pacific Fleet in early 1920s, 53-55

News Media
Questioning President Franklin D. Roosevelt during his press conferences in 1942, 278-281; coverage of the battleship Iowa's (BB-61) commissioning at New York Navy Yard in February 1943, 296-297

New York Navy Yard
Site of the commissioning of the battleship Iowa (BB-61) in February 1943, 293-298

New York, USS (BB-34)
Battleship that served with the British during World War I, 1, 41-51; condition of in World War I, 91; present for surrender of German fleet after World War I, 99-100; officers McCrea served under while on board, 1915-19, 126-127

Nicaragua
  A citizen's view of the country's penchant for revolution in the 1930s, 113-114

Nimitz, Fleet Admiral Chester W., USN (USNA, 1905)
  McCrea's boss (1945-47) as Chief of Naval Operations, 135; sent McCrea to Hyde Park national memorial dedication in 1945, 210; although Nimitz backed Admiral William H. P. Blandy for Chief of Naval Operations in 1947, Admiral Louis E. Denfeld was chosen, 301-302; assigned McCrea to odd jobs in OpNav shortly after World War II, 322-323, 331-332; reorganized OpNav during his tenure as CNO, 1945-47, 330-331

North Pacific Force
  McCrea used the light cruiser Richmond (CL-9) as his flagship while conducting operations in the Aleutians and Kuriles in 1944-45, 316-320

Osterhaus, Lieutenant Commander Hugo W., USN (USNA, 1900)
  Kindness in the face of McCrea's grief over his father's death in 1914, 32-33

Pacific War Council
  British Prime Minister Winston Churchill addressed members of the Pacific War Council at a meeting in Washington, D.C., circa 1942, 211

Palmer, Commander Leigh C., USN (USNA, 1896)
  Executive officer of the New York (BB-34) in 1915 and McCrea's idol, 47-49; his style of leadership, 127

Panama
  McCrea passed the canal zone bar exam around 1930, 110-113; Panamanians have gained more control of the Panama Canal as a result of the 1977 treaty, 116-117

Pan American World Airways
  Assistance from the Navy on Guam in 1930s, 179-184, 189-190

Pay and Allowances
  Theodore Roosevelt's policy of extra pay for sailors shortly after the beginning of the 20th century if they were American citizens, 20-21; pay of the crew of the USS Massachusetts (BB-2) in 1912, 21

Pearson, Andrew R.
  President Franklin D. Roosevelt asked press secretary Steve Early to pick up this columnist's press pass in 1942, but Early declined, 279-281; attacked Secretary of Defense James Forrestal in his newspaper column in the late 1940s, 338-339

Pennsylvania, USS (BB-38)
    Fleet flagship visited by Secretary of the Navy Charles Edison in 1940, 50-51, 76; junior officers in May 1940 needed a pep talk about preparing for war, 87-90; advantages of being executive officer, 133; McCrea made a capable landing alongside a tender at San Pedro, 250

Personnel
    Demobilization right after World War I diminished the U.S. Navy's ability to perform its missions, 54-56

Philippine Islands
    Admiral Harold Stark's role in sending Navy dependents home from the Philippines in the summer of 1941, 355-357

Philippine Sea, Battle of
    Operations of the battleship Iowa (BB-61) during this battle in June 1944, 307-308

Post, Commander Nathan W., USN (USNA, 1904)
    McCrea's discussion with about laying up the USS Babbitt (DD-128) in 1922, 72-73

Potomac, USS (AG-25)
    Franklin D. Roosevelt's presidential yacht that provided furnishings for Shangri-la retreat in 1942, 154-156

Quiggle, Commander Lynne C., USN (USNA, 1930)
    Exemplary gunnery officer aboard the Iowa in 1943-44, later committed suicide, 99, 308

Raby, Lieutenant Commander James J. (USNA, 1895)
    Member of Naval Academy Board of Examiners in 1911, 15-16

Radar
    Rear Admiral William H. P. Blandy made a presentation at the White House in 1942 on the capabilities of radar, 300

Radford, Admiral Arthur W., USN (USNA, 1916)
    Sharp-penned writer as Vice Chief of Naval Operations under Nimitz in mid-1940s, 331-332; as Commander in Chief Pacific Fleet, discussions with McCrea regarding the latter's remaining as his deputy in May 1949, 345-347

Ramapo, USS (AO-12)
    McCrea as executive officer for tour in the Pacific in early 1920s, 75-76

Ramsey, Admiral DeWitt C., USN (USNA, 1912)
    Pacific Fleet Commander in Chief pushed around by General Douglas MacArthur in May 1948, 190-191; McCrea's interaction with when Ramsey was Commander in Chief Pacific Fleet, 1948-49, 341-344

Refueling
    Examples of battleships refueling destroyers at sea in the 1940s, 76-77

Rescue at Sea
    The minesweeper Bittern (AM-36) provided assistance to the commercial passenger ship SS Irene near Chefoo, China, in July 1925, 101-105; the destroyer Trever (DD-339) picked up aviators lost from the carrier Lexington (CV-2) in the Pacific in the early 1930s, 213-214; on direction from the battleship Iowa (BB-61), a destroyer rescued a downed American pilot during the Battle of the Philippine Sea in June 1944, 307-308

Richardson, Admiral James O., USN (USNA, 1902)
    As Commander in Chief U.S. Fleet, conferred with McCrea in late 1940 about new war plans, 85-86

Richmond, USS (CL-9)
    McCrea's flagship in Aleutian waters and the Japanese Kuriles in 1944-45, 316-320

Rochester, USS (ACR-2)
    Served as the flagship of the Special Service Squadron in the Caribbean in the early 1930s, 113-116

Rodman, Admiral Hugh, USN (USNA, 1880)
    As rear admiral, commanded six battleships assigned to the British Grand Fleet in World War I, 41-42; Commander in Chief Pacific Fleet, 1919-22, 42; on board the New Mexico (BB-42) in 1919, 51-57; McCrea's opinion of as a naval officer, 58-61; Admiral Ernest King's critique of, 128-130, 212; chatted with banker James Drake around 1920 on quarterdeck of the USS New Mexico (BB-40), 271

Roosevelt, Eleanor
    Demonstrated a great deal of kindness toward people in the early 1940s when she was First Lady, 264; attended the launching of the Iowa (BB-61) at New York in 1942, 285-286; sent a dispatch to her sons in April 1945 to tell them President Roosevelt had died, 320

Roosevelt, President Franklin Delano
    Asked McCrea to walk with Princess Juliana of the Netherlands at Hyde Park, New York, in the summer of 1942, 71-72; schemed to get British Prime Minister Winston Churchill to Hyde Park in June 1942, 140-144; teased Churchill about the Russians at the Casablanca Conference in January 1943, 145-146; sensitivity in renaming an American ship the Canberra (CA-70), 146-149; renamed a destroyer The Sullivans (DD-537) after the sinking of the Juneau (CL-52) in November 1942, 151; commissioned a team that set up Shangri-La as a retreat closer than Hyde Park to Washington, D.C., early 1942,

152-155; good humor over magazine cartoon, 156; remembered by McCrea as quick-witted and loquacious, 156-157, 275-276; interviewed Samuel E. Morison to write the naval history of World War II, 159-162; reaction to news of lost cruisers at Savo Island in August 1942, 169-170; sensitivity to displacing Admiral Vice Admiral Robert Ghormley in the summer of 1942, 170-171; kissed McCrea's daughter on the cheek on her 16th birthday, 203-204; solicited a story with "drama and pathos" for a "fireside chat" in 1942, 204-206; made Atlantic crossing in the battleship Iowa (BB-61) for the Teheran conference in November 1943, 218-219, 222-235; sent a hand-knitted afghan to McCrea aboard the Iowa (BB-61) in 1943, 263; bonds of affection for McCrea and his wife, 264-265; impressed McCrea at the Naval Academy in 1913, 265-266; his confidence in Admiral Harold Stark and General George Marshall, 267; concern about public opinion, 275-279; interaction with Steve Early as his press secretary, 279-282; criticism of Roy Howard when head of United Press, 282-284; secured an assignment for McCrea after his service as naval aide, 284-288; discussions with McCrea in 1942 about a North African conference, 289-291; air travel arrangements for reaching the Casablanca Conference in January 1943, 312-313; asked that Under Secretary of State Sumner Welles be invited to a White House lunch in 1942 because of superstition, 326-328; expressed interest in a squabble between Under Secretary James Forrestal and the Navy Judge Advocate General early in World War II, 334-336; Forrestal quizzed McCrea about Roosevelt's World War II dealings with the Soviet Union, 337-338

Roosevelt, President Theodore
Policy of extra pay for sailors shortly after the beginning of the 20th century if they were American citizens, 20-21; reference to Wister's biography of, 118-119

Root, Captain Edmund S., USN (USNA, 1905)
McCrea's commanding officer on board the Astoria (CA-34) in the mid-1930s, 134; conversations with McCrea in the 1930s about Guam, 173-174

Rosenman, Samuel I.
Communications to McCrea about a possible appointment as President Harry Truman's naval aide in 1945, 129, 320; present in Shangri-La when McCrea reported to President Franklin D. Roosevelt on the sinking of the cruiser Astoria (CA-34) in August 1942, 170

Royal Navy
Augmented by six U.S. battleships in 1917-18, 41-43; comparison of British and American warships in World War I, 90-91, 96-98; contact with McCrea in November 1943

after the battleship <u>Iowa</u> (BB-61) reached Oran, 238-240; performance of the cruiser <u>Ajax</u> in fighting the German battleship <u>Graf Spee</u> in 1939, 295-296

Savo Island
    President Franklin D. Roosevelt's reaction to news of four Allied cruisers sunk off of in August 1942, 169-170

Seibert, Midshipman Walter, USN (USNA, 1913)
    High school companion of McCrea who preceded him to the Naval Academy in 1909, 8-11; failed first entrance exam, 8, 13-14; pitched a no-hitter as a midshipman baseball player, 9

Sherman, Admiral Forrest P., USN (USNA, 1918)
    Excellent, ambitious officer who apparently had his goal set for a long time on becoming Chief of Naval Operations, which he did in 1949, 323-324; shortly before his death in 1951, made a vague promise to McCrea about a future billet, 324

Shangri-La
    Establishment of this camp in the spring of 1942 as a presidential retreat for Franklin D. Roosevelt, 152-154; camp furnishings came from the yacht <u>Potomac</u> (AG-25), 154-156

Sherman, Rear Admiral Frederick C., USN (USNA, 1910)
    Expressed gratitude in early 1944 for having the antiaircraft capability of <u>Iowa</u> (BB-61)-class battleships available in carrier task groups, 251

Ship Handling
    While executive officer of the battleship <u>Pennsylvania</u> (BB-38) around 1940, McCrea made a capable landing alongside a tender at San Pedro, 250

Smedberg, Vice Admiral William R. III, USN (USNA, 1926)
    As Chief of Bureau Personnel in the early 1960s, his interaction with McCrea concerning Naval Academy candidates, 80

<u>South Carolina</u> (BB-26)
    Picked up midshipmen in Veracruz, Mexico, in 1913 en route to the Phildelphia Navy Yard, 25

Soviet Union
    Secretary of the Navy James Forrestal quizzed McCrea shortly after World War II about President Franklin D. Roosevelt's wartime dealings with the Soviet Union, 337-338

Special Service Squadron
    Represented the interests of the United States in Central

America in the early 1930s, 113-118

Spruance, Vice Admiral Raymond A., USN (USNA, 1907)
Embarked in the New Jersey (BB-62) when McCrea, in the Iowa (BB-61), sank a Japanese cruiser in 1944, 248-250; consideration of the Iowa as his flagship in 1944, 255-257; McCrea's speculation about discord between Spruance and Vice Admiral Frank Jack Fletcher in 1944-45, 321

Standley, Admiral William H., USN (USNA, 1895)
McCrea's destroyer commander while in the Trever (DD-339) in 1932, 190, 196-197; McCrea's opinion of and President Franklin D. Roosevelt's affection for, 196, 198; compared with Admiral Husband Kimmel, 197-198

Stark, Admiral Harold R., USN (USNA, 1903)
McCrea's service as aide while Stark was Chief of Naval Operations, 1940-42, 80, 120-121; sent McCrea to deliver war plans to Pacific commanders, 1940-41, 85-86; Admiral Husband Kimmel accused Stark of perjury in connection with the post-World War II hearings on Pearl Harbor, 93; relationship to Admiral Kimmel, 95; commended McCrea as presidential naval aide in 1942, 136-138; replaced Vice Admiral Robert Ghormley in London in April 1942, 170-171; FDR's opinion of, 267; role in sending Navy dependents home from the Philippines in the summer of 1941, 355-357

Starling, Edmund W.
As supervisor of the White House Secret Service detail in 1942, was not told by McCrea of President Franklin D. Roosevelt's impending trip to the Casablanca Conference, 309-311

Sullivan, R. O. D.
Pan American Airways pilot who flew to Guam in the 1930s, 184-185

Sumatra
Visited by American scientific observers in the mid-1920s, 65-71

Teel, Roland M.
Instructor at Robert L. Werntz School in 1911, founder of the Severn School, 14

Tennessee, USS (Armed Cruiser Number 10)
Sent to Europe to rescue stranded Americans at outbreak of World War I in 1914, 28

Theobald, Lieutenant Robert A., USN (USNA, 1907)
Baseball coach at U.S. Naval Academy circa 1912, 38

The Sullivans, USS (DD-537)
Destroyer named in 1943 for brothers lost when the

cruiser Juneau (CL-52) sank in November 1942, 150-152

Tigan, Midshipman Walter J., USN
Dismissed from U.S. Naval Academy in 1912 for hazing, 39-40

Trever, USS (DD-339)
Pacific Fleet destroyer that improved condition under McCrea's command in 1932, 123-128

Truk Atoll
Japanese surface ships tangled with the battleships Iowa (BB-61) and New Jersey (BB-62) at Truk in February 1944, 248-250

Truman, Harry S.
Selected Captain James Vardaman as his naval aide in 1945, 129, 320; retained name of Shangri-La for presidential retreat, 155; McCrea's complete file of messages between FDR, Truman, Stalin, and Chiang Kai-shek, 167; recalled General Douglas MacArthur from the Far East in 1951, 193-195; Dutch Ambassador Alexander Loudon's view of, 210-211; reliance on Admiral Leahy, 301, 341; reluctance about calling reserves for Korean War, 353-354; lost respect for Dwight D. Eisenhower because he tolerated attacks on George Marshall, 355

Turner, Captain Richmond Kelly, USN (USNA, 1908)
Director of Navy war plans at the outset of World War II, 121; McCrea's opinions about his drinking and style of leadership, 122-123

United Fruit Company
Provided schools, medical services for the peoples of Central and South America in the 1930s, 114

Vardaman, Captain James K., USNR
Naval Reserve captain appointed as naval aide to President Harry Truman in 1945, 129

Wallace, Mrs. Ilo Browne
As sponsor of the battleship Iowa (BB-61), attended the launching in 1942 but not the commissioning in 1943, 286, 291-292

Wasmuth, USS (DD-338)
Operations with the aircraft carrier Lexington (CV-2) in the Pacific in the early 1930s, 212-213

Wassell, Lieutenant Commander Corydon, MC, USNR
The story of his medical exploits in the Dutch East Indies in 1942 became the subject of a "fireside chat" by President Franklin D. Roosevelt and later inspired a Hollywood movie, 204-206

Welles, Sumner
    Under Secretary of State who was invited to a White House lunch in 1942 because of superstition, 326-328

Wilhelmina, Queen
    The Dutch queen lived in the United States during World War II, visited Hyde Park, New York, in 1942, 71-72; presented a decoration to Admiral Thomas C. Hart in August 1942 for his role in the Far East at the beginning of World War II, 207-208

William D. Porter, USS (DD-579)
    Inadvertently fired a live torpedo at the battleship Iowa (BB-61) during a crossing of the Atlantic in November 1943, 232-235

Willson, Rear Admiral Russell, USN (USNA, 1906)
    Served as superintendent of the Naval Academy, 1941-42, then ordered to the staff of Admiral Ernest J. King, 138

Wister, Owen
    Reference to the biography he wrote of his Harvard classmate Theodore Roosevelt, 118-119

Wollcott, Alexander
    Famous journalist who encountered McCrea during a visit to the White House in 1942, 269-270

World War I
    The Greek Navy bought the USS Idaho (BB-24) from the U.S. Navy as war was starting in the summer of 1914, 26-29; U.S. battleships formed the Sixth Battle Squadron of British and American warships, 90-91, 96-98

www.ingramcontent.com/pod-product-compliance
Lightning Source LLC
Chambersburg PA
CBHW080623170426
43209CB00007B/1500